Best Editorial Cartoons of the Year

BEST EDITORIAL CARTOONS OF THE YEAR

1977 EDITION

Edited by
CHARLES BROOKS

Foreword by DRAPER HILL

A FIREBIRD PRESS BOOK

PELICAN PUBLISHING COMPANY
Gretna 1998

Copyright © 1977
By Charles G. Brooks
All rights reserved
ISBN: 0-88289-170-7 Hardcover
ISBN: 1-56554-514-1 Paperback

Manufactured in the United States of America
Published by Pelican Publishing Company, Inc.
1000 Burmaster Street, Gretna, Louisiana 70053

Contents

Foreword 7
Award-Winning Cartoons 12
1976 Election 15
Ford Administration and Campaign 33
Reagan and the Primaries 41
Presidential Debates 48
U.S. Congress 53
Wayne Hays Scandal 57
Playboy Magazine 65
Southern Africa 72
Bicentennial Celebration 81
Energy and World Resources 86
The Middle East 93
Death of Mao 96
Viking I and II 100
International Affairs 103
Medicaid and Malpractice Charges 114
Crime 117
Russia 121
Olympics 123
The Post Office 126
Morality 129
U.S. Defense 134
Education 136
The Economy 138
Swine Flu 143
Earl Butz 145
...And Other Issues 148
Past Award Winners 155
Index 159

The Bench, by William Hogarth, first published September 4, 1758. From the fifth and final state, which shows that the "Townshend problem" obsessed Hogarth to the end of his life (note the last line). His "dedication" to Townshend beneath the subtitle was deleted from the copperplate almost immediately after the initial impression.

Foreword

"You are Max Beerbohm?" murmured Rudyard Kipling with obvious approval as he was introduced to the twenty-two-year-old writer-caricaturist. "So young to have a style."

"Style is bunk; some of these young artists take two hours to sign their name. It's the idea that counts."
Bill Mauldin

What is this thing called style? How does it serve the men (and women) who produce the supercharged ideograms that we have come to call editorial cartoons? Is it distinguishable from technique? From manner? Is it some mystical personal quality that gets through the nervous system, down the arm, and out of the pen point without troubling the labors of the mind? Can it be invented, constructed, blended, borrowed, or lifted? Or must style evolve gradually and unconsciously, a seamless web of personality, passion, experience, influence, and philosophy? You will not be surprised to learn that there is room for discussion on this subject, particularly inside a trade whose artistic family trees tend occasionally to entwine.

The debate is further enlivened by breathless talk of a "new breed" of pictorial satirist and of how these Young Turks are revamping the body and spirit of their profession. Without disputing for an instant the presence of an impudent, welcome breeze, freshly gusting through editorial passageways these days, one really must point out that it was ever thus. Since William Hogarth first established our Anglo-American heritage of free and lively graphic comment on morality and politics (c. 1730-1764), new breed has challenged old breed every couple of decades with the comforting regularity of a pendulum.

If one "school" favored preaching, teaching, and moral uplift, it would invite competition from another that preferred slash, puncture, and general good fun. If one age leaned toward license, the next might well tilt toward dignity and responsibility. The first representative of a "new breed" was George Townshend, hot-tempered member of Parliament for Norfolk. In the sweltering political summer of 1756, Townshend began to supply a cooperative publisher with deft, highly partisan *caricatura* prints, scarely bigger than playing cards, which planted the real seed for the eventual development of the modern newspaper cartoon. Where Hogarth's great tableaux had been painstakingly conceived and elaborately engraved in full tone, Townshend struck like a hornet, employing wit, irony, and personal exaggeration. His pen sketches were

FOREWORD

translated into print by the lighter, less mannered process of etching. Townshend caught on immediately, and Hogarth was not amused.

Two years later the older artist's irritation with the new vogue came to a boil in an extended lecture on the distinction between "Character" (what *he* did), "Caracature" (what Townshend thought *he* was doing), and "Outre" ("degenerate" French distortion). Hogarth argued, somewhat unconvincingly, that the manner "which has, of late years, got the name of *Caracatura* [must be] totally divested of every stroke that hath a tendency to Good Drawing" to realize its purposes. "All the humorous Effects of the fashionable manner of Caricaturing chiefly depend on the surprize we are under at finding ourselves caught with any sort of Similitude in objects absolutely remote." Hogarth's pioneer How-to-do-it guide, offered as an extended caption to a plate of September, 1758 (*The Bench*, see page 6), was pointedly *"Address'd to the Honble Coll T[own]s[hen]d."* At length, in 1762, Townshend's publisher Mary Darly responded with a counter manual on *Caricatura* "for the use of Young Gentlemen and Ladies." Darly urged her readers to let it all hang out. "Keep constantly practising from this book," she recommended, "till drawing in this manner becomes familiar and is attended with pleasure."

The next breed hit about 1780. James Gillray and Thomas Rowlandson were the first English cartoonists who could and did benefit from the availability of formal artistic training on their home turf. They were also the first to have the additional advantages of a full-fledged, pretentiously high-minded art establishment against which to rebel. Their excesses and successes over the next three decades spread to a small host of disciples and imitators throughout the realm, across Europe, and gradually into the former colonies on the other side of the Atlantic. There was very little that Gillray and Rowlandson were not game to tackle, from the royal boudoir to the ministerial privy. The good, gray spirit of Victorian fair play put a stop to that sort of thing, and the action moved elsewhere.

Inevitably, style is affected by techinque and the realities of reproduction. The Georgian cartoonist drew with a needle on copper. He had to—it was the only game in town. From the third decade of the nineteenth century, the availablity and increasing popularity of the lithographic crayon permitted both the lustrous textural effects of Gavarni and the potent appeals to emotion and mood of Daumier's middle and later years. A restless, inventive draftsman like Thomas Nast apparently chafed at the need to have his pencil renderings cut into wood blocks by other hands. When photomechanical reproduction became practical in the early 1880s, Nast was one of the first major figures to abandon wood for pen and ink. Ten years later, again he was one of the earliest to plunge wholeheartedly into chalk surfaces, grained papers, and mechanical benday patterns. Nast may well have felt, as others have

FOREWORD

since, that it is all too easy to become trapped, imprisoned, within the confines of one's own style. Not the least drawback to an elaborate, highly individual manner is that it can force its possessor into self-parody (assuming that it doesn't first tax his sanity, sobriety, or eyesight). Experimentation with approach and materials is not always helpful; in Nast's case it tended to dilute the forcefulness that won him his greatest celebrity. This shift was variously attributed to disillusion, age, or an unlucky choice of pens. However, it is possible to regard his homogenization as a considered adjustment to a new political climate.

Bill Mauldin says that he has always been "antistyle" and that he sees a cartoon simply as an instrument for moving an idea. Before World War II, Mauldin recalls, he used to worry more about shading and wrinkles. During the war, working with worn-out Italian engraving equipment—and occasionally obliged to swipe unused coffin linings for plates—he changed direction:

> *What I started doing, because they couldn't reproduce this fancy thing—I started drawing with a very bold and simple brushstroke. I did it for purely mechanical reasons. I suddenly realized this is a good way to draw the war—it's very stark, very bold, very rough black and white and so on. Then after the war these things tended to jump off the page at the readers. I was dealing with politics. There are more shades of gray in politics than there are in the violence of war. That kind of style—or whatever you call it—technique didn't seem suited, so I went back to using more gray.*

Mauldin comments that he draws primarily for himself and that he is not trying to be "artistic" or "to worry about an audience":

> *If people want large, complicated, involved pictures, they can find them in galleries, they can find them in photographs, they can find them in a lot of places. A drawing should be somewhat like a play. There shouldn't be a line in it, or a motion in it, or a figure in it that doesn't contribute directly to putting across the idea.*

The dictionary tells us that style is "the way in which something is said or done, as distinguished from its substance"—the singer, not the song. A difficulty presented by Mauldin's definition is that, in a cartoon the absence or denial of style *is* style incarnate and calls for a particular verve and virtuosity to make it work. The irony of Kipling's 1895 salutation to Beerbohm is that we don't know whether the compliment was intended for Max's audacious, slightly precious essays or for his caricatures. Practically from the outset, the latter were revolutionary, expressive blueprints for a new way of looking at people. In the best of them, the style was indivisibly the substance and truth.

Twenty years after the death of Honore Daumier, the reigning French cartoonist was J. L. Forain (1852-1931), pioneer of the powerful crayon-on-paper technique that we associate with the subsequent work of Robert Minor, Rollin Kirby, and Daniel Fitzpatrick. Forain had a fondness for studies of lawyers, judges, bohemians, and political hacks that invited comparison with his great predecessor. His ferocious

FOREWORD

conservatism kept him well supplied with enemies, particularly among his fellow artists. On one splendidly wicked occasion, the painter Degas, aged and half-blind, tottered into a preview of an exhibition of drawings. "Qu'est-ce que c'est?" he exclaimed in a deafening whisper, fixing his attention on a luckless drawing at the other end of the room. "Qu'est-ce que c'est?" Degas quavered forward. "Is it a bad Daumier? . . . Is it a bad Daumier?" He arrived at the picture, thrust his nose forward, squinted closely, and announced, "Mais non! It is an EXCELLENT Forain." Forain never lived it down.

Each generation of editorial cartoonists grows out of the one that precedes it. There seems to be no other way to learn. George Cruikshank began as a carbon-copy Gillray. Fitzpatrick's early work was in the middle-American pen technique popular at the turn of the century. Looking at scrapbooks of David Low's work in Sydney (1911-1919), one can virtually pinpoint the day that he first saw, and responded to, the cartoons of Oscar Cesare in the New York *World*. The formative impulse for Paul Conrad, who grew up in Iowa, came from the examples of Ding Darling of the Des Moines *Register*. Out of the brush and crayon manner prevalent in Chicago in the twenties, Herblock forged one of the most direct, devastating weapons in the history of communications. Unfortunately, any attempt to encapsulate the interlocking "apprenticeships" of the past half-century is bound to result in the omission of fifteen or twenty vital links in the chain. The last "new breed" before the current one, Hugh Haynie and Bill Sanders, began their careers with brief stylistic homages to Herb Block before they found stars of their own to sail by. In the sixties, impulses generated in the London of Ronald Searle, Carl Giles, *Private Eye* magazine, Ralph Steadman, and Gerald Scarfe began to take root on these insular shores. Lively schools of satire in Canada and Australia have hardly been without their effect, as well.

In 1965 *Holiday* magazine quoted the editor of one major (cartoonistless) paper to the effect that the editorial cartoon, "with a bare handful of exceptions," had "shot its wad." Now, more than a decade later, the art is probably more vigorous, healthy, and popular than it has ever been. Today's cartoonist no longer subscribes to the instruction-book dictum of 1904 that "nothing . . . must offend readers or advertisers in any way." Most of us would differ with Rube Goldberg's advice of 1956 that the cartoon "must carry dignity and conviction—even though, at times, it might be humorous." Nor would we all agree with Rube that the job is "a constant search for symbols" or that these provide a cushion of "familiar elements to fall back on whenever necessary."

Today's cartoon is probably closer to the spirit of Townshend and Gillray. If there is a common denominator it probably lies in a willingness to put more trust in the expressive qualities of line and form. Where titles used to stand apart, providing a secondary punch, currently

FOREWORD

there is apt to be more unity between literary and visual elements, with the visual predominating. Dignity is out of fashion. For the younger cartoonists, sentiment is so suspect as to be virtually taboo. Artistically, there is more willingness to take risks, to draw and redraw spontaneously over a light board, to employ such blunt and indelible tools as Magic Markers. The disciplines of the action painter are making themselves felt.

Although there is still latitude for the expression of rage and moral indignation, the cartoonist as jester or "fool" is enjoying a special popularity. The jacket blurb on one recent anthology speaks of the cartoonist "jumping from subject to subject with the grace of a scatterbrained hare, pokin' fun at everyone and everything." This is some distance down the road from David Low's reflection that "the list of the great caricaturists is also a list of philosophers, whose pictorial satire was but the vehicle for interpreting and exhibiting their own passions." The difference may rest in what Mike Peters perceptively calls the distinction between cartoonists who are "audience oriented" and cartoonists who are "victim oriented."

As arts go, ours is still a young one. The entire span from Townshend to the present can still be covered by three lifetimes: Rowlandson's, John Tenniel's, and Herblock's. The bicentennial feast year, which this collection helps to commemorate, is also the 220th anniversary of the craft itself. The great-granddaddy of the volume you are holding was a collection of seventy-five mini-satires published in book form in 1758. *A Political and Satirical History of the Years 1756 and 1757* was presented as "a series of Humorous and Entertaining Prints . . . containing all the most remarkable Transactions, Characters and Caricatures, of those memorable Years." It came complete with "An explanatory Key to every Print; rendering the Whole full and significant."

That, one hopes, is more than you will need to recapture the flavor of this political and satirical history of the year 1976.

Award-Winning Cartoons

1976 PULITZER PRIZE

'O beautiful for spacious skies
For amber waves of grain...'

TONY AUTH

Editorial Cartoonist
Philadelphia Enquirer

Born in Akron, Ohio, 1943, graduate of the University of California at Los Angeles, 1965; worked six years as a medical illustrator; joined *Philadelphia Enquirer* as editorial cartoonist, 1971; work appears five times weekly and is syndicated by the *Washington Post*; winner of the 1975 Sigma Delta Chi Award for editorial cartooning.

1975 SIGMA DELTA CHI AWARD
(Selected in 1976)

TONY AUTH

Editorial Cartoonist
Philadelphia Enquirer

1975 NATIONAL NEWSPAPER AWARD/CANADA

(Selected in 1976)

ROY PETERSON

Editorial Cartoonist
Vancouver Sun

Born in Winnipeg, Manitoba, in 1936; began freelancing for magazines in Canada and U. S., 1962; has worked primarily for the *Vancouver Sun*; editorial cartoons, social comment cartoons, illustrations; work has appeared in every major magazine in Canada and in many U. S. publications; writer; book cover designer; previous winner of National Newspaper Award, 1968; first in world competition, International Salon of Cartoons, Montreal, 1973.

1976 Election

On November 2, American voters weighed the record of the Ford administration against the campaign promises of a somewhat obscure former governor of Georgia, Jimmy Carter, and decided it was time for a change. The closest electoral vote in sixty years elevated Carter to the presidency and put a man from the Deep South in the White House for the first time since the Civil War.

President Gerald Ford staged an amazing comeback late in the campaign, cutting what had seemed an insurmountable Carter lead to almost a dead heat. He was the first incumbent to be defeated since Herbert Hoover was swept from office by the Great Depression in 1932.

A month before the first primary, eleven candidates had announced for the Democratic nomination. But all but one of them—Wallace, Byrd, Sanford, Udall, Harris, Shriver, Shapp, Bayh, Church, and Brown—fell by the wayside. Senator Hubert Humphrey merely warmed up on the sidelines.

Carter positioned himself to the right of the Democratic party's left wing throughout the primaries and allowed the liberal candidates to eliminate each other. Then, in Florida, he dealt George Wallace's hopes a deathblow. With the strong support of organized labor, Carter sailed on to victory, winning eighteen primaries along the way.

GENE BASSET
Courtesy Scripps-Howard Newspapers

"FIRST OFF, TELL THE STATE DEPARTMENT TO ESTABLISH DIPLOMATIC RELATIONS WITH THE WEST"

JOHN FISCHETTI
Courtesy Chicago Daily News

"I'VE BEEN INVITED TO A COME-AS-YOU-ARE PARTY IN NEW YORK"

"Sometimes I think I oughta get outta the rat race an' move from Plains."

JIM BERRY
©NEA

JEFF MACNELLY
Richmond News Leader
©Chicago Tribune—New York News Syndicate

THE UNDECIDED VOTER

BOB ENGLEHART
Courtesy Dayton Journal Herald

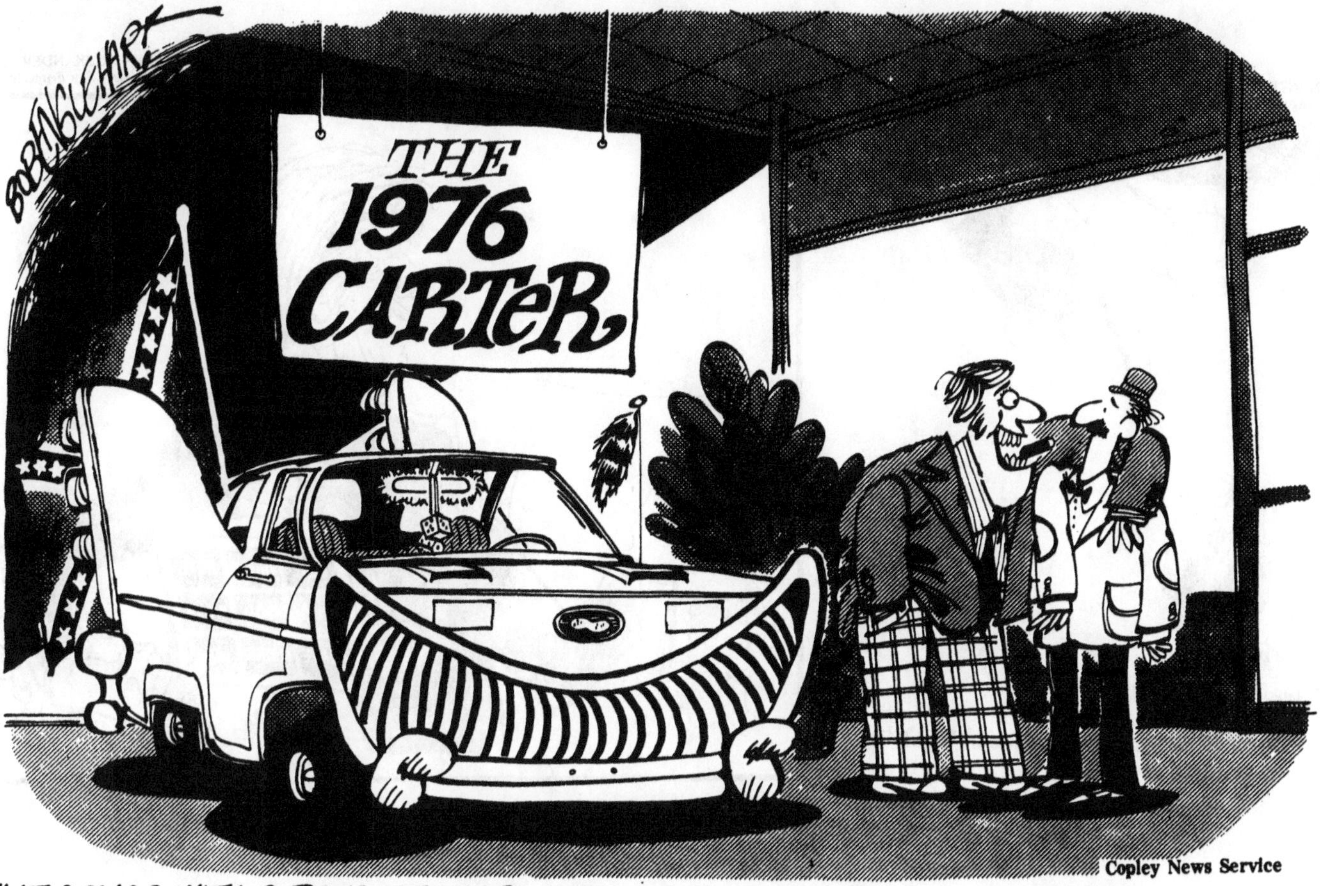
BOB ENGLEHART
THE 1976 CARTER
Copley News Service

"IT COMES WITH A REVOLUTIONARY NEW PURCHASE PLAN. YOU DON'T FIND OUT HOW MUCH IT COSTS UNTIL **AFTER** YOU BUY IT!"

HERE'S WHERE I STAND

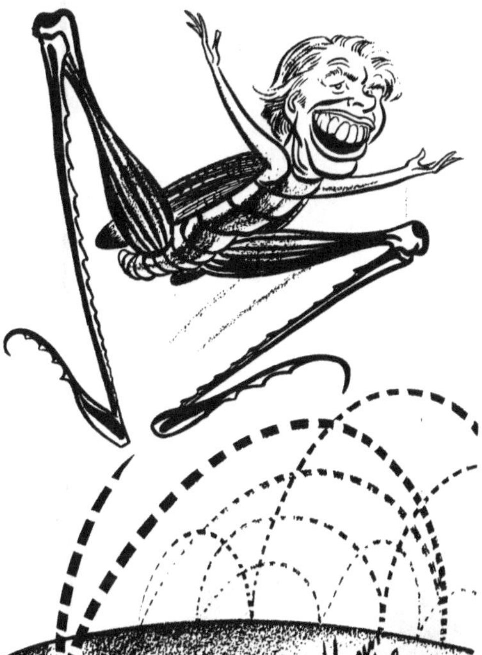
Warren King

WARREN KING
Courtesy N.Y. Daily News

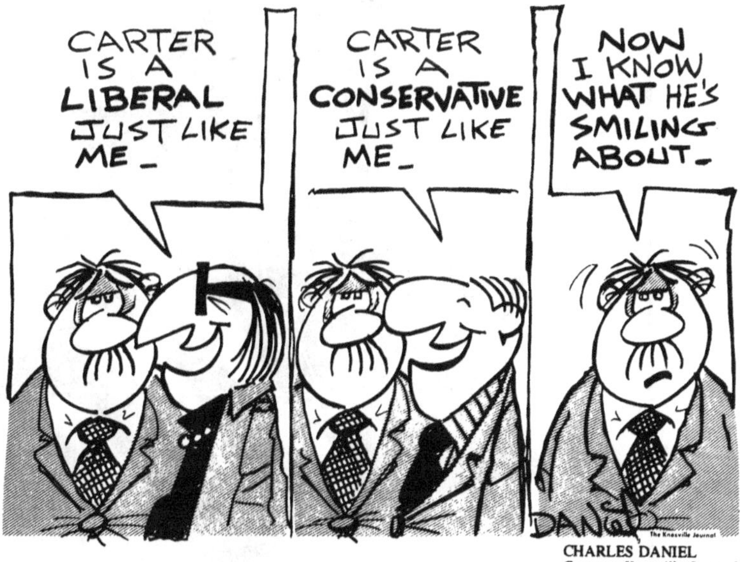
CARTER IS A **LIBERAL** JUST LIKE ME_
CARTER IS A **CONSERVATIVE** JUST LIKE ME_
NOW I KNOW WHAT HE'S SMILING ABOUT_
DANIEL

CHARLES DANIEL
Courtesy Knoxville Journal

FRANK INTERLANDI
©Los Angeles Times Syndicate

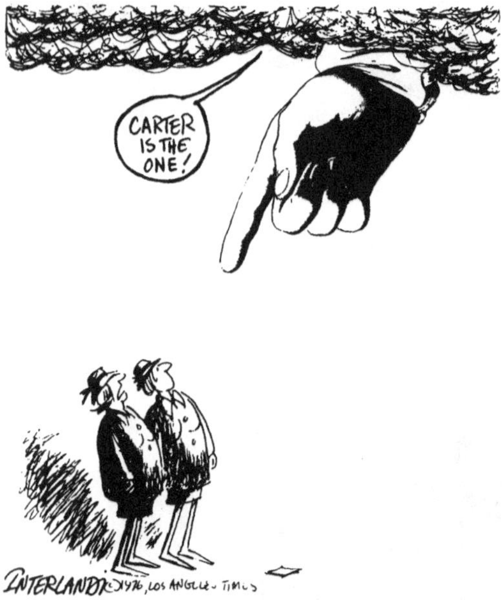
CARTER IS THE ONE!

"Wow! What a campaign organization he's got!"

KEN ALEXANDER
Courtesy San Francisco Examiner

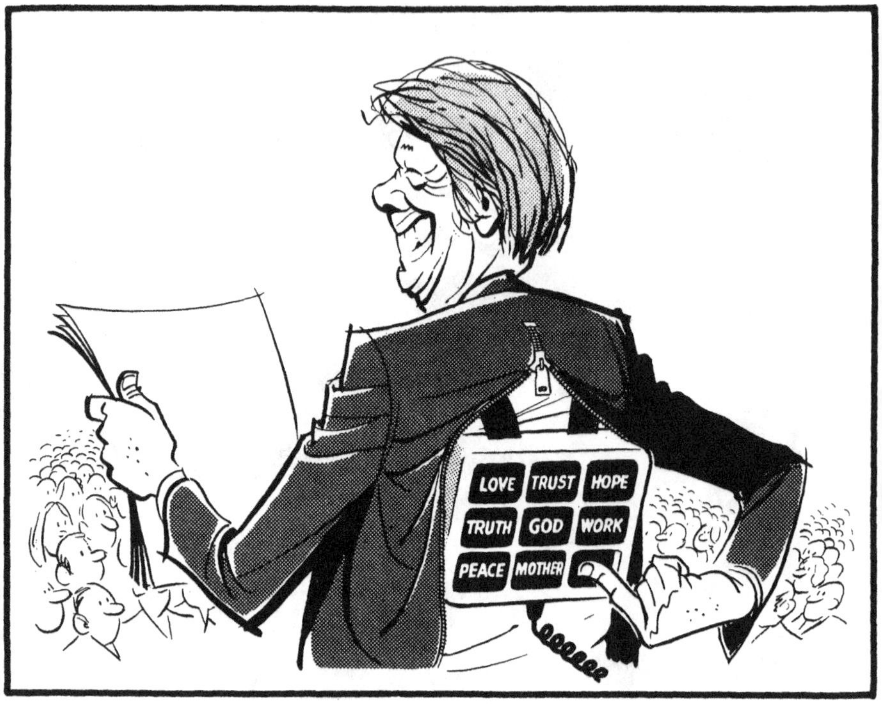
LOVE TRUST HOPE
TRUTH GOD WORK
PEACE MOTHER

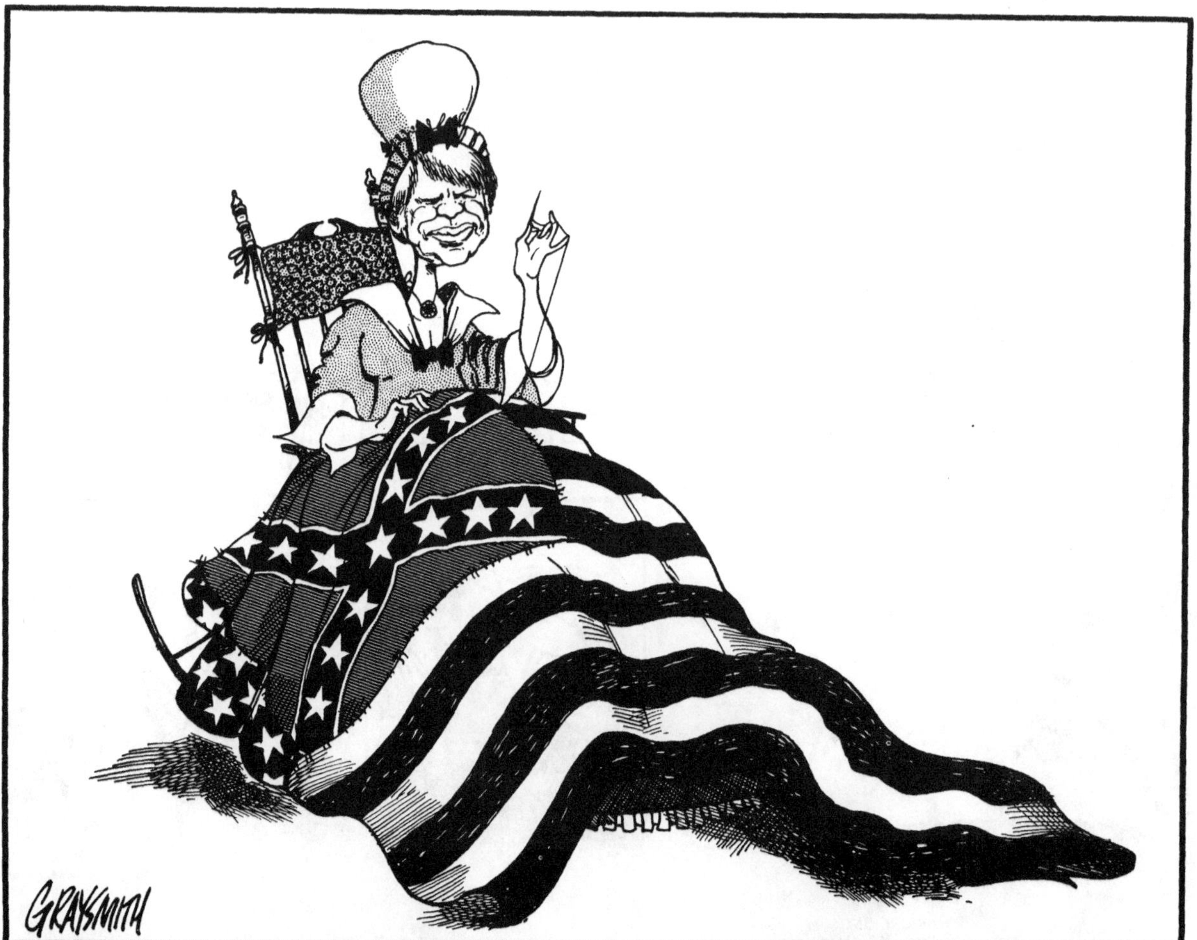
GRAYSMITH

ROBERT GRAYSMITH
Courtesy San Francisco Chronicle

MERLE CUNNINGTON
Courtesy Valley News (Calif.)

SPLINTER PARTY CANDIDATE

JACK McLEOD
Courtesy Buffalo Evening News

JON KENNEDY
Courtesy Arkansas Democrat

Born-again candidate

JOHN CRAWFORD
Courtesy Alabama Journal

V. ROSCHKOV
Courtesy Windsor Star

JACK McLEOD
Courtesy Buffalo Evening News

'... EXCITEMENT ON THE FLOOR—A DOZING DELEGATE FELL INTO THE AISLE.'

CALVIN GRONDAHL
Courtesy Deseret News

"Oh, 'trick-or-treating' in Plains isn't so bad if you can eat 150 pounds of peanuts."

JEFF MACNELLY
Richmond News Leader
©Chicago Tribune—New York
News Syndicate

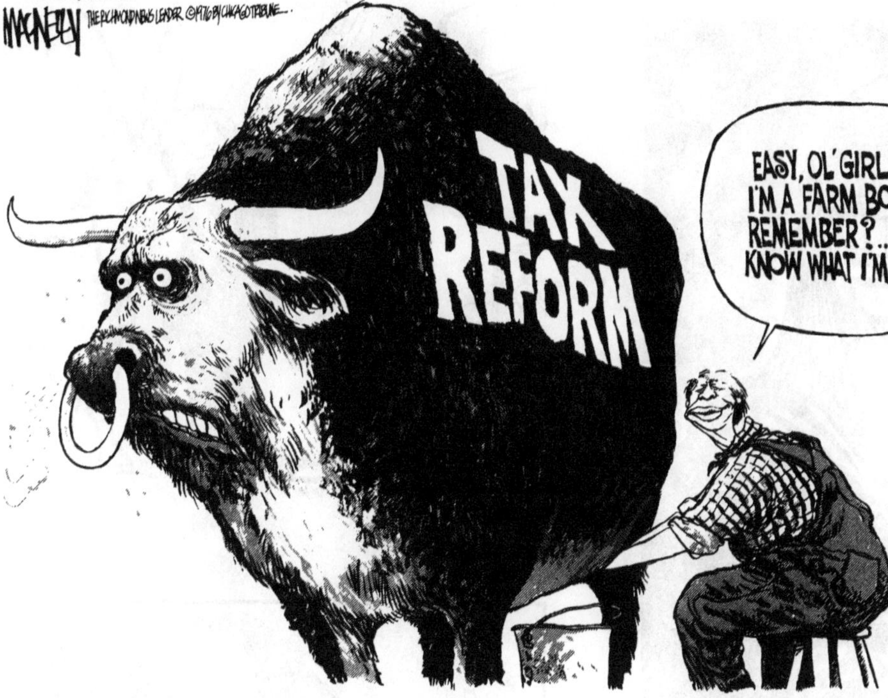
MACNELLY
TAX REFORM
EASY, OL' GIRL! I'M A FARM BOY, REMEMBER?... I KNOW WHAT I'M DOIN'...

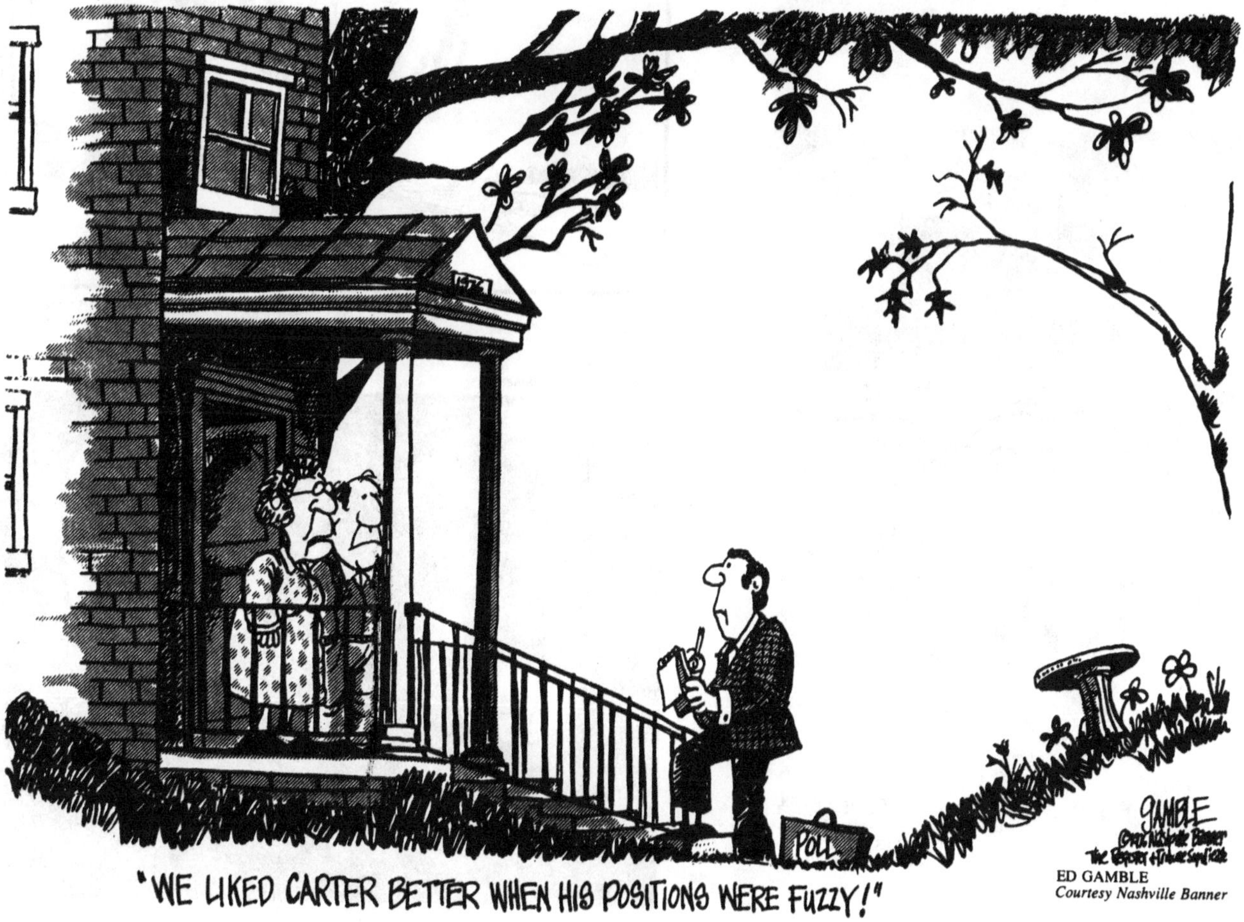
POLL
GAMBLE

"WE LIKED CARTER BETTER WHEN HIS POSITIONS WERE FUZZY!"

ED GAMBLE
Courtesy Nashville Banner

THAT ENIGMATIC SMILE

KARL HUBENTHAL
Courtesy Los Angeles Herald-Examiner

CHARLES WERNER
Courtesy Indianapolis Star

"SMILE"

TOM FLANNERY
Courtesy Baltimore Sun

BILL GARNER
Courtesy The Commercial Appeal

DAVID SIMPSON
Courtesy Tulsa Tribune

DICK WALLMEYER
Long Beach Press-Telegram
©Register and Tribune Syndicate

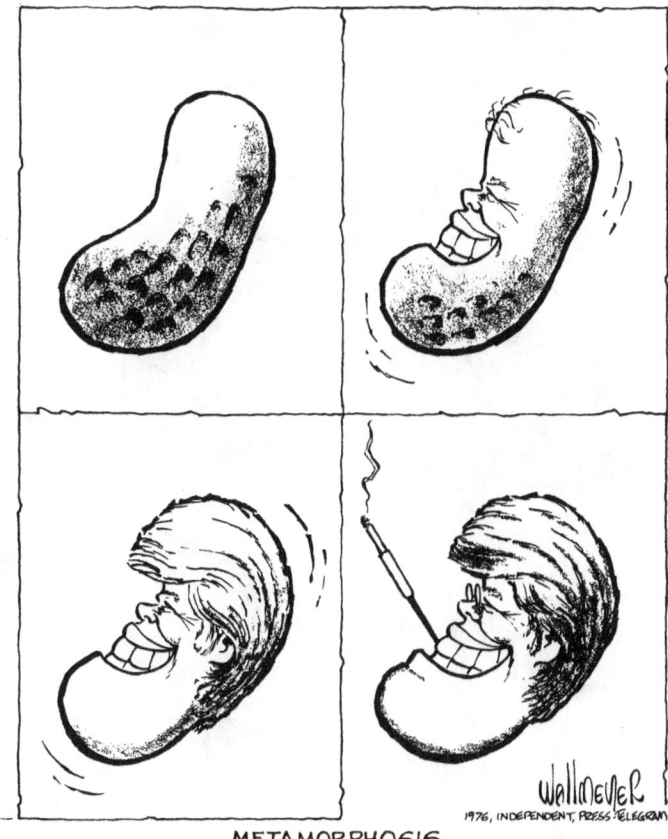

METAMORPHOSIS

JACK JURDEN
Courtesy Wilmington Evening Journal-News

WAYNE STAYSKAL
Courtesy Chicago Tribune

"SORRY, MR. ROCKEFELLER... PRESIDENT'S ORDERS!"

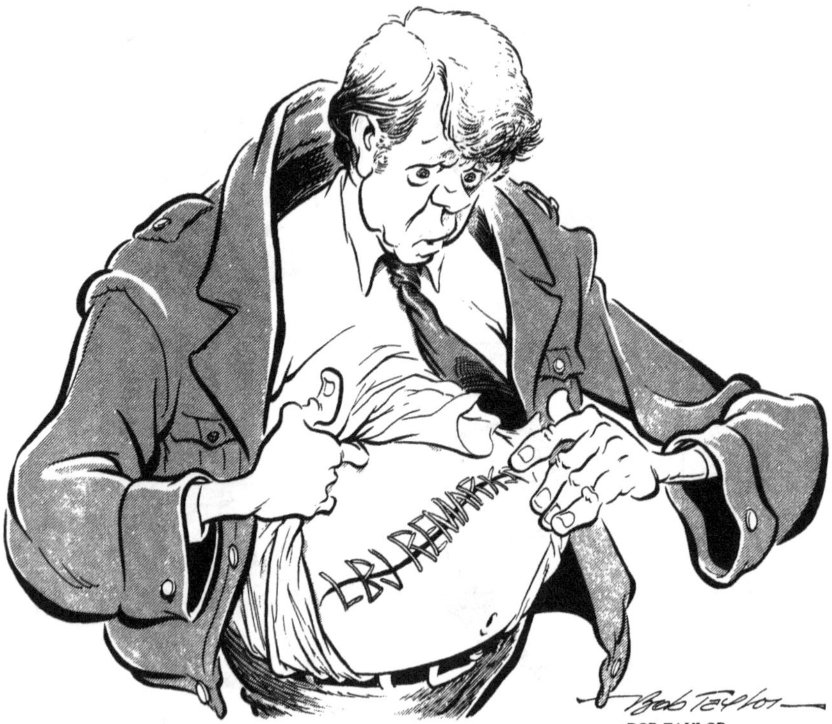
LBJ REMARKS

BOB TAYLOR
Courtesy Dallas Times Herald

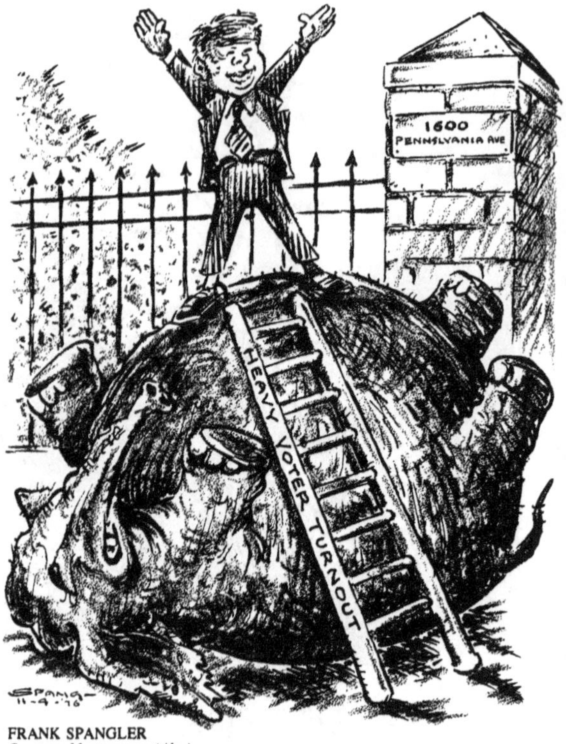
1600
PENNSYLVANIA AVE
HEAVY VOTER TURNOUT

FRANK SPANGLER
Courtesy Montgomery (Ala.) Advertiser

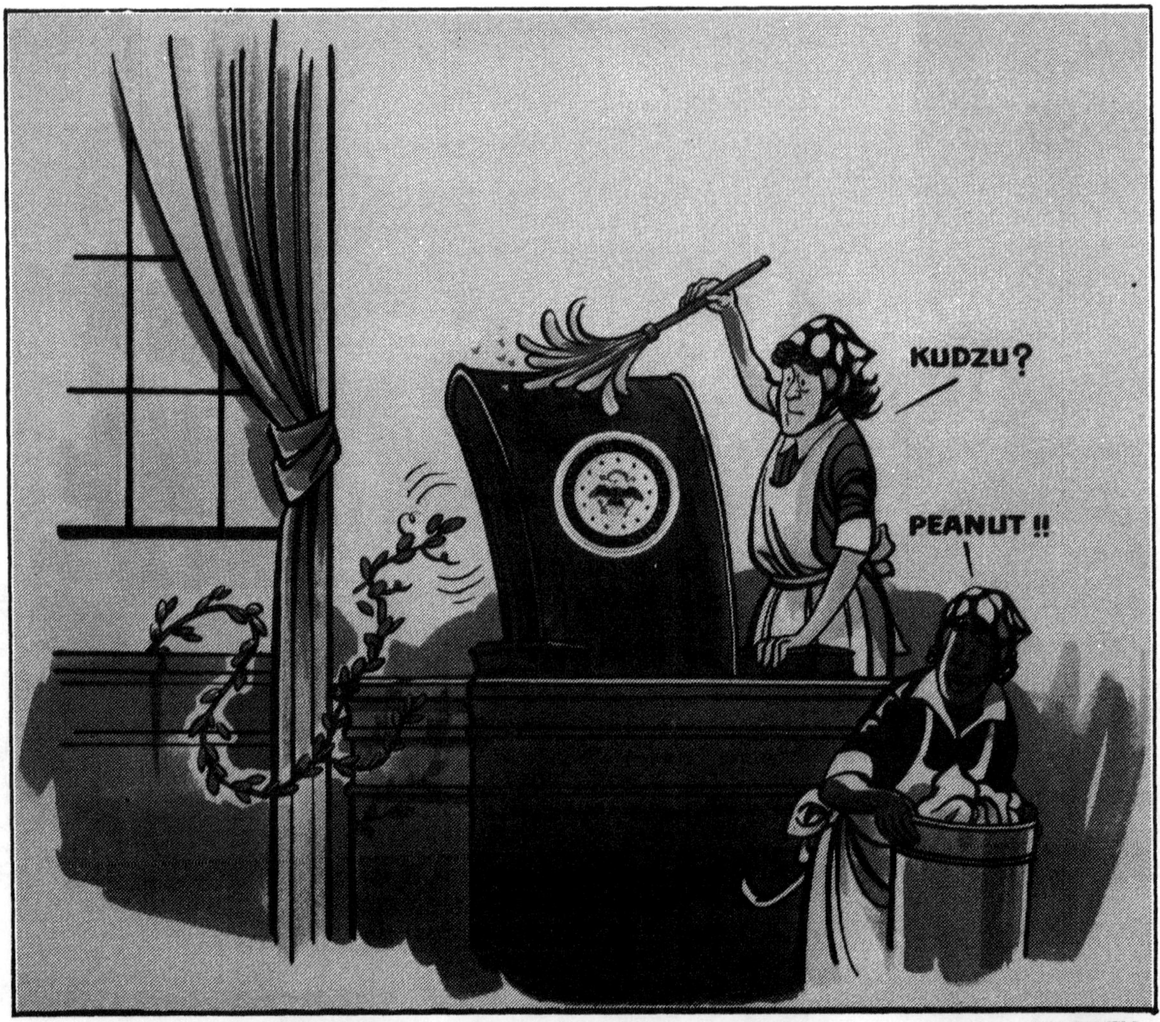
KUDZU?
PEANUT !!

BILL DANIELS
Courtesy WSB-TV

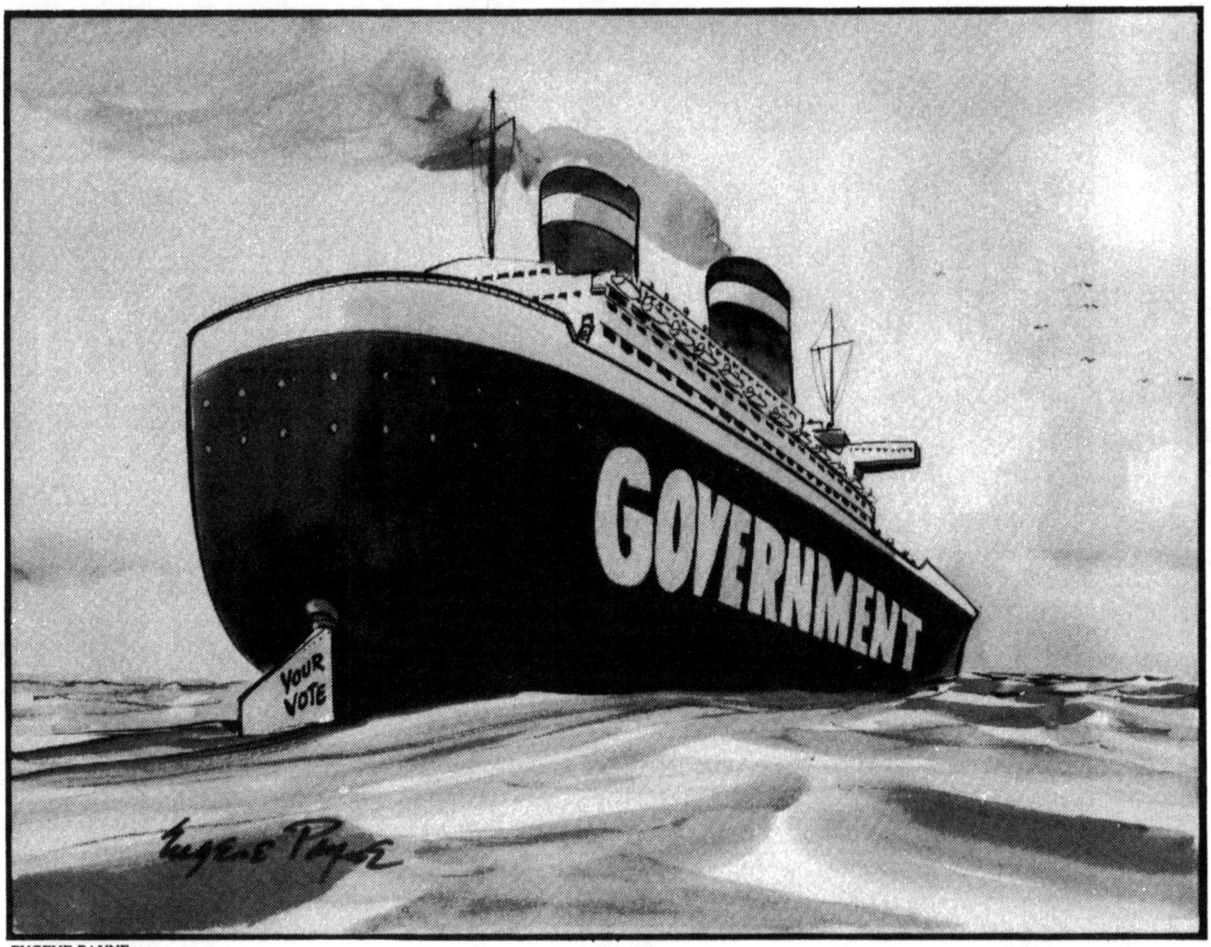
GOVERNMENT
YOUR VOTE
EUGENE PAYNE

EUGENE PAYNE
Courtesy WSOC-TV, Charlotte

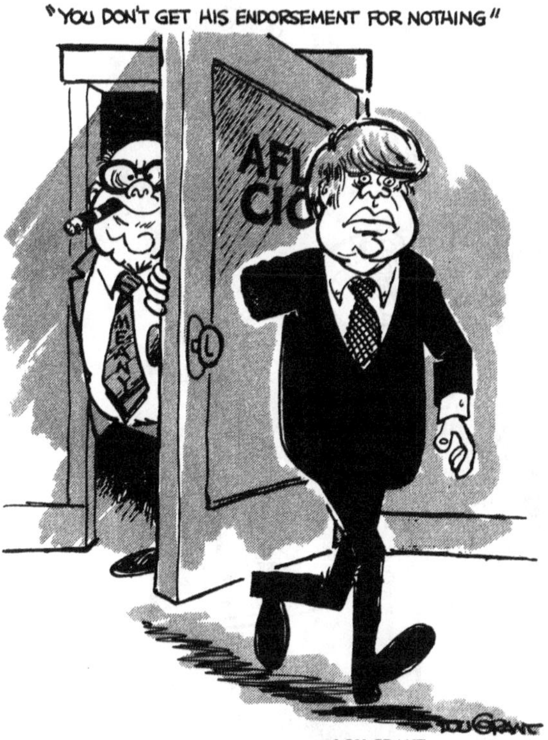
"YOU DON'T GET HIS ENDORSEMENT FOR NOTHING"
AFL CIO
MEANY
LOU GRANT

LOU GRANT
Oakland Tribune
©Los Angeles Times Syndicate

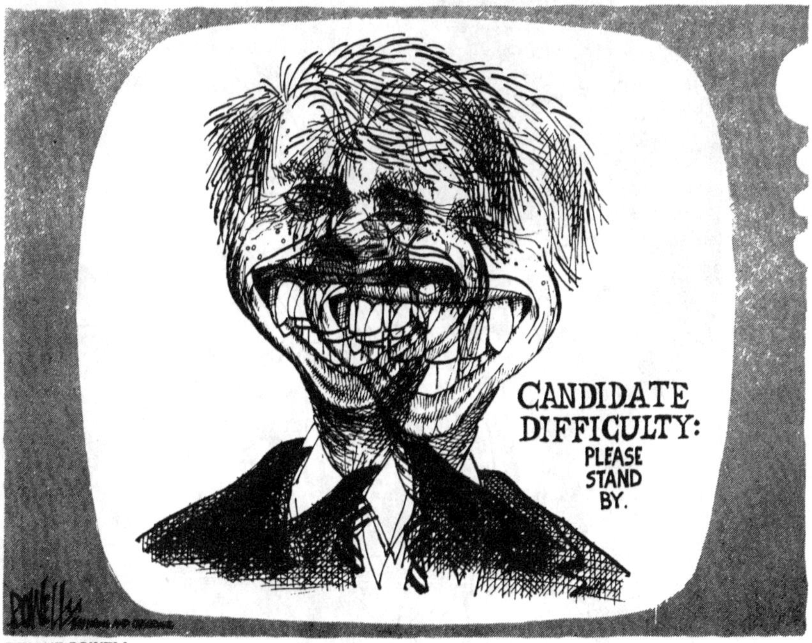
CANDIDATE
DIFFICULTY:
PLEASE
STAND
BY.
POWELL

DWANE POWELL
Courtesy News and Observer

PAT MCCARTHY
Courtesy Amarillo Globe-News

JERRY ROBINSON
©Chicago Tribune-N.Y. News Syndicate

CALVIN GRONDAHL
Courtesy Deseret News

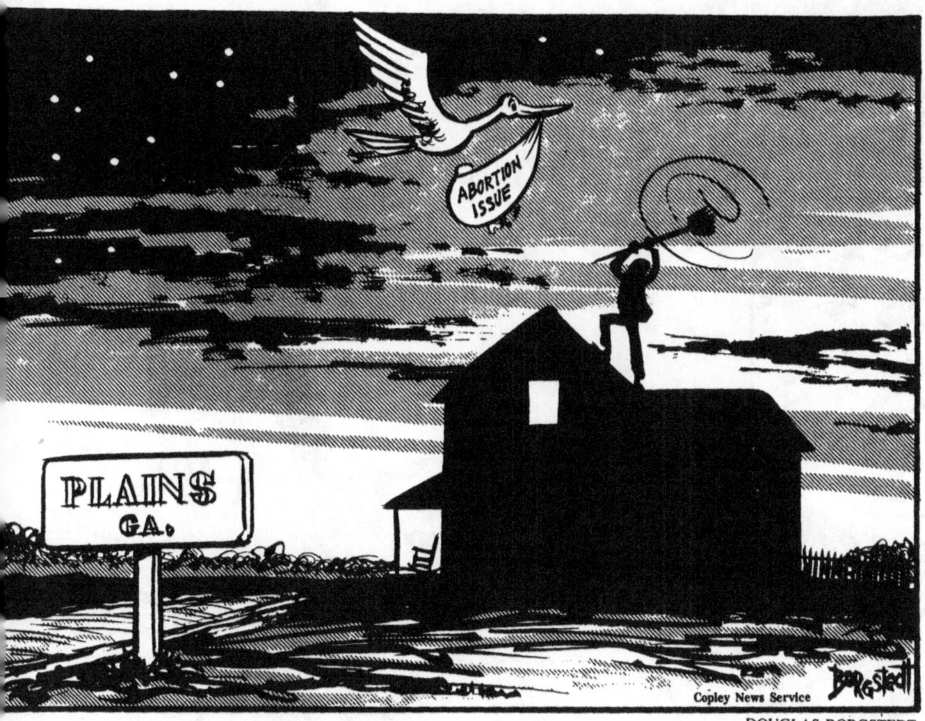
ABORTION ISSUE
PLAINS GA.
Copley News Service
BORGSTEDT

DOUGLAS BORGSTEDT
©Copley News Service

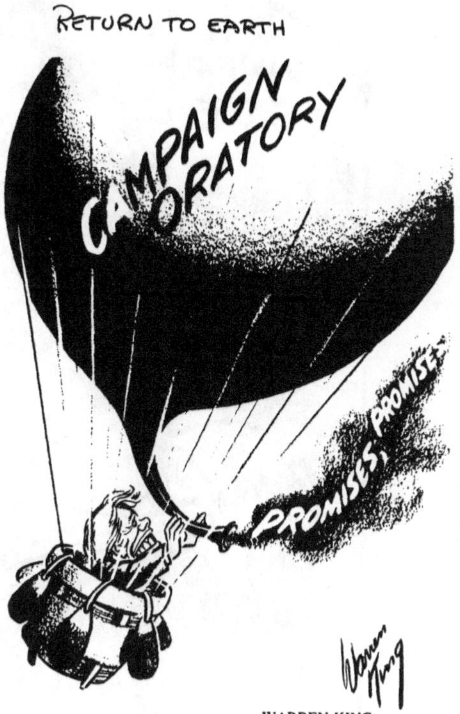
RETURN TO EARTH
CAMPAIGN ORATORY
PROMISES, PROMISES

WARREN KING
Courtesy N.Y. Daily News

HUGH HAYNIE
Louisville Courier-Journal
©Los Angeles Times Syndicate

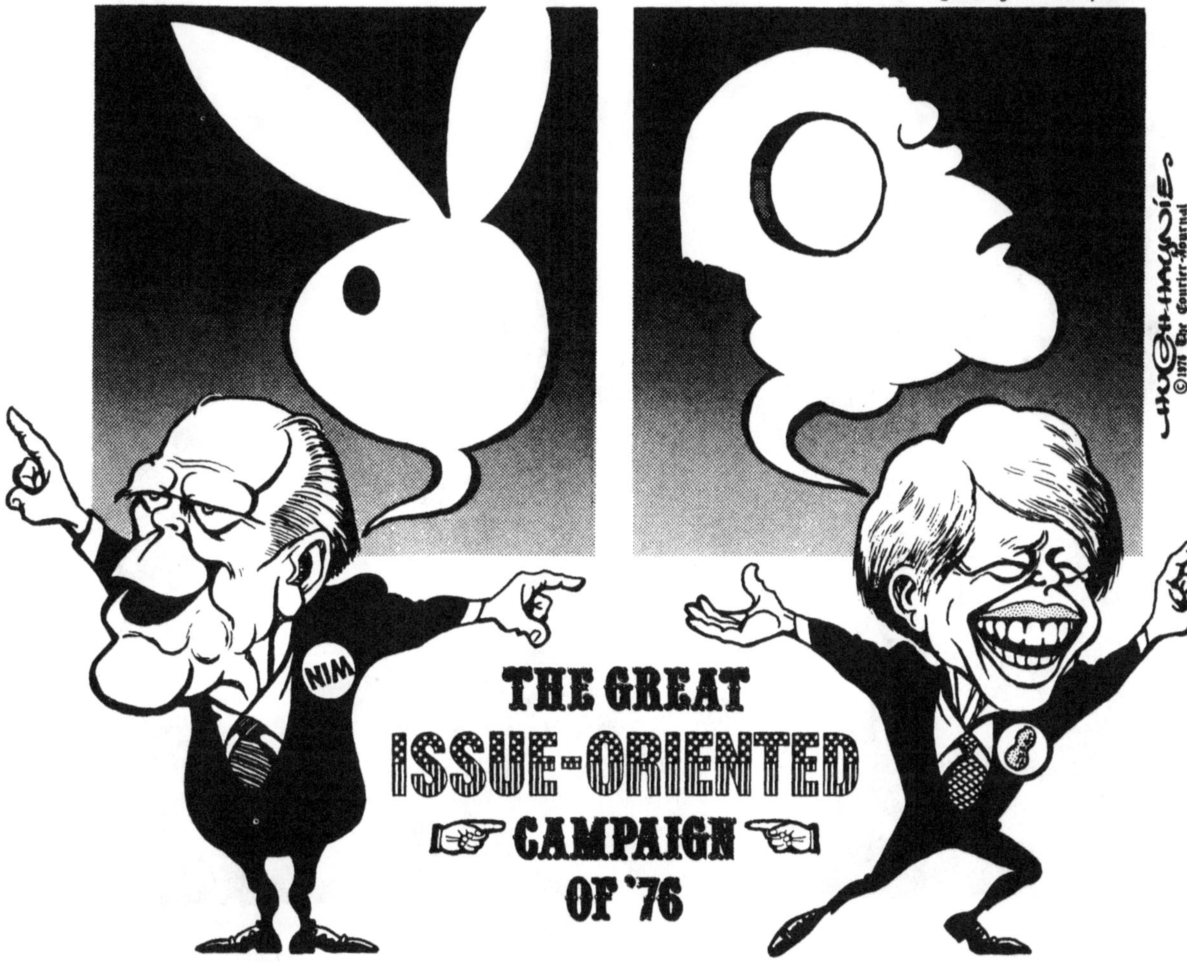
NIM
THE GREAT
ISSUE-ORIENTED
CAMPAIGN
OF '76
HUGH HAYNIE
©1976 The Courier-Journal

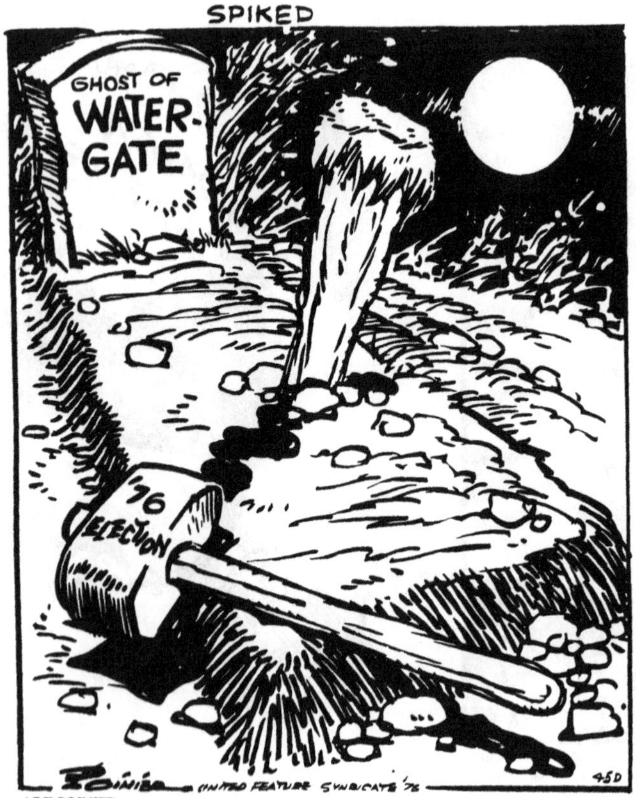
SPIKED
GHOST OF WATER-GATE
'76 ELECTION
UNITED FEATURE SYNDICATE '76

ART POINIER
© United Feature Syndicate

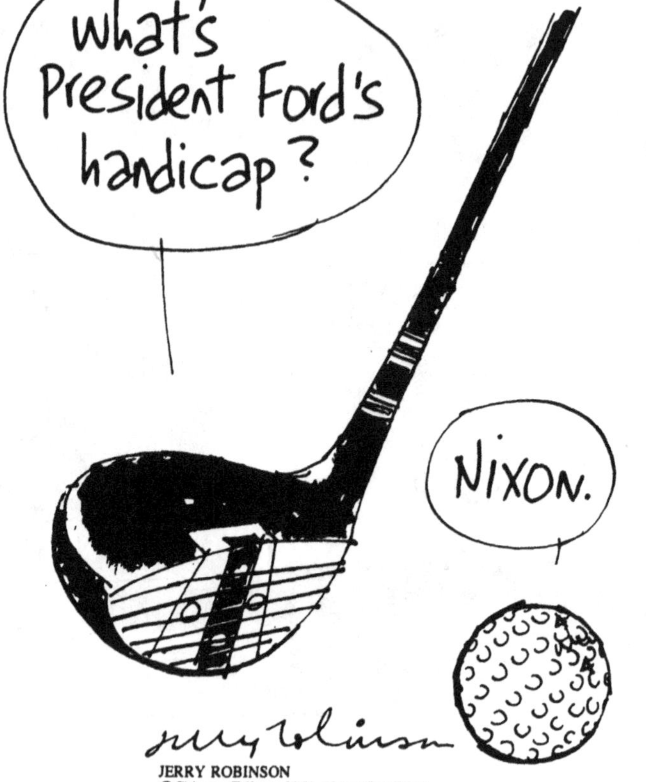
what's President Ford's handicap?
NIXON.

JERRY ROBINSON
©Chicago Tribune-N.Y. News Syndicate

S. C. RAWLS
Courtesy Palm Beach Post

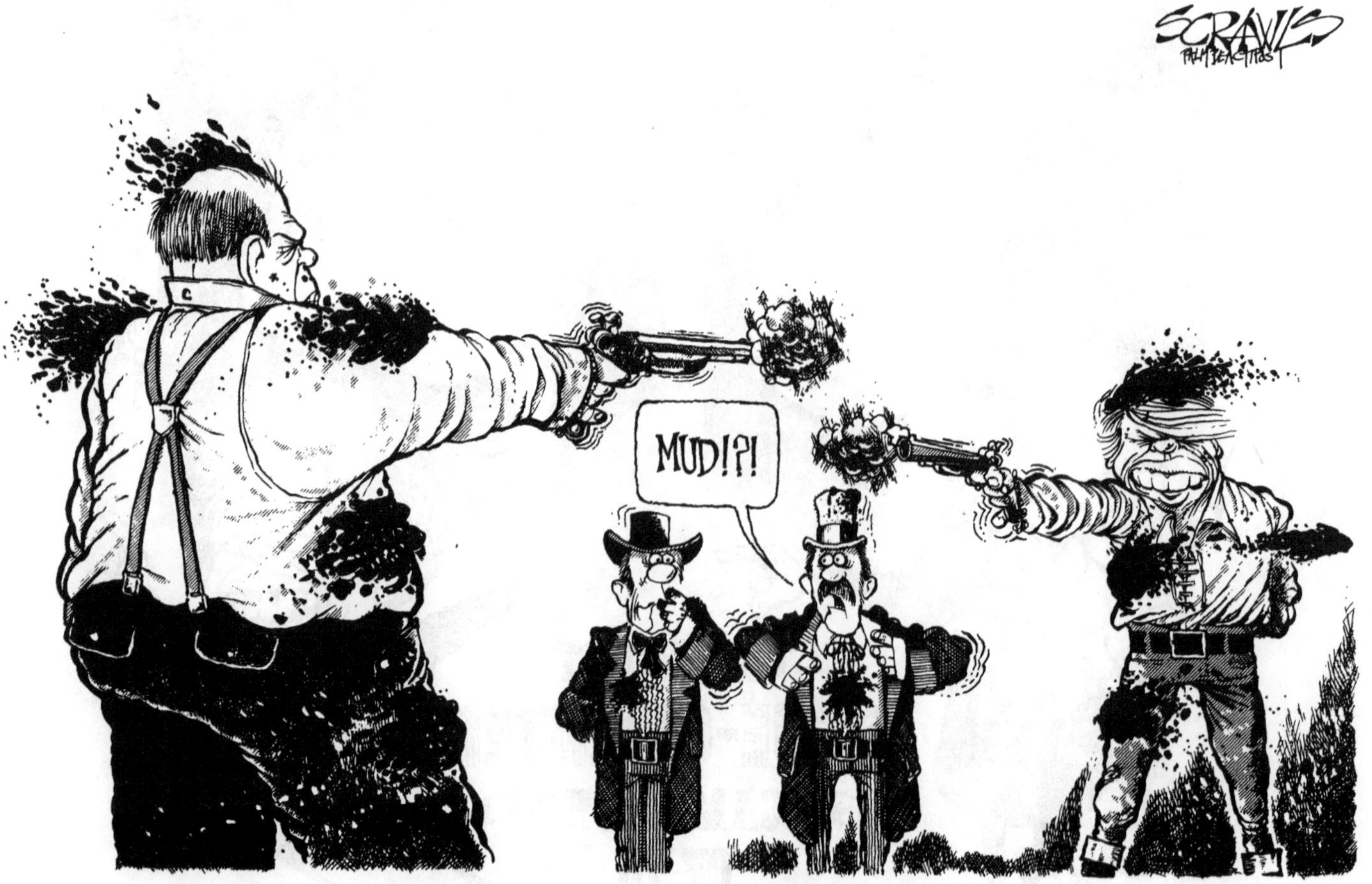
MUD!?!

CLYDE PETERSON
Courtesy Houston Chronicle

"OUR FIRST ORDER OF BUSINESS WILL BE TO TEACH IT WHO'S BOSS."

ART WOOD
Courtesy U. S. Independent Telephone Assn.

JON KENNEDY
Courtesy Arkansas Democrat

'May I cut in?'

DANNY AGUILA
Courtesy BanClub Digest

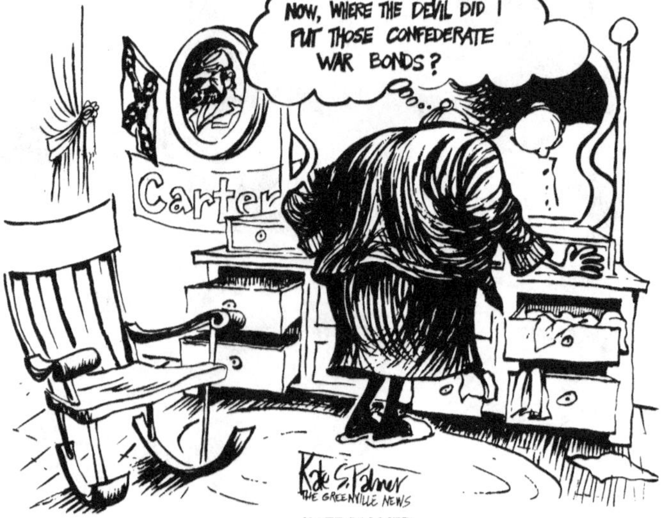
NOW, WHERE THE DEVIL DID I PUT THOSE CONFEDERATE WAR BONDS?
Carter
Kate S. Palmer
THE GREENVILLE NEWS
KATE PALMER
Courtesy Greenville (S.C.) News

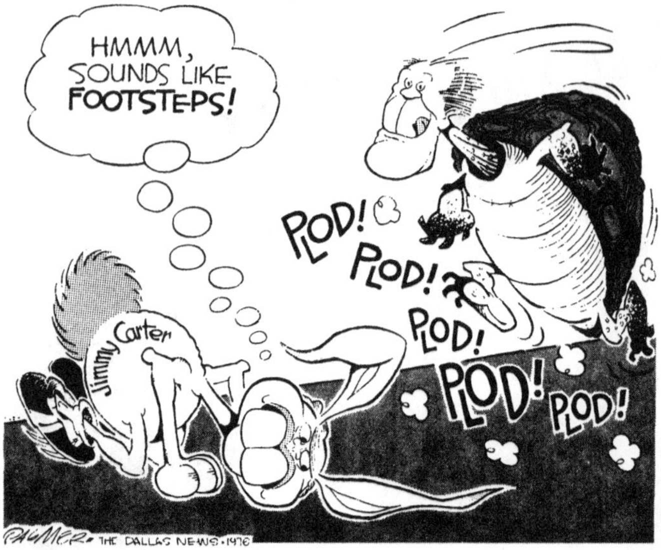
HMMM, SOUNDS LIKE FOOTSTEPS!
Jimmy Carter
PLOD! PLOD! PLOD! PLOD! PLOD!
PALMER • THE DALLAS NEWS • 1976
JIM PALMER
Courtesy Dallas News

BILL GARNER
Courtesy The Commercial Appeal

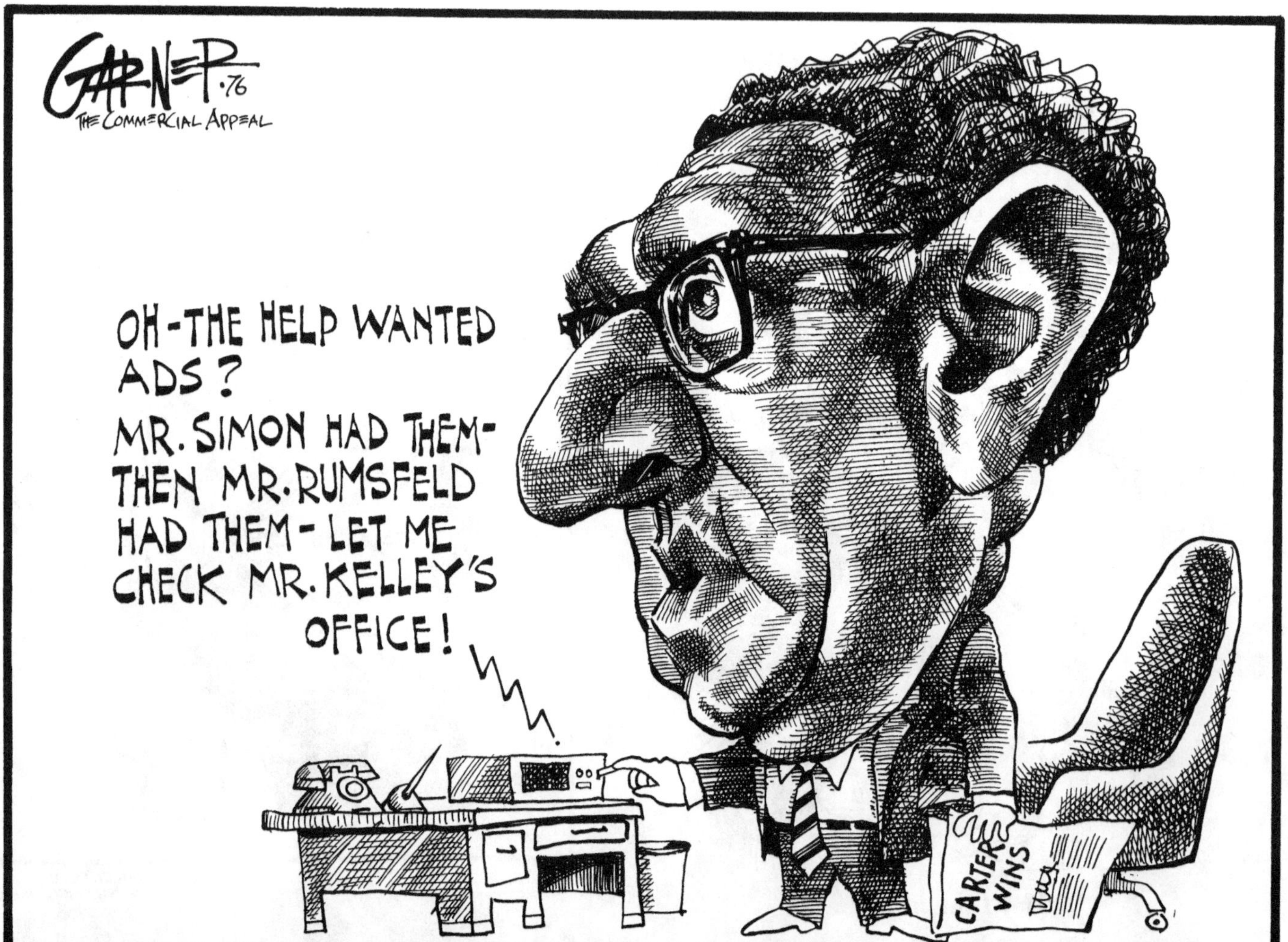
GARNER •76
THE COMMERCIAL APPEAL
OH-THE HELP WANTED ADS? MR. SIMON HAD THEM-THEN MR. RUMSFELD HAD THEM-LET ME CHECK MR. KELLEY'S OFFICE!
CARTER WINS

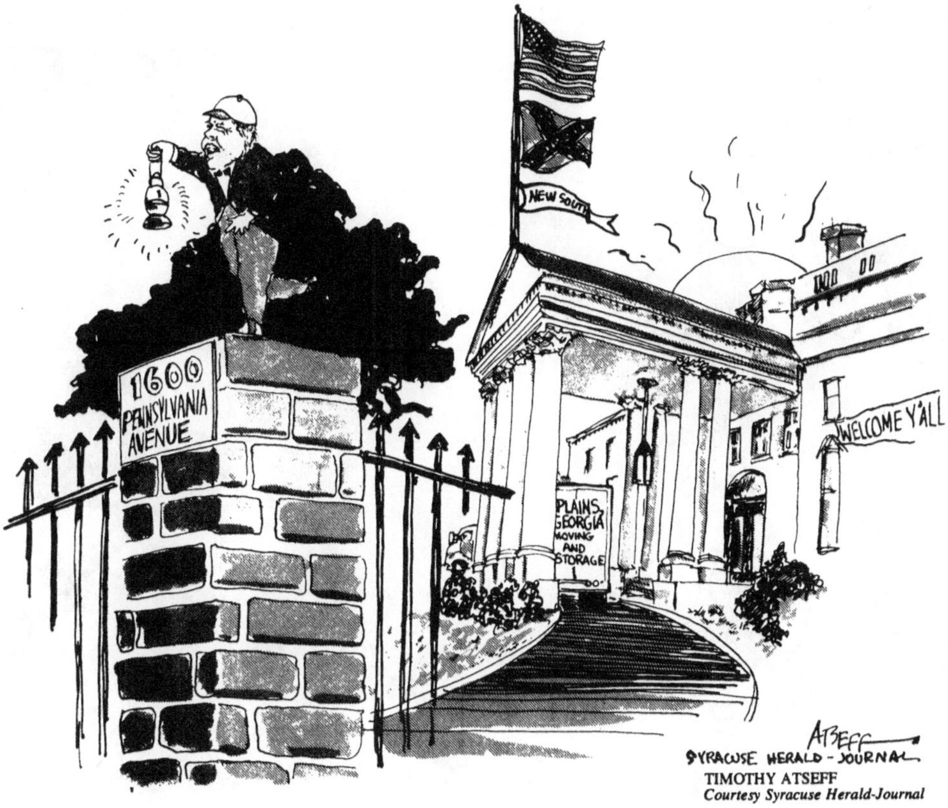
1600
PENNSYLVANIA
AVENUE
NEW SOUTH
WELCOME Y'ALL
PLAINS, GEORGIA MOVING AND STORAGE
ATSEFF
SYRACUSE HERALD-JOURNAL

TIMOTHY ATSEFF
Courtesy Syracuse Herald-Journal

MIKE PETERS
Courtesy Dayton Daily News

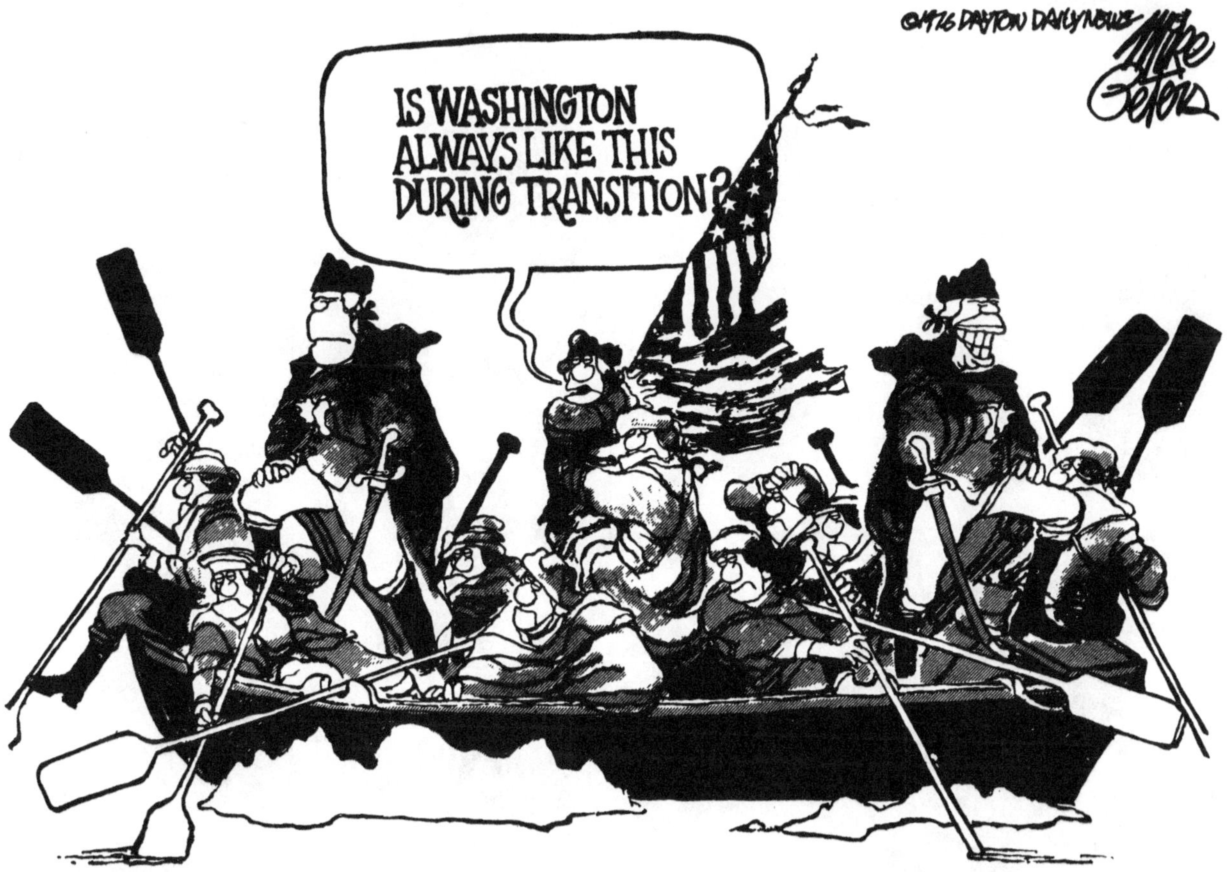
©1976 DAYTON DAILY NEWS
MIKE PETERS
IS WASHINGTON ALWAYS LIKE THIS DURING TRANSITION?

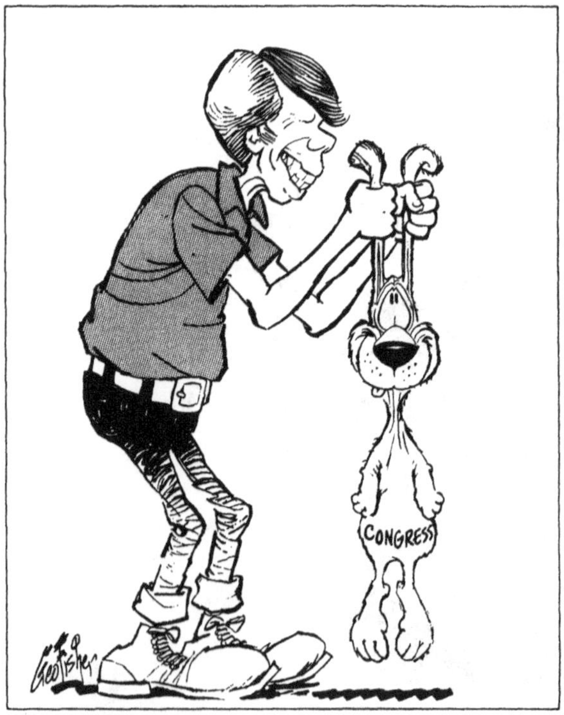
CONGRESS

GEORGE FISHER
Courtesy N. Little Rock Times

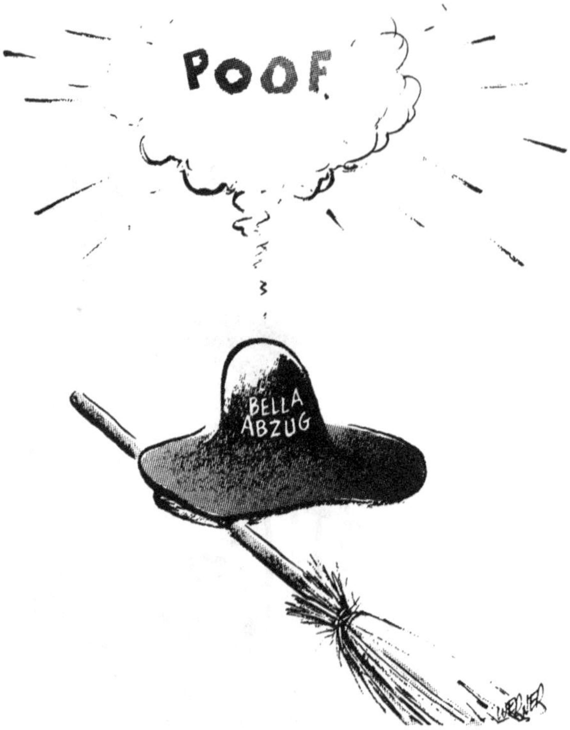
POOF
BELLA ABZUG

CHARLES WERNER
Courtesy Indianapolis Star

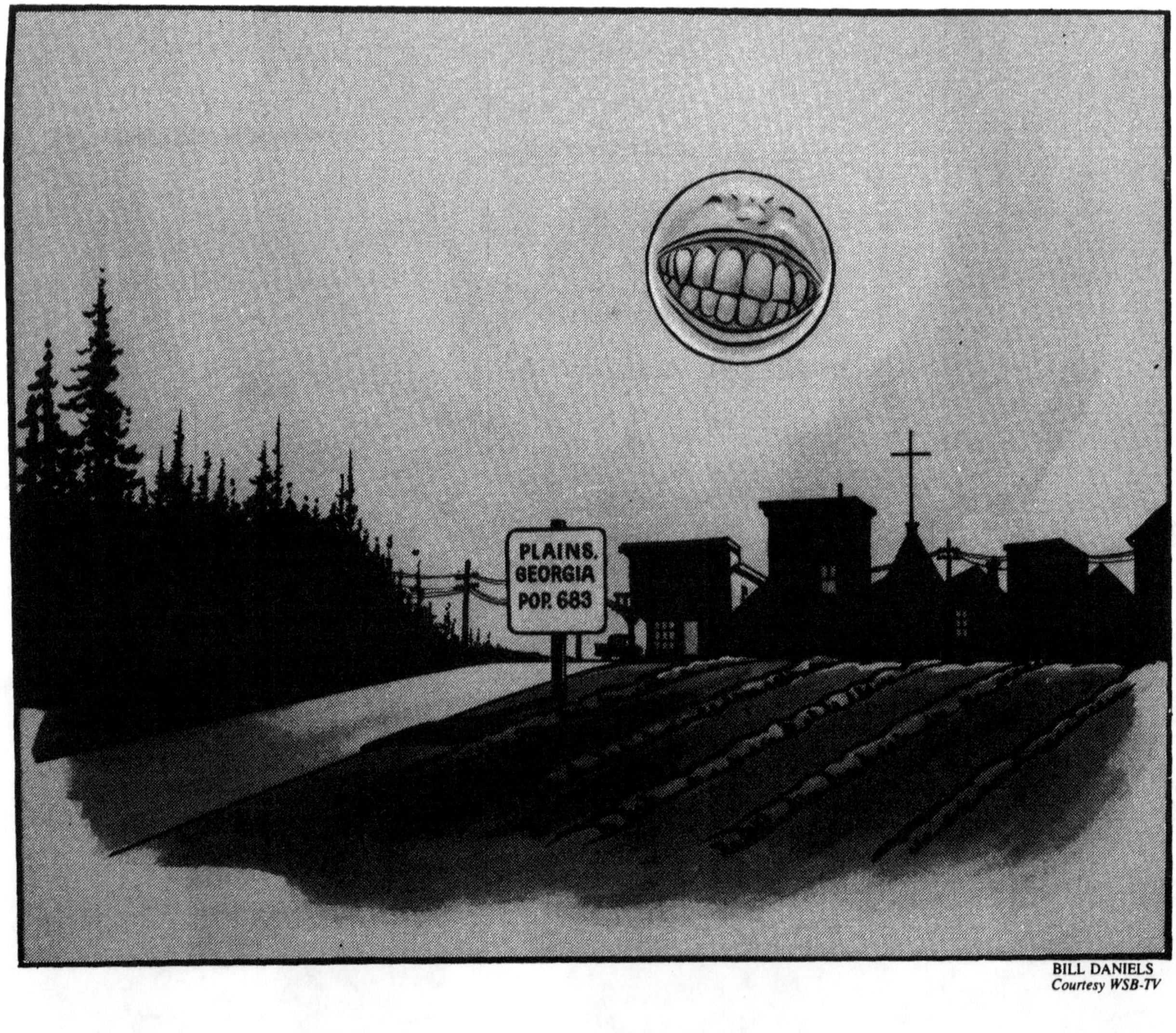
PLAINS, GEORGIA POP. 683

BILL DANIELS
Courtesy WSB-TV

Ford Administration and Campaign

Reversing his early position that he had no intention of becoming a candidate in the 1976 presidential campaign, Gerald Ford took on Ronald Reagan in the snows of New Hampshire in the GOP's opening primary and won a narrow victory. He widened the margin in Florida, where Reagan's hopes were high, and after nine primaries seemed well on his way to an easy nomination.

However, stunning victories by Reagan in Texas, Alabama, Georgia, and Indiana slowed Ford's momentum, and shortly before convention time the race seemed virtually deadlocked. A hundred or so uncommitted delegates, believed to be leaning toward Ford, held the key. In a desperate ploy to win the uncommitted, the Reagan forces sponsored a proposal that would have forced Ford to name his vice-presidential choice before the presidential balloting. The proposal was defeated, thus ending Reagan's hopes for the nomination.

Ford named Senator Robert Dole as his running mate. While the president remained in the White House much of the time, Dole criss-

JEFF MACNELLY
Richmond News Leader
©Chicago Tribune—New York News Syndicate

'THAT MUST BE PRESIDENT FORD AGAIN .... MERLE'S AN UNCOMMITTED DELEGATE, Y'KNOW...'

FORD ADMINISTRATION AND CAMPAIGN

crossed the country on the attack, but he failed to cut into Jimmy Carter's strength in the South.

Although going down in defeat, Ford could point to several major achievements. He succeeded in lowering the rate of inflation from 12 per cent in 1974 to about 4.8 per cent in 1976. His policies helped reduce tension in the perilous Middle East. But, perhaps most importantly, he gave the country stable leadership, provided middle-of-the-road direction, and restored confidence in the presidency.

KEN ALEXANDER
Courtesy San Francisco Examiner

"Hello, Spiro?... Dick... Any calls from Kansas City yet?... me neither"

DAVID SIMPSON
Courtesy Tulsa Tribune

CHESTER COMMODORE
Courtesy Chicago Daily Defender

RUNNING MATE

BOB TAYLOR
Courtesy Dallas Times Herald

Phantom of the Opera

ERIC SMITH
Courtesy Capital-Gazette (Md.) Newspapers

AND THE RACE IS ON...

V. ROSCHKOV
Courtesy Windsor Star

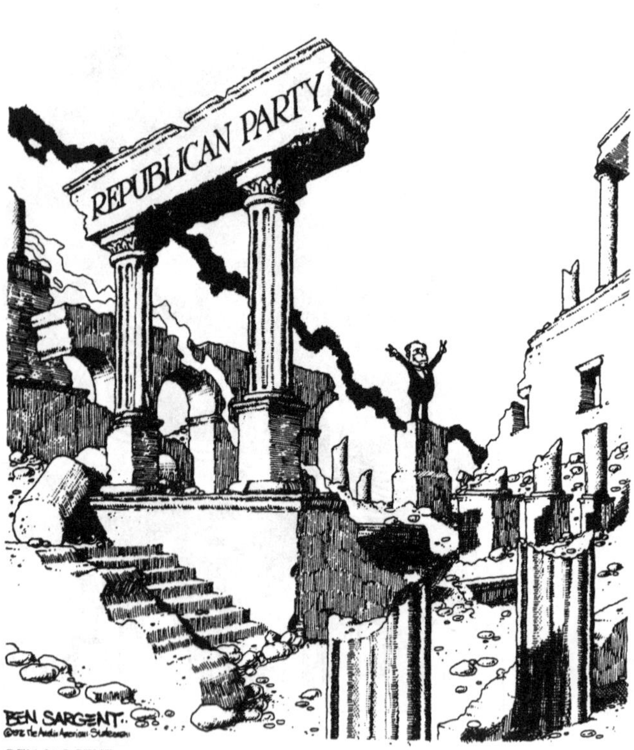
REPUBLICAN PARTY
BEN SARGENT

BEN SARGENT
Courtesy Austin American

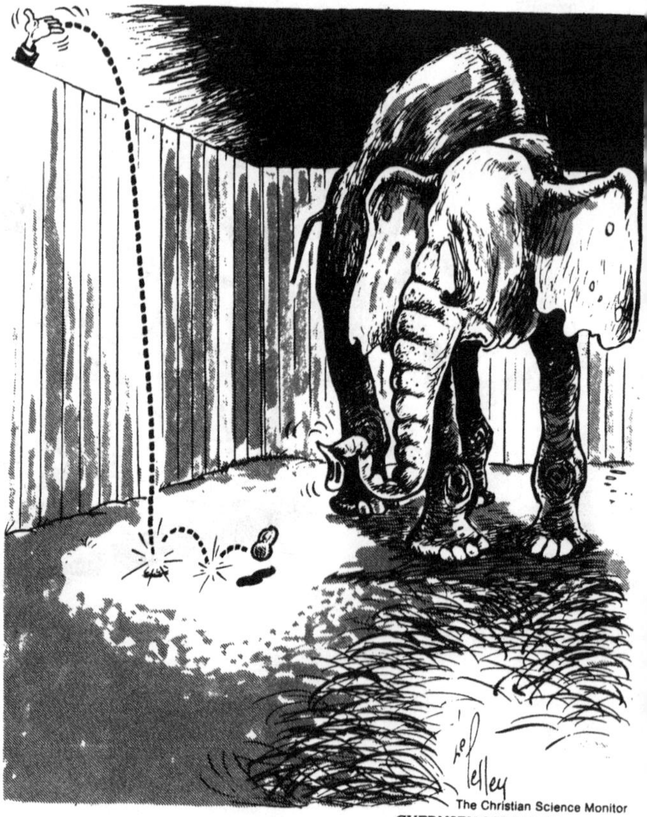
The Christian Science Monitor

GUERNSEY LEPELLEY
Courtesy Christian Science Monitor

GENE BASSET
Courtesy Scripps-Howard Newspapers

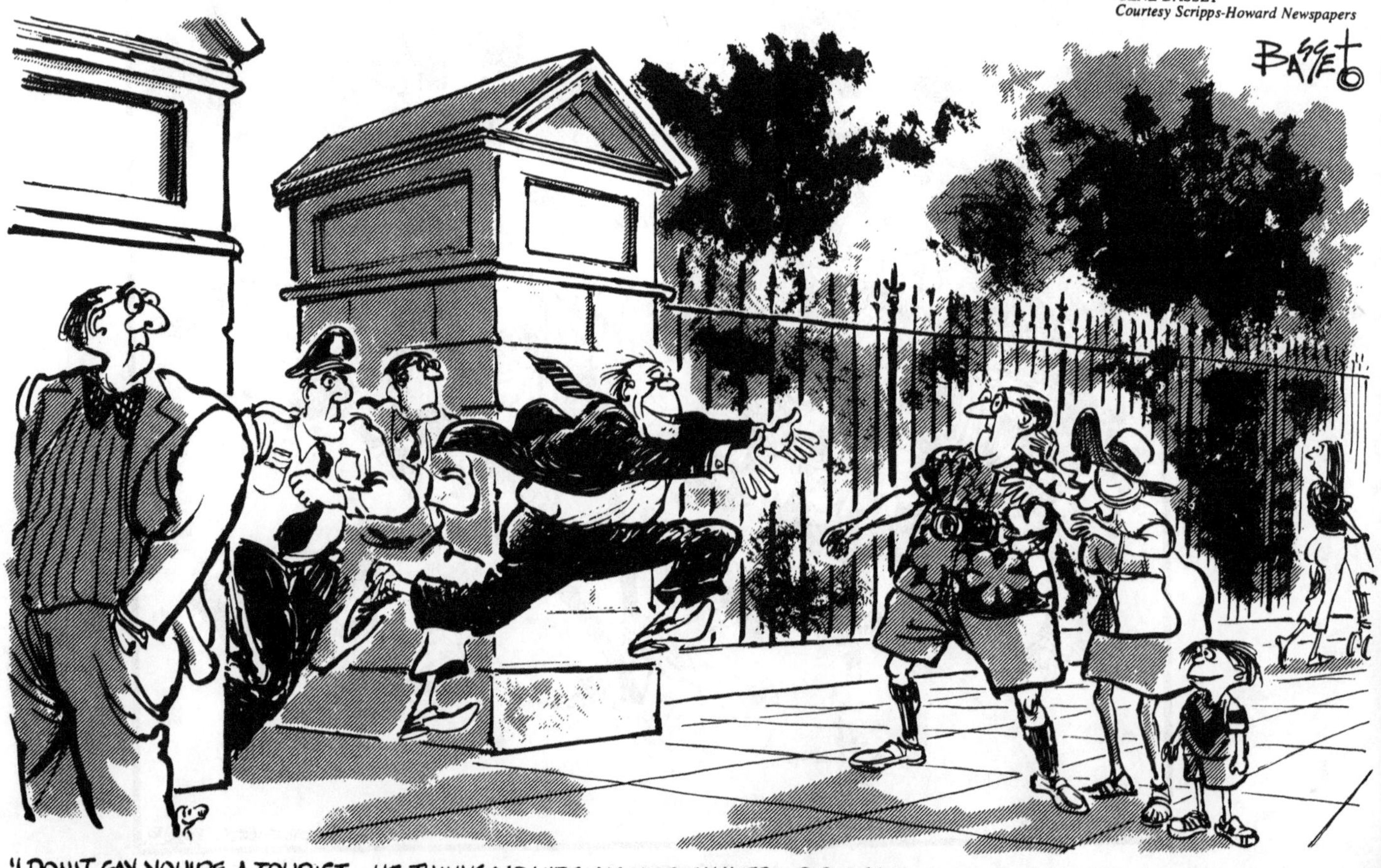
BASSETT

"DON'T SAY YOU'RE A TOURIST... HE THINKS YOU'RE AN UNCOMMITTED DELEGATE AND HE'LL INVITE US TO LUNCH"

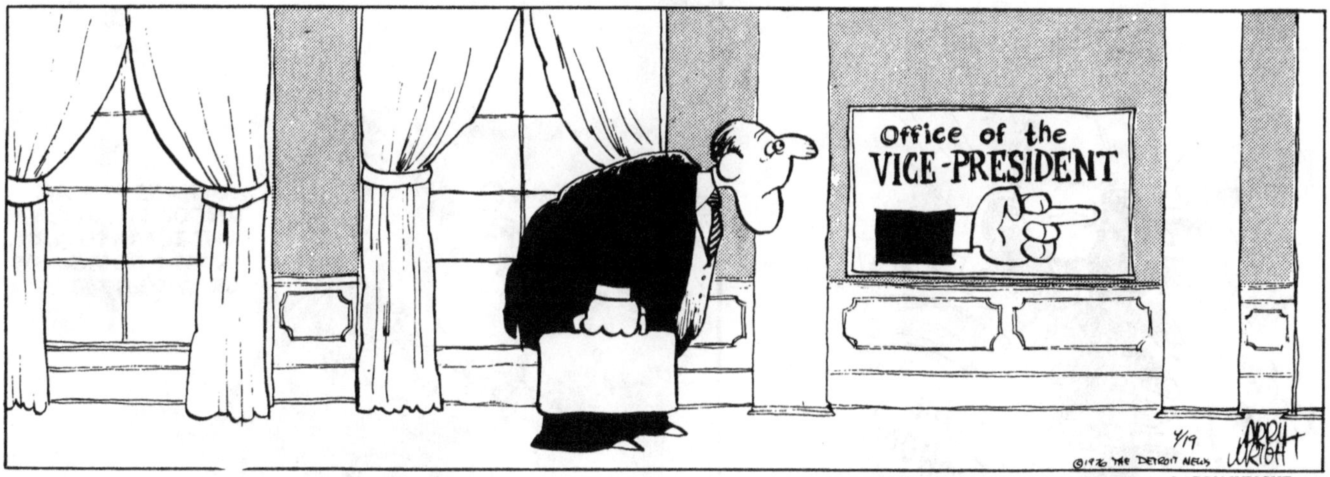
Office of the
VICE-PRESIDENT
4/19
©1976 The Detroit News
LARRY WRIGHT

LARRY WRIGHT
Courtesy Detroit News

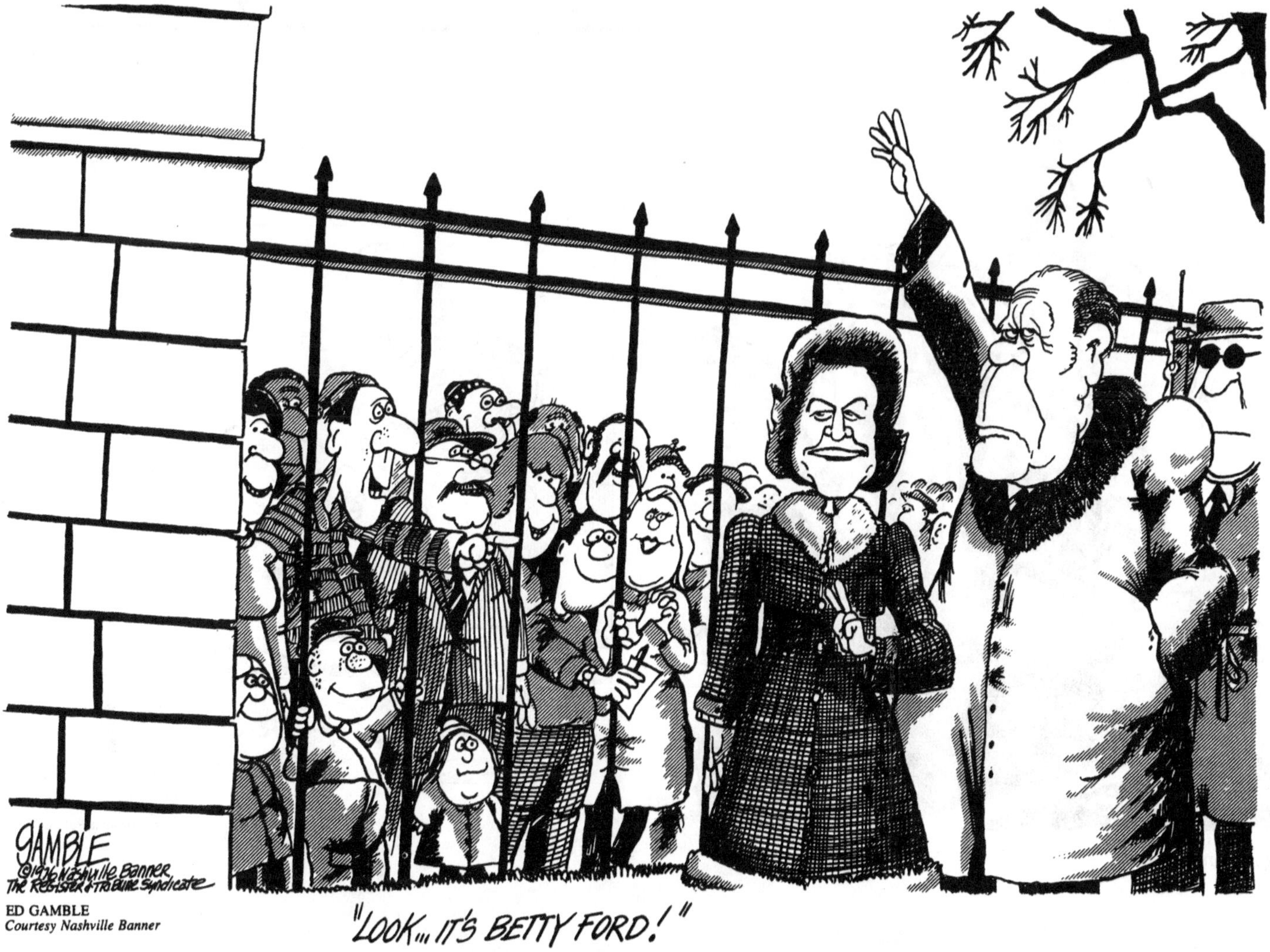
GAMBLE
©1976 Nashville Banner
The Register & Tribune Syndicate

ED GAMBLE
Courtesy Nashville Banner

"LOOK... IT'S BETTY FORD!"

FRANK SPANGLER
Courtesy Montgomery (Ala.) Advertiser

BILL DANIELS
Courtesy WSB-TV

DAVID SIMPSON
Courtesy Tulsa Tribune

JIM LANGE
The Daily Oklahoman
©The Oklahoma Publishing Co.

SCOTT LONG
Courtesy Minneapolis Tribune

LOU GRANT
Oakland Tribune
©Los Angeles Times Syndica

MIKE PETERS
Courtesy Dayton Daily News

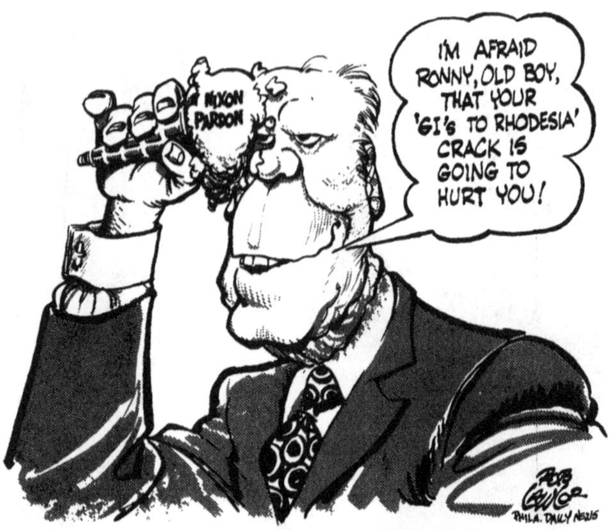
NIXON PARDON
I'M AFRAID RONNY, OLD BOY, THAT YOUR 'GI'S TO RHODESIA' CRACK IS GOING TO HURT YOU!

ROB LAWLOR
Courtesy Philadelphia Daily News

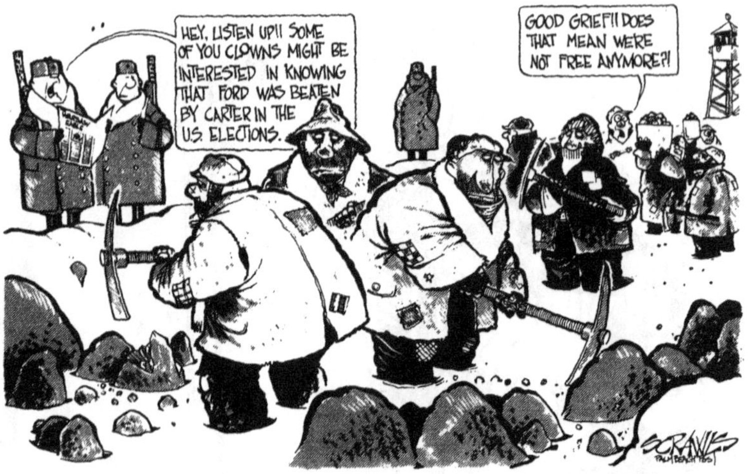
HEY, LISTEN UP!! SOME OF YOU CLOWNS MIGHT BE INTERESTED IN KNOWING THAT FORD WAS BEATEN BY CARTER IN THE U.S. ELECTIONS.
GOOD GRIEF!! DOES THAT MEAN WE'RE NOT FREE ANYMORE?!

S. C. RAWLS
Courtesy Palm Beach Post

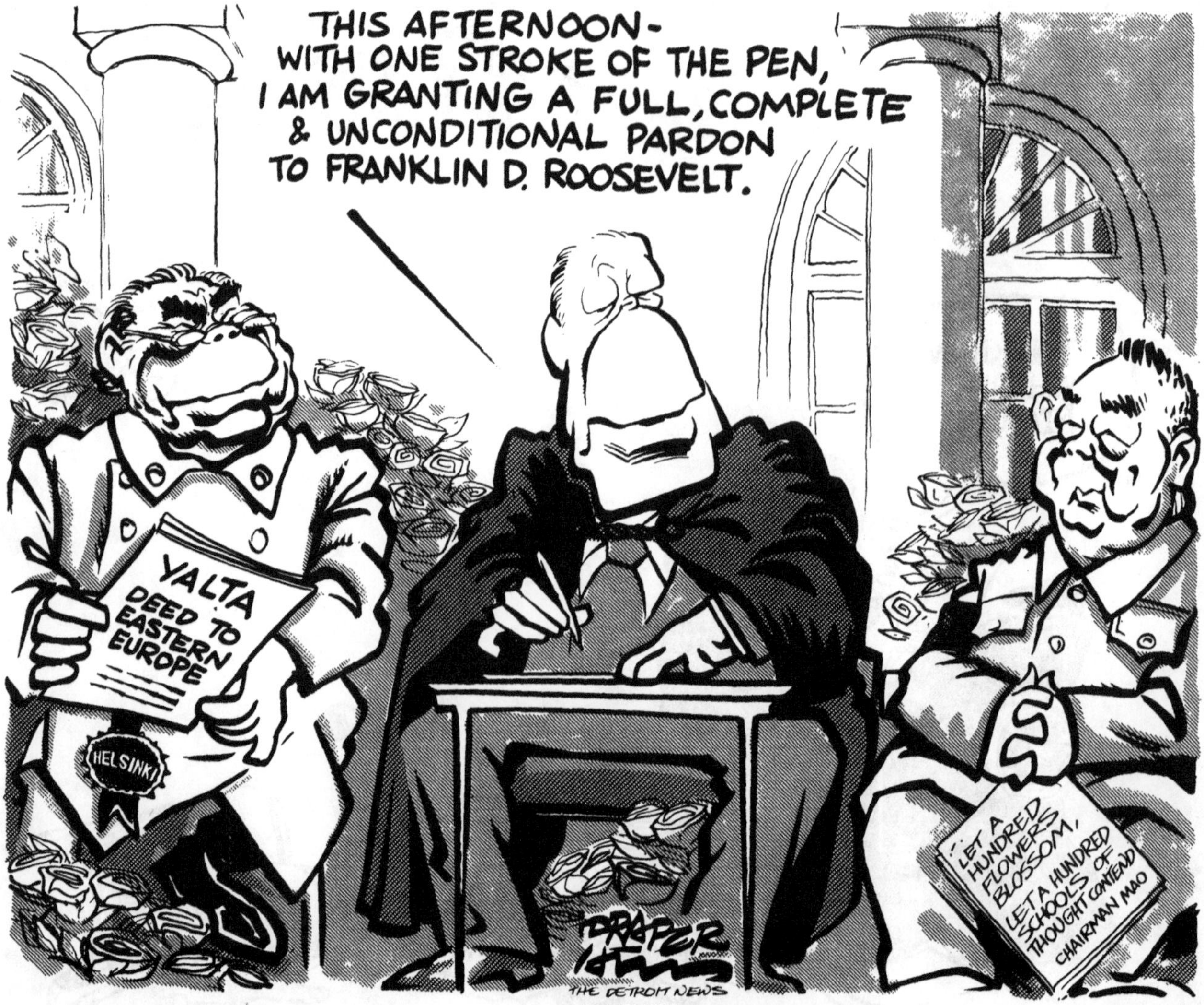
THIS AFTERNOON- WITH ONE STROKE OF THE PEN, I AM GRANTING A FULL, COMPLETE & UNCONDITIONAL PARDON TO FRANKLIN D. ROOSEVELT.
YALTA DEED TO EASTERN EUROPE
HELSINKI
LET A HUNDRED FLOWERS BLOSSOM, LET A HUNDRED SCHOOLS OF THOUGHT CONTEND CHAIRMAN MAO
THE DETROIT NEWS

DRAPER HILL
Courtesy Detroit News

Reagan and the Primaries

Despite the overwhelming odds against successfully opposing an incumbent, Ronald Reagan waged an exciting campaign against Gerald Ford for the GOP presidential nomination—and missed the coveted prize by a whisker.

Following a heated campaign that saw Ford grab a quick lead and then lose four straight primaries to Reagan, the race narrowed down to a hundred uncommitted delegates shortly before the convention. Ford began making inroads among the uncommitted, and it appeared he might clinch the nomination before the convention convened. In an unprecedented and controversial move, Reagan announced on July 26 that Senator Richard Schweiker, a liberal Republican from Pennsylvania would be his running mate. It was a last-ditch strategy to woo liberal delegates from the Northeast.

The nomination was finally decided at the convention when the Reagan camp demanded a floor vote on a proposal that would have forced Ford also to name his running mate before the presidential balloting. The bid failed by a vote of 1,180 to 1,069 and ended Reagan's chances for victory.

Richard Nixon, secluded in San Clemente, was not invited to attend the convention.

DICK WALLMEYER
Long Beach Press-Telegram
©Register and Tribune Syndicate

JON KENNEDY
Courtesy Arkansas Democrat

Nearing high noon . . .

JERRY FEARING
Courtesy St. Paul Dispatch

'OLD SOLDIERS...'

BERT WHITMAN
Courtesy Phoenix Gazette

TOM CURTIS
Courtesy Milwaukee Sentinel

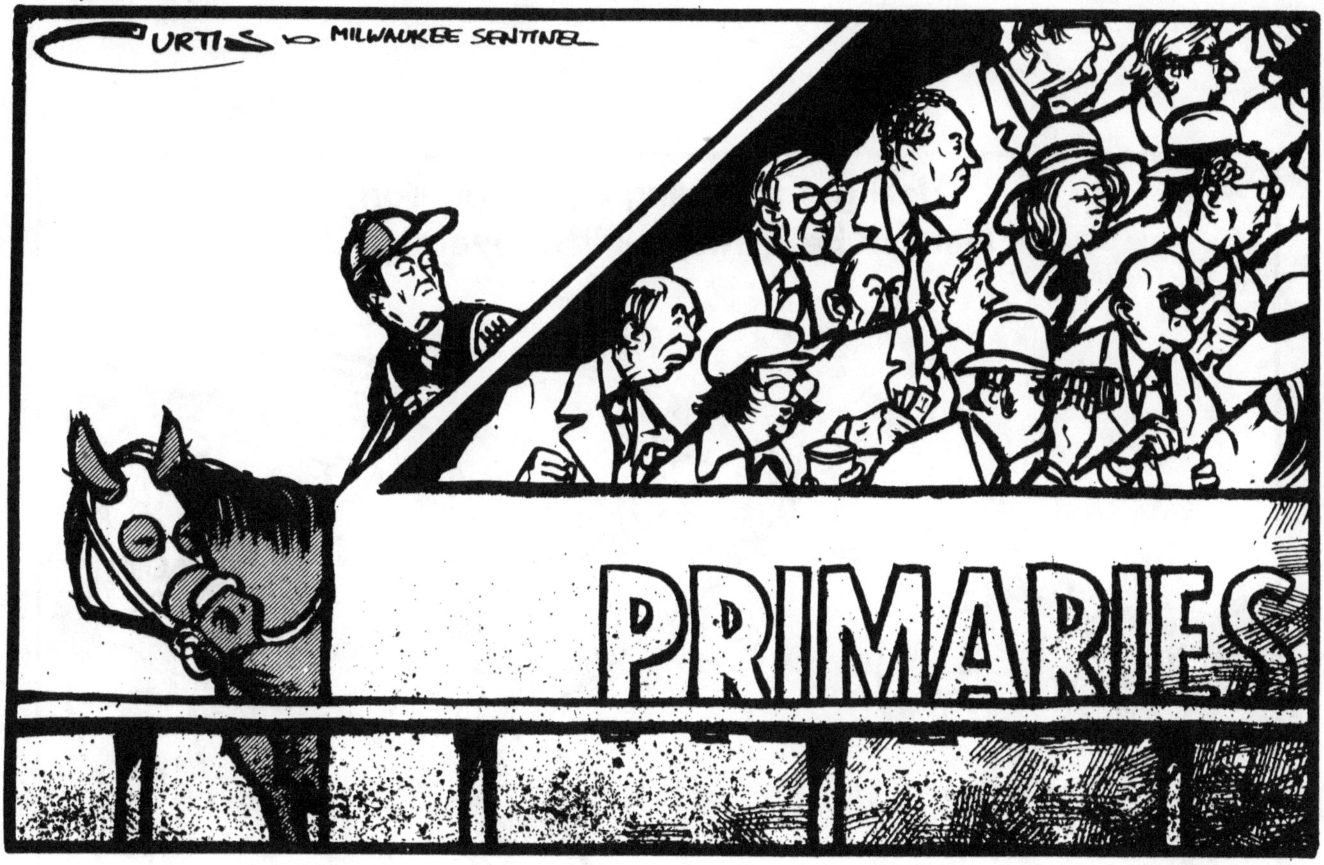
CURTIS © MILWAUKEE SENTINEL
PRIMARIES

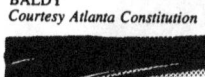

BALDY
Courtesy Atlanta Constitution

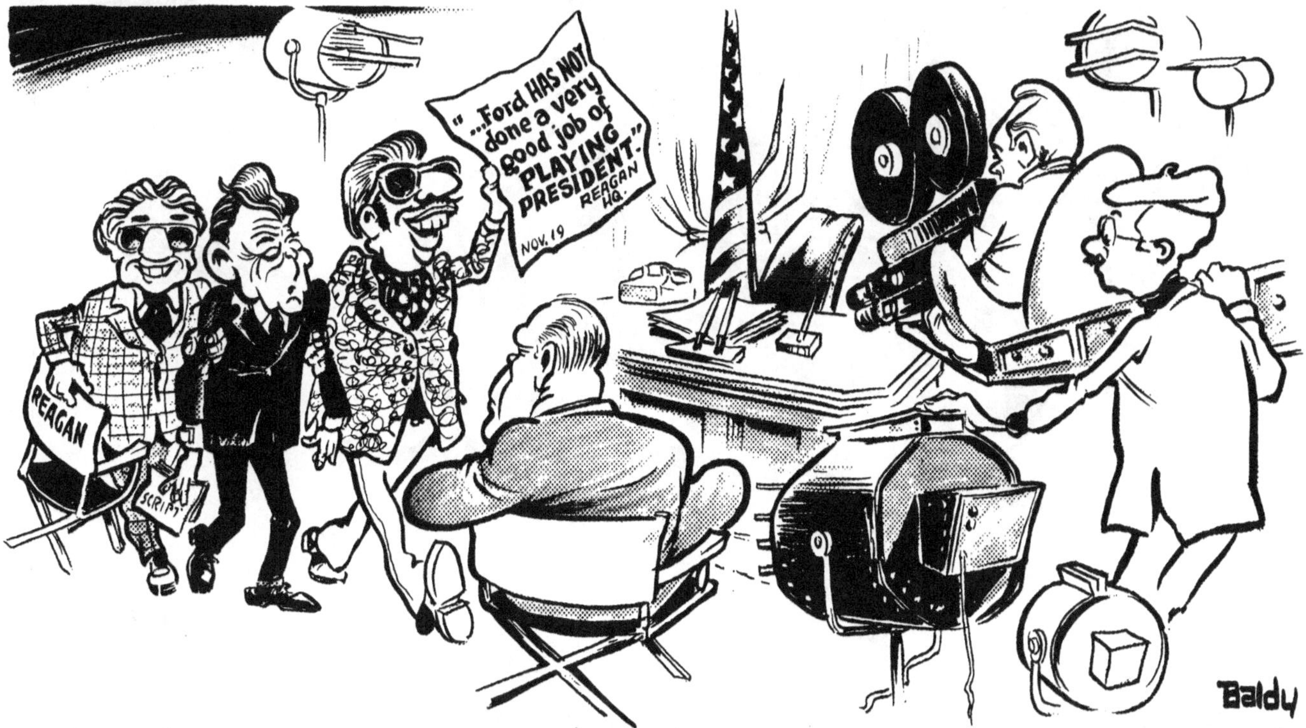
"...Ford HAS NOT done a very good job of PLAYING PRESIDENT." REAGAN HQ. NOV. 19
REAGAN
SCRIPT
Baldy

"...HERE'S JUST TH MAN FOR THE PART! SHOW 'EM YOUR ACTOR'S GUILD CARD, RONNIE, BABY!"

GEORGE FISHER
Courtesy N. Little Rock Times

BEN SARGENT
Courtesy Austin American

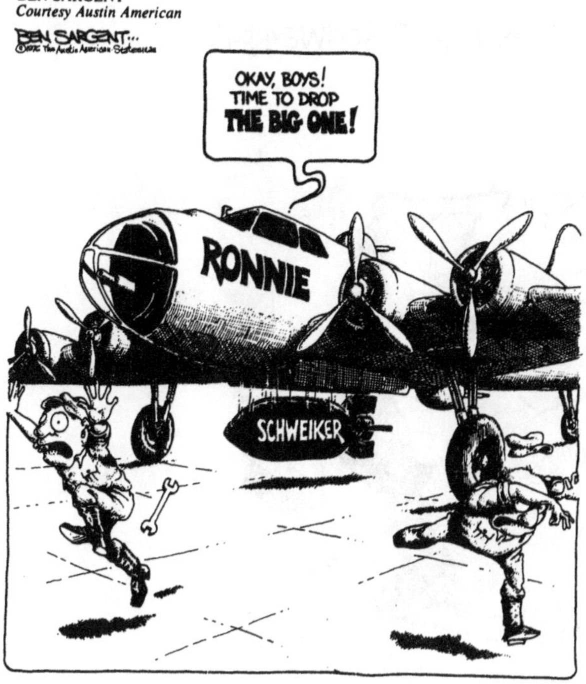
BEN SARGENT...
OKAY, BOYS! TIME TO DROP THE BIG ONE!
RONNIE
SCHWEIKER

BOB ALEXANDER
Courtesy Lawrence (Mass.) Eagle-Tribune

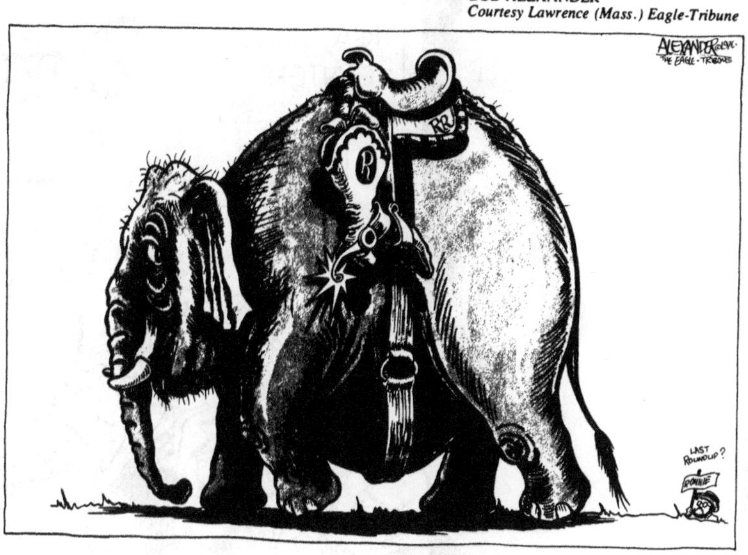
ALEXANDER
THE EAGLE-TRIBUNE
RR
R
LAST ROUNDUP?
RONNIE

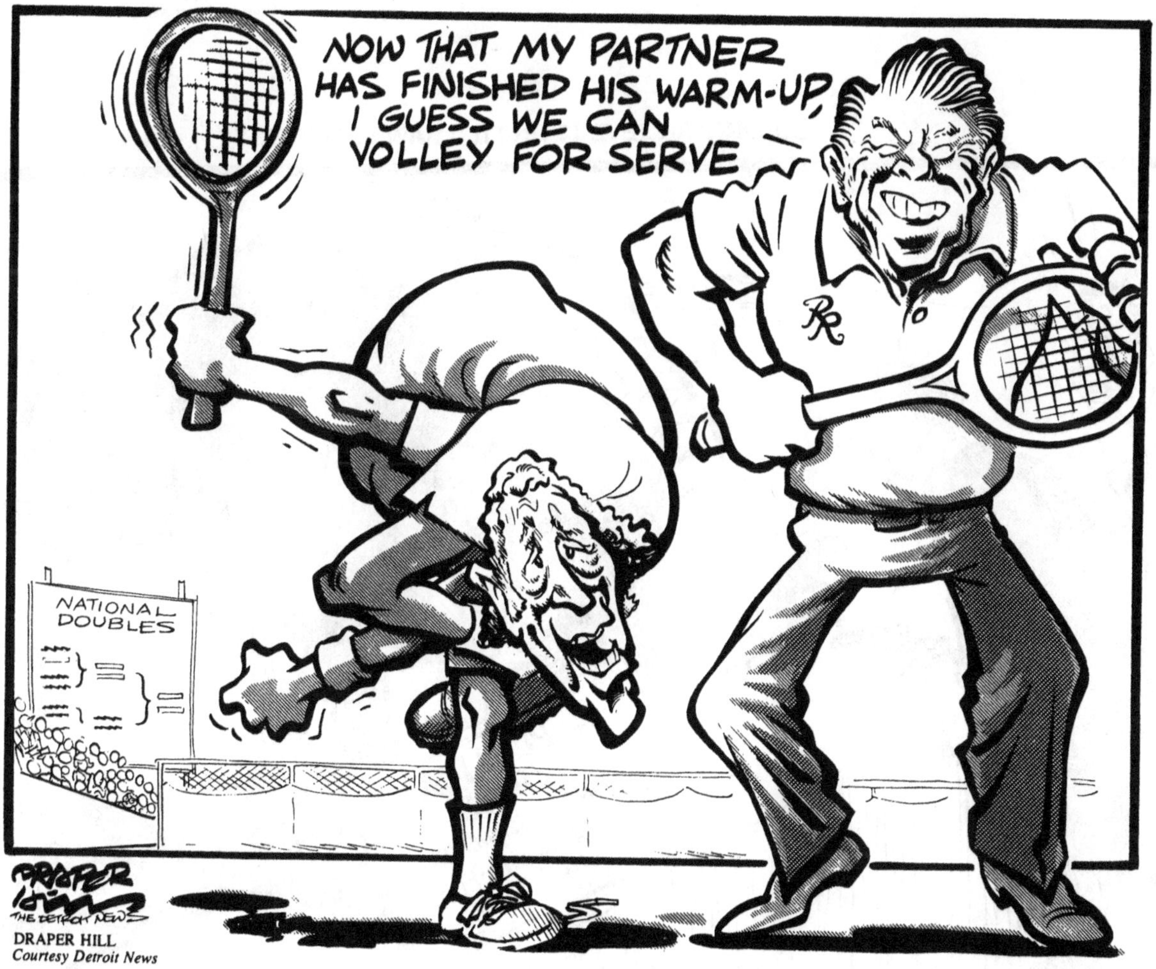
NOW THAT MY PARTNER HAS FINISHED HIS WARM-UP, I GUESS WE CAN VOLLEY FOR SERVE
RR
NATIONAL DOUBLES
DRAPER HILL
THE DETROIT NEWS

DRAPER HILL
Courtesy Detroit News

JIM PALMER
Courtesy Dallas News

KARL HUBENTHAL
Courtesy Los Angeles
Herald-Examiner

CHOMP . . . CHOMP . . . CHOMP

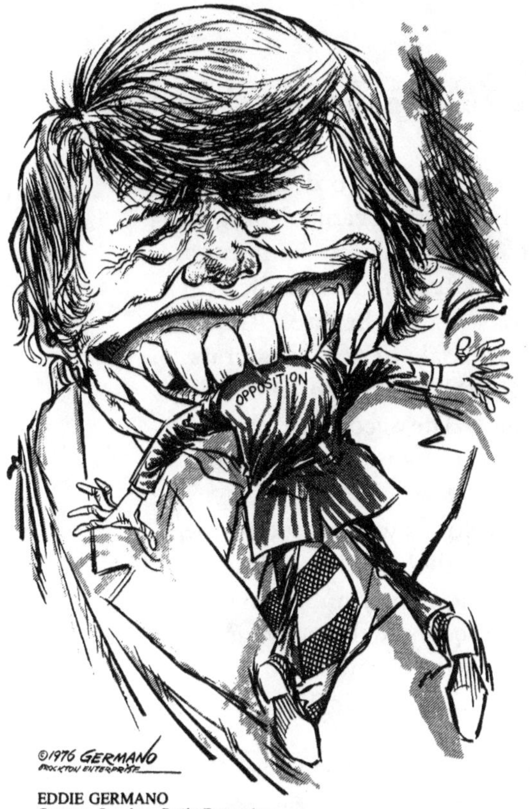
OPPOSITION
©1976 GERMANO

EDDIE GERMANO
Courtesy Brockton Daily Enterprise

BALDY
Courtesy Atlanta Constitution

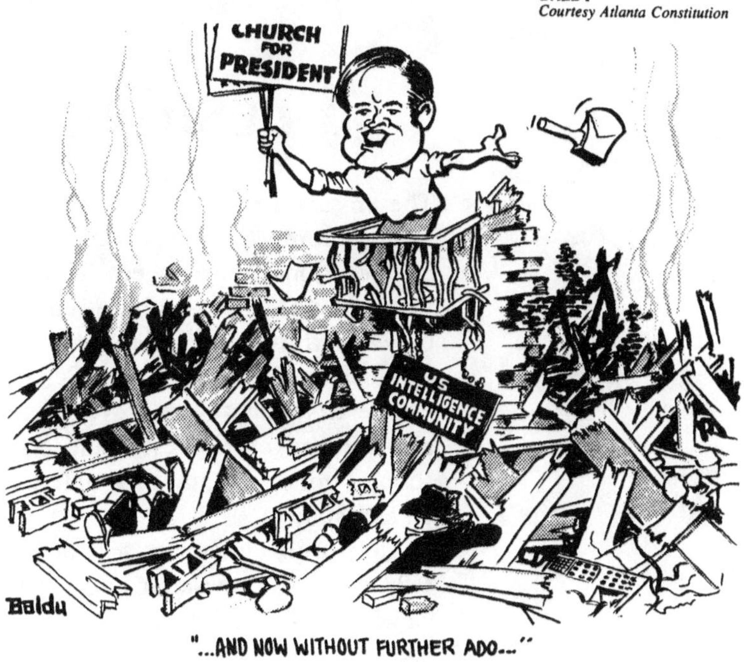
CHURCH FOR PRESIDENT
US INTELLIGENCE COMMUNITY
Baldy

"...AND NOW WITHOUT FURTHER ADO..."

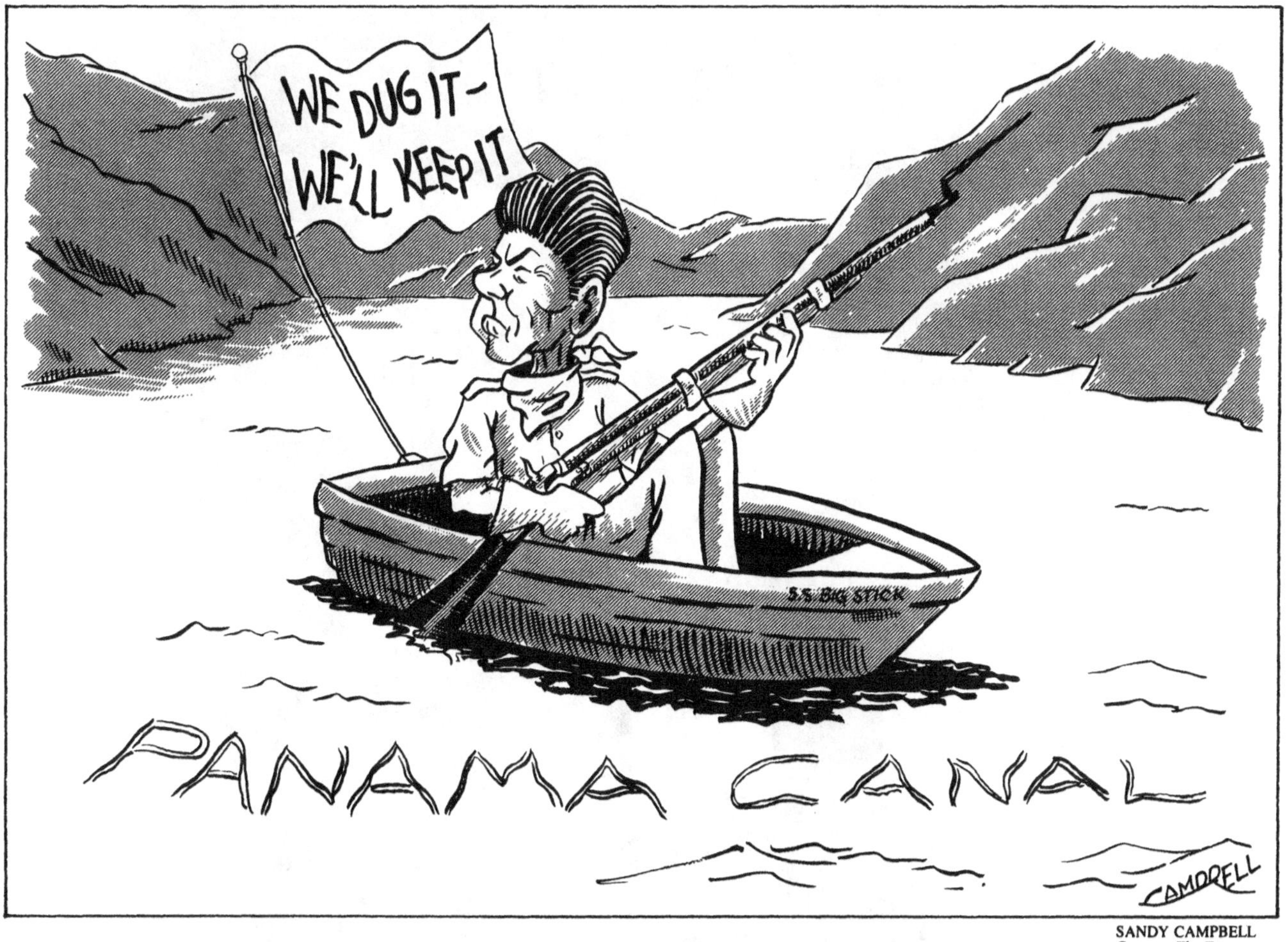
WE DUG IT-
WE'LL KEEP IT
S.S. BIG STICK
PANAMA CANAL
CAMPBELL

SANDY CAMPBELL
Courtesy The Tennessean

Presidential Debates

The so-called Great Debates between President Gerald Ford and challenger Jimmy Carter overshadowed most of the other campaigning as election time approached. The League of Women Voters sponsored three televised debates between the two candidates and added a fourth between the vice-presidential candidates—conservative Senator Robert Dole of the GOP and liberal Senator Walter Mondale of the Democrats.

The first ninety-minute confrontation took place on September 23 and focused on domestic and economic issues. The second dealt with foreign policy and national defense, and the third was open to questions on any subject.

The forums were not true debates, since questions were posed to the candidates by newsmen and newswomen. Nevertheless, they attracted viewing audiences estimated between seventy and ninety million Americans. Pollster George Gallup reported that the second debate, generally believed to have been won by Carter, stopped the Democratic candidate's downward plunge in the polls and turned the election around.

"AND IN REBUTTAL, LET ME SAY..."

KARL HUBENTHAL
Courtesy Los Angeles

ANDY DONATO
Courtesy Toronto Sun

PAUL SZEP
Courtesy Boston Globe

JIM BORGMAN
Courtesy Cincinnati Enquirer

DENNIS RENAULT
©McClatchy Newspapers

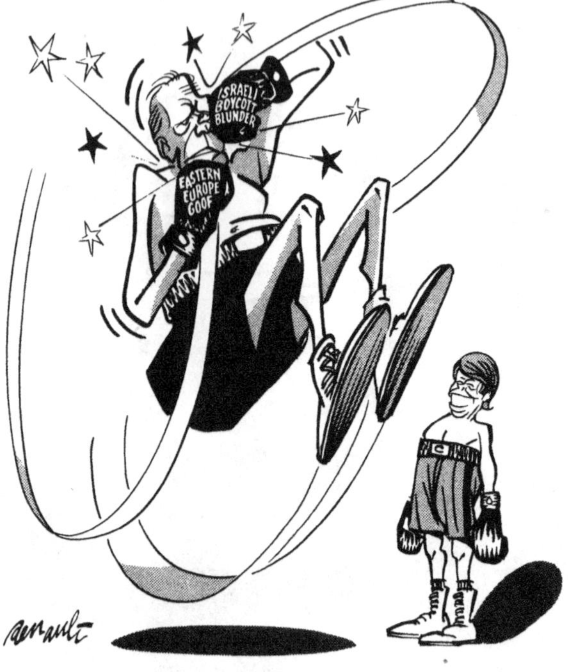
ISRAELI BOYCOTT BLUNDER
EASTERN EUROPE GOOF

'Take THAT! And THAT! And . . . . !'

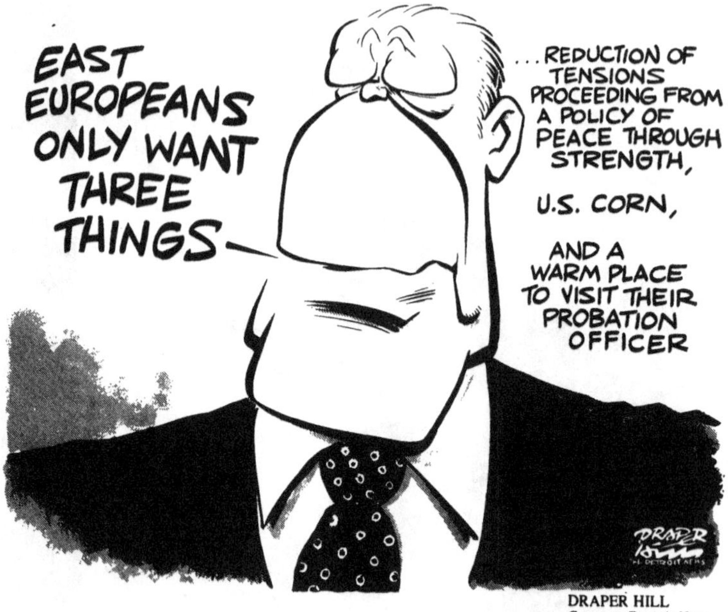
EAST EUROPEANS ONLY WANT THREE THINGS
...REDUCTION OF TENSIONS PROCEEDING FROM A POLICY OF PEACE THROUGH STRENGTH,
U.S. CORN,
AND A WARM PLACE TO VISIT THEIR PROBATION OFFICER

DRAPER HILL
Courtesy Detroit News

DWANE POWELL
Courtesy News and Observer

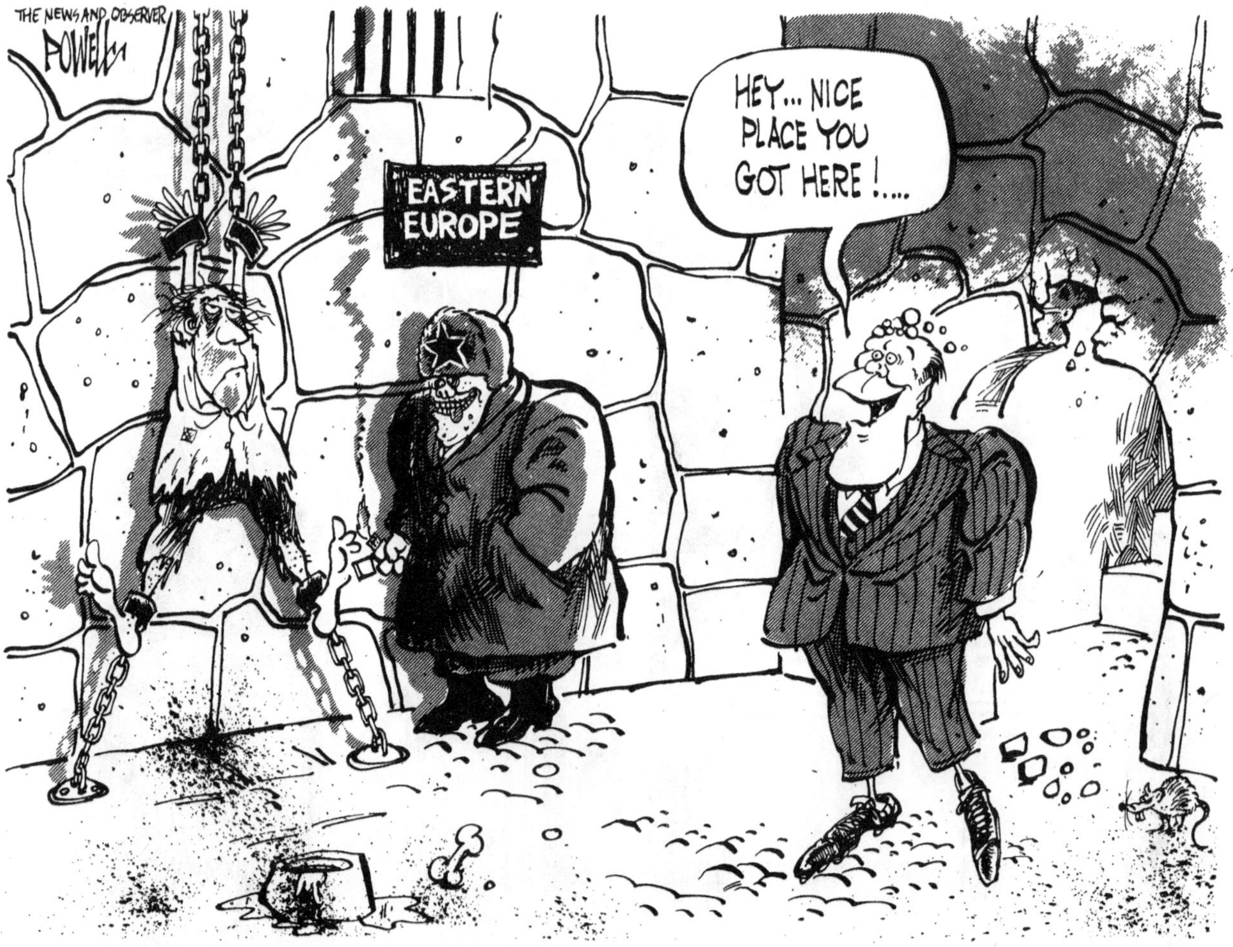
THE NEWS AND OBSERVER
POWELL
EASTERN EUROPE
HEY... NICE PLACE YOU GOT HERE !....

ANDY DONATO
Courtesy Toronto Sun

JIM IVEY
Orlando Sentinel Star
©Rothco Cartoons, Inc.

MICHAEL KONOPACKI
©Rothco Cartoons

KEN ALEXANDER
Courtesy San Francisco Examiner

LARRY WRIGHT
Courtesy Detroit News

ED FISCHER
Courtesy Omaha World-Herald

MICHAEL KONOPACKI
©Rothco Cartoons

"Let's hear it for freedom of choice!"

PAUL SZEP
Courtesy Boston Globe

MIKE KEEFE
Courtesy Denver Post

"...TEN PACES, TURN, THEN WAFFLE AT WILL!"

U.S. Congress

The Ninety-fourth Congress, which began in 1975 with high expectations, was at best a disappointment in many areas. A partisan body that at times played unabashed politics, Congress battled the president head-on time and again. It ignored Ford's proposed $395 billion ceiling on spending, blocked foreign policy measures such as aid to pro-Western forces in the Angolan civil war, and conducted the most searching investigation of the Central Intelligence Agency in years.

The House proposed a tough tax-reform bill, but the Senate tacked on so many special provisions that observers called it a "Christmas tree" with something for everybody. Congress compromised with Ford on the energy problem, reducing domestic oil prices instead of removing controls as he had asked.

Ford applied his veto power thirty-three times during the two-year session and was overridden by Congress eight times. Many of the veto battles brought into sharp focus the differing philosophies of a Democratic Congress and a Republican president on how best to lift the economy out of a recession without promoting runaway inflation.

In the final hours of the session, Ford agreed to sign bills appropriating money for a jobs program and continuing an existing program providing for 260,000 public service jobs.

"Zzzzzzzzzzz ..."

PAUL SZEP
Courtesy Boston Globe

"HERE, NOW YOU CAN MAKE A HABIT OF IT"

C. F. MORSE
©Hearst Newspapers

JIM ORTON
Courtesy Roll Call

'Do you mind if he goes first? He's our best customer'

"HEY, YOU KNOW WHAT?"

HERC FICKLEN
Courtesy Dallas Morning News

ART HENRIKSON
Courtesy Des Plaines (Ill.) Herald

Super chisel: Further adventures of the famous sculptor.

"DON'T WORRY ABOUT YOUR CHICKENS....I'M ON GUARD...BURP"

BOB PALMER
Courtesy Springfield (Mo.)
Leader-Press

"YOU CAN REST EASY — THEY'LL BE RUNNING THE CIA FROM NOW ON!"

CHARLES BROOKS
Courtesy Birmingham (Ala.) News

DAVID LEVINE
Courtesy David Levine

THE DWELLERS ON MOUNT OLYMPUS

VIC RUNTZ
Courtesy Bangor Daily News

'OLDER PEOPLE LIVE MORE EXCITING LIVES NOWADAYS!'

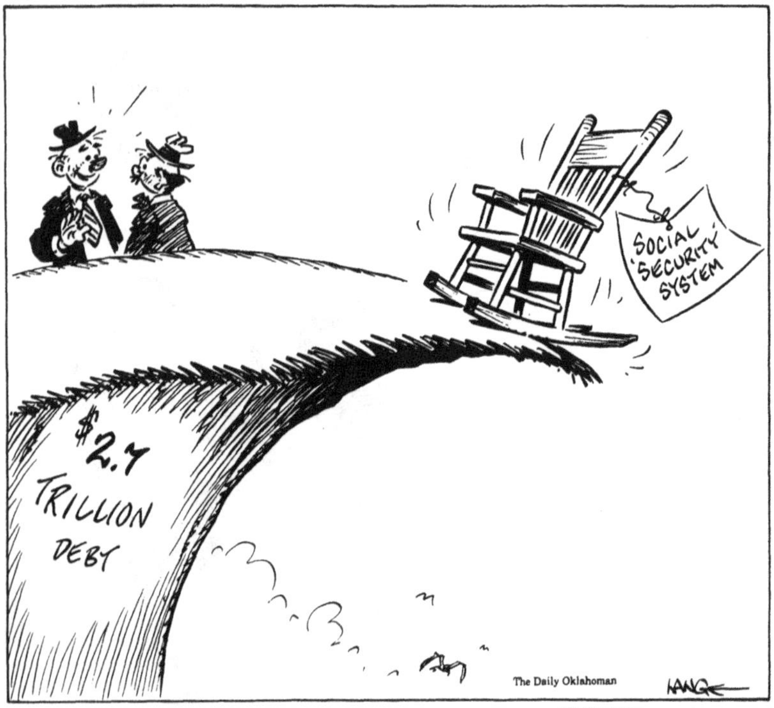
SOCIAL 'SECURITY' SYSTEM
$2.7 TRILLION DEBT
The Daily Oklahoman
LANGE

JIM LANGE
The Daily Oklahoman
©The Oklahoma Publishing Co.

But, Admiral Columbus—

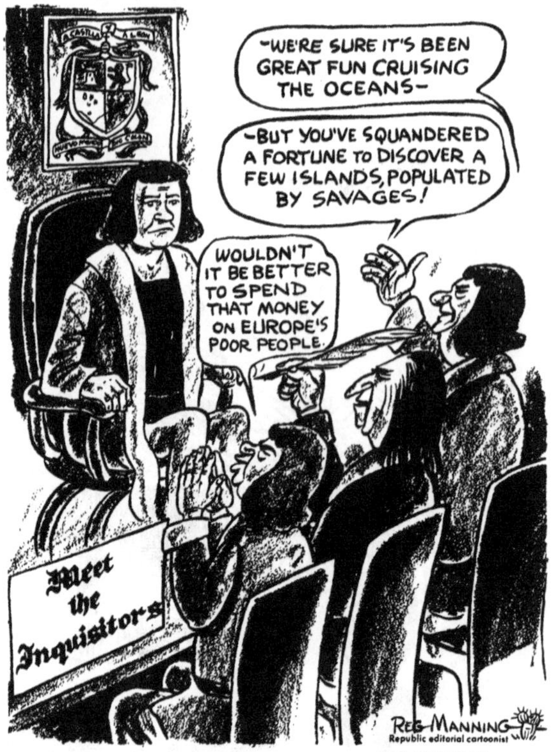
-WE'RE SURE IT'S BEEN GREAT FUN CRUISING THE OCEANS-
-BUT YOU'VE SQUANDERED A FORTUNE TO DISCOVER A FEW ISLANDS, POPULATED BY SAVAGES!
WOULDN'T IT BE BETTER TO SPEND THAT MONEY ON EUROPE'S POOR PEOPLE.
Meet the Inquisitors
REG MANNING
Republic editorial cartoonist

REG MANNING
Courtesy Arizona Republic

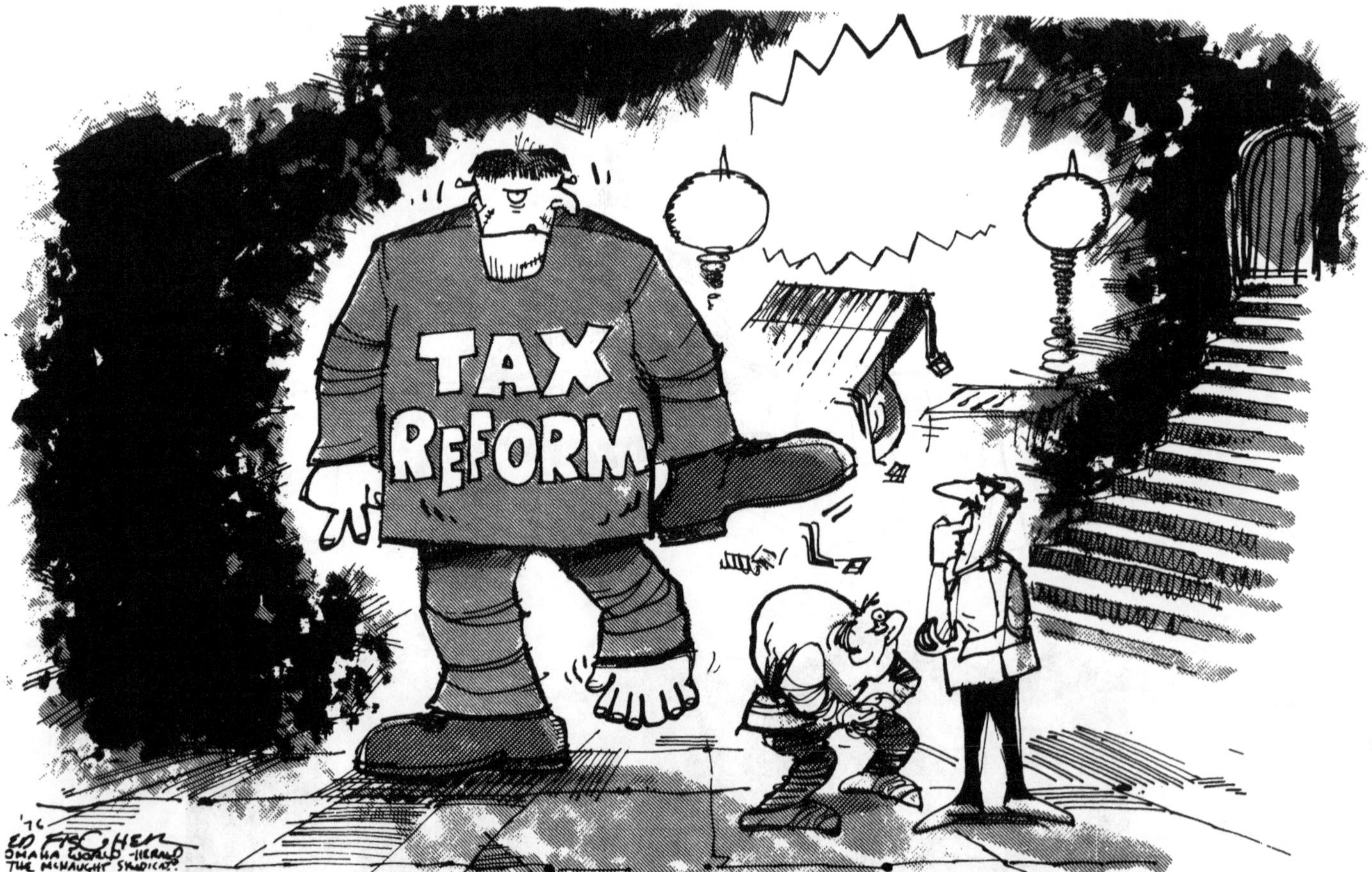
TAX REFORM
'76
ED FISCHER
OMAHA WORLD-HERALD
THE McNAUGHT SYNDICATE

ED FISCHER
Courtesy Omaha World-Herald

'DON'T VORRY, DOKTOR CONGRESSTEIN—ONE OF THESE YEARS YOU'LL GET IT RIGHT'

Wayne Hays Scandal

Wayne Hays, a sixty-five-year-old Democratic congressman from Ohio, in May found himself at the center of one of the Capitol's biggest scandals, one that ended his political career. Elizabeth Ray, a sometime model and onetime staff member in Hays's office, told a Washington *Post* reporter that she had been carried on Hays's payroll solely to provide him with sexual favors.

The newly married congressman denied all at first, then admitted that he had indeed had an affair with Ray. But he insisted she had performed regular secretarial duties for her $14,000 yearly salary.

Yielding to pressure from his congressional colleagues, Hays first resigned as chairman of the powerful House Administration Committee and as chairman of the Democratic party's House Democratic Campaign Committee. Finally, on September 1, faced with the prospect of a formal hearing into his conduct by the House Ethics Committee, he resigned from Congress.

Shortly after Hays's activities came to light, another Democratic congressman, Allan T. Howe of Utah, was arrested in Salt Lake City and charged with soliciting sex acts from two female police decoys. Howe charged that he was framed, but he was defeated for reelection.

HY ROSEN
Courtesy Albany Times-Union

"I WAS JUST THE BAIT. HE CAUGHT HIMSELF!"

VIC RUNTZ
Courtesy Bangor Daily News

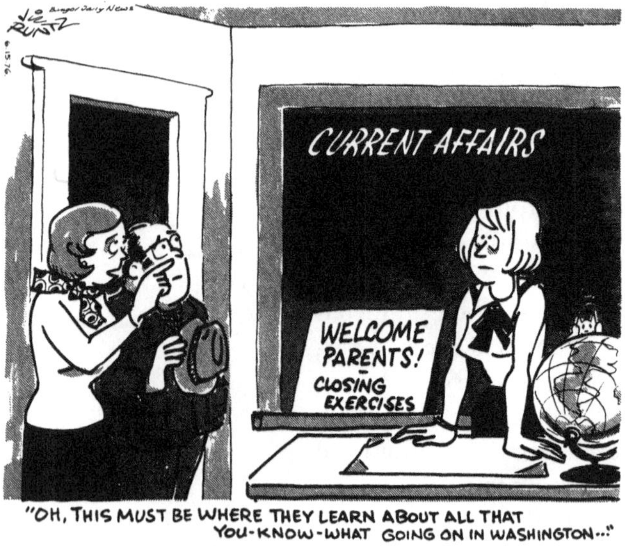
CURRENT AFFAIRS
WELCOME PARENTS! CLOSING EXERCISES
"OH, THIS MUST BE WHERE THEY LEARN ABOUT ALL THAT YOU-KNOW-WHAT GOING ON IN WASHINGTON..."

BOB TAYLOR
Courtesy Dallas Times Herald

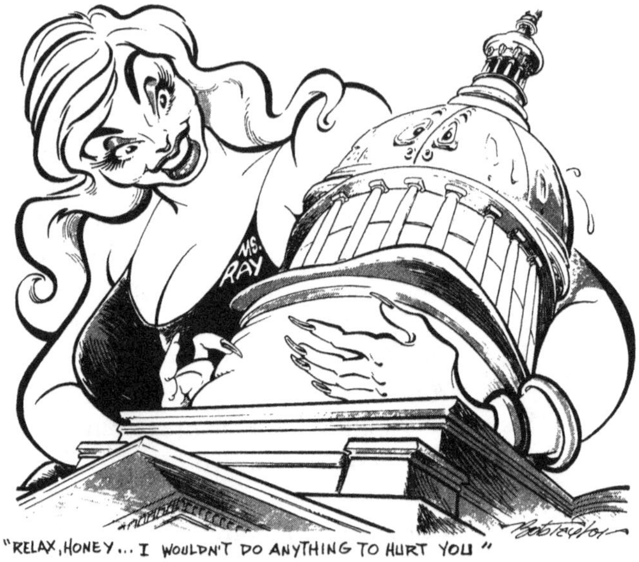
MS. RAY
"RELAX, HONEY... I WOULDN'T DO ANYTHING TO HURT YOU"

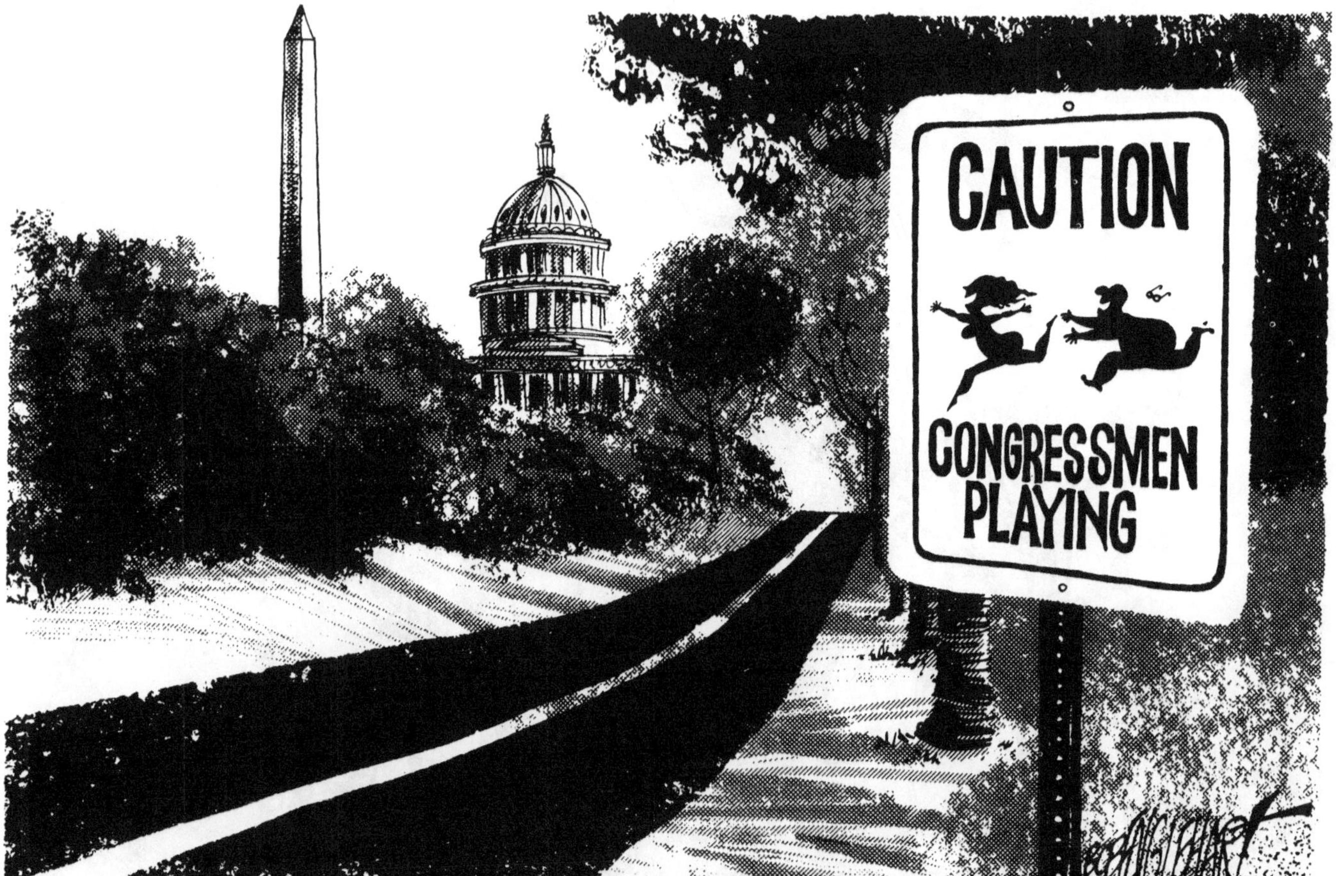
CAUTION
CONGRESSMEN PLAYING

BOB ENGLEHART
Courtesy Dayton Journal Herald

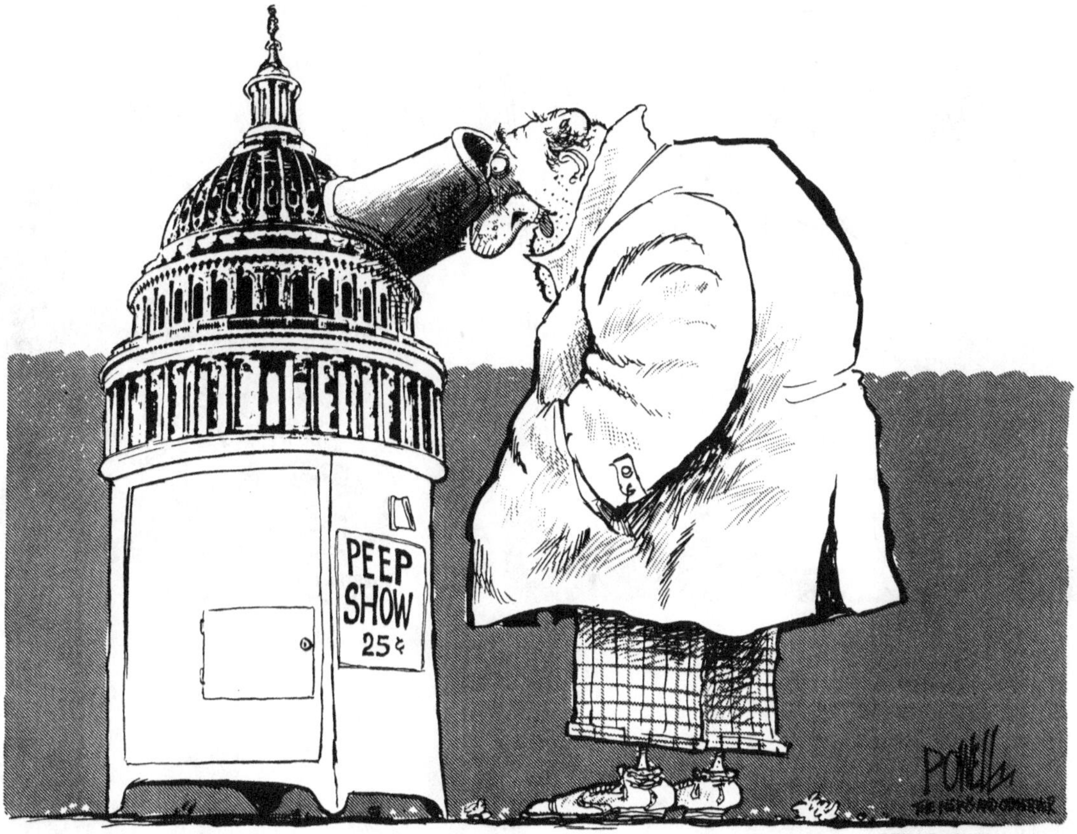
PEEP
SHOW
25¢
POWELL

DWANE POWELL
Courtesy News and Observer

WAYNE STAYSKAL
Courtesy Chicago Tribune

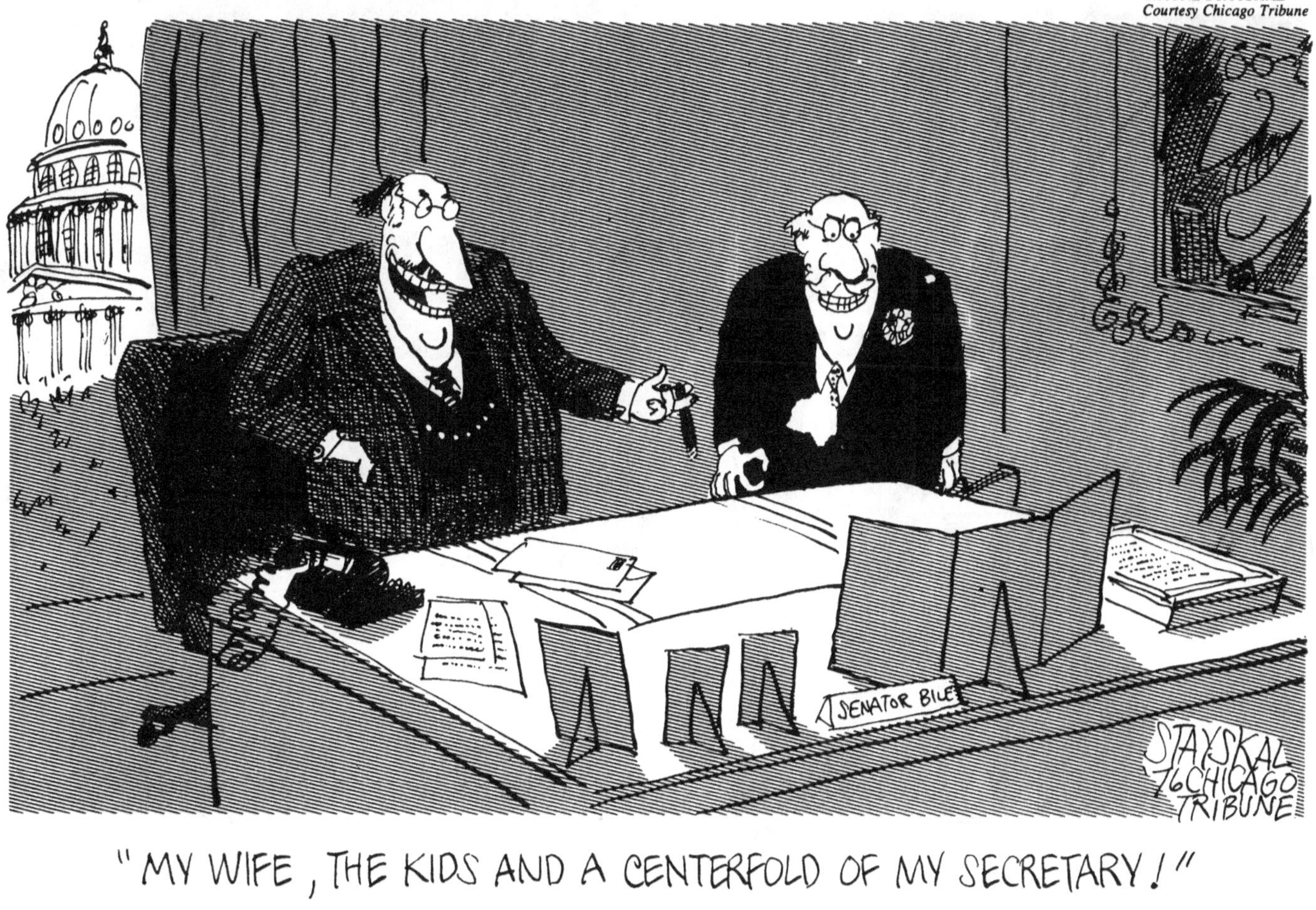
SENATOR BILE
STAYSKAL
76 CHICAGO
TRIBUNE

"MY WIFE, THE KIDS AND A CENTERFOLD OF MY SECRETARY!"

BERT WHITMAN
Courtesy Phoenix Gazette

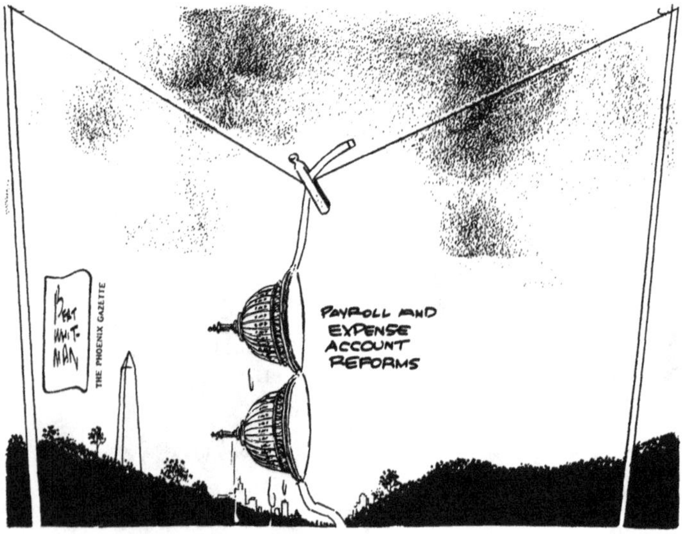
THE PHOENIX GAZETTE
PAYROLL AND EXPENSE ACCOUNT REFORMS

WASH DAY

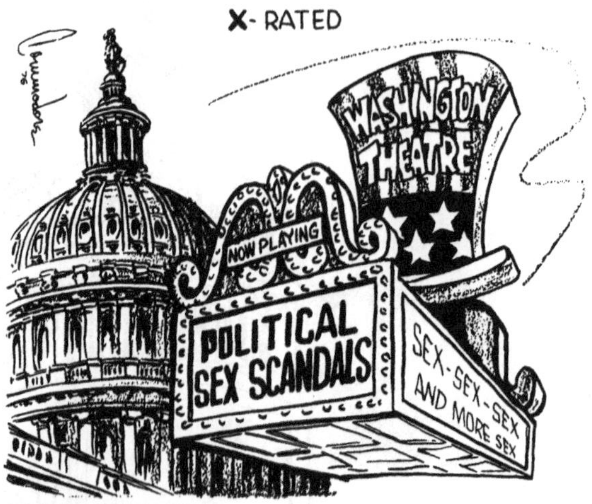
X- RATED
WASHINGTON THEATRE
NOW PLAYING
POLITICAL SEX SCANDALS
SEX-SEX-SEX AND MORE SEX

CHESTER COMMODORE
Courtesy Chicago Daily Defender

JIM BORGMAN
Courtesy Cincinnati Enquirer

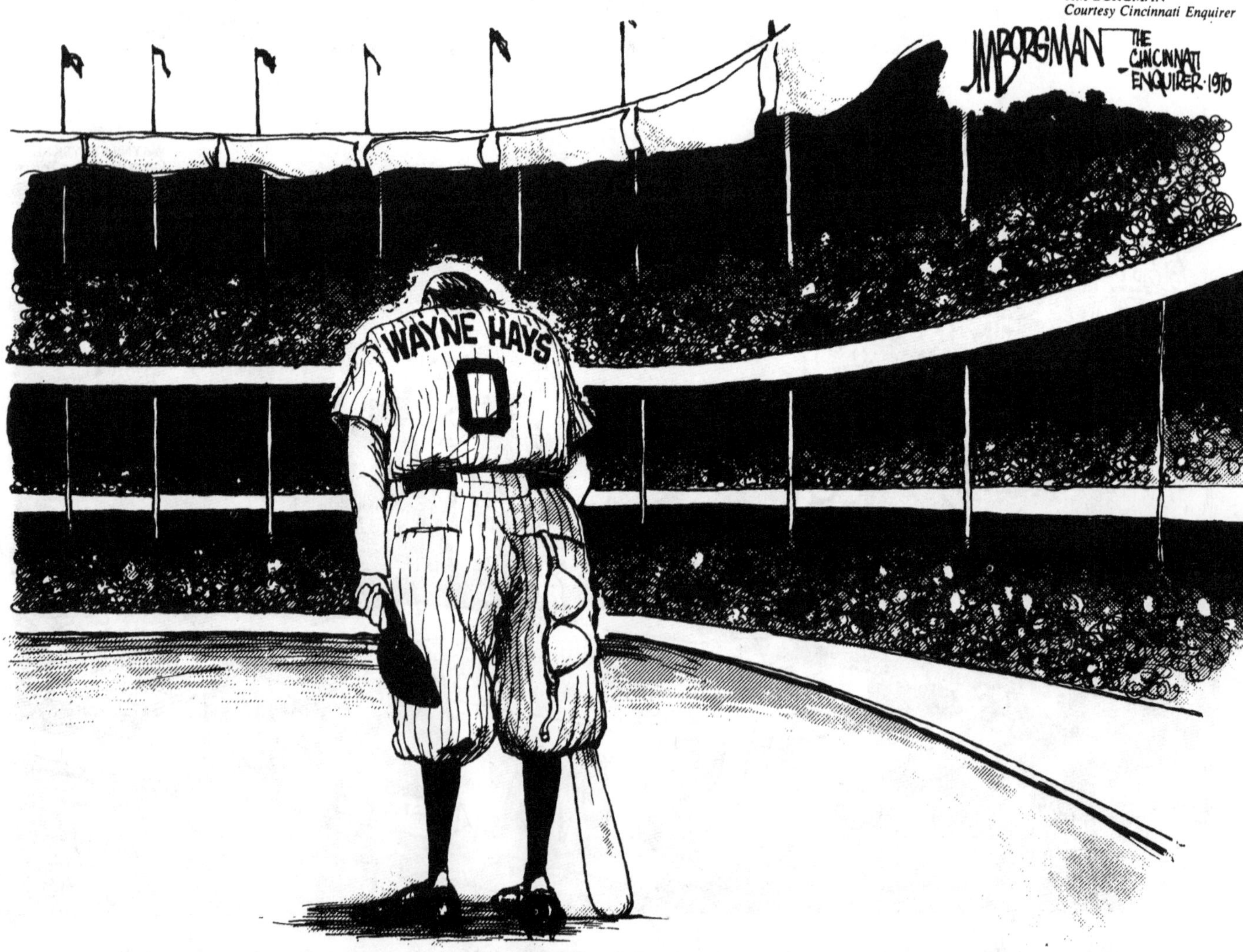
JMBORGMAN THE CINCINNATI ENQUIRER 1976
WAYNE HAYS
0

VERN THOMPSON
Courtesy Lawton (Okla.) Constitution

YOUR TAX DOLLAR

A. NATIONAL DEFENSE
B. DOMESTIC PROGRAMS
C. PAPER CLIPS & CARBON PAPER
D. "SECRETARIES" WHO DON'T TYPE OR ANSWER THE TELEPHONE

MIKE KEEFE
Courtesy Denver Post

TOM CURTIS
Courtesy Milwaukee Sentinel

"I'm getting worried about our national image, Mr. Speaker!"

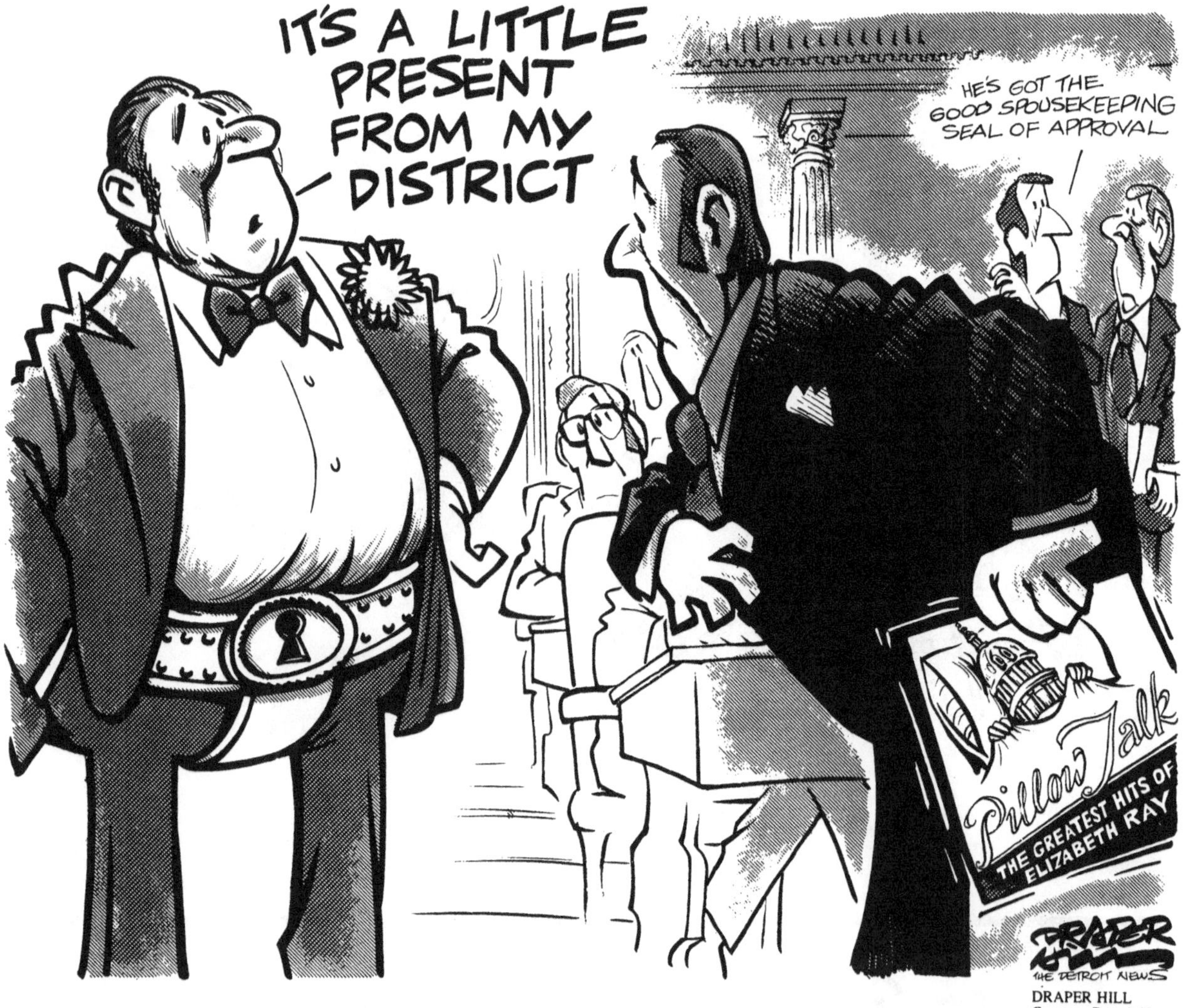
IT'S A LITTLE PRESENT FROM MY DISTRICT
HE'S GOT THE GOOD SPOUSEKEEPING SEAL OF APPROVAL
Pillow Talk
THE GREATEST HITS OF ELIZABETH RAY
DRAPER HILL
THE DETROIT NEWS

DRAPER HILL
Courtesy Detroit News

AL LIEDERMAN
Courtesy Long Island Press

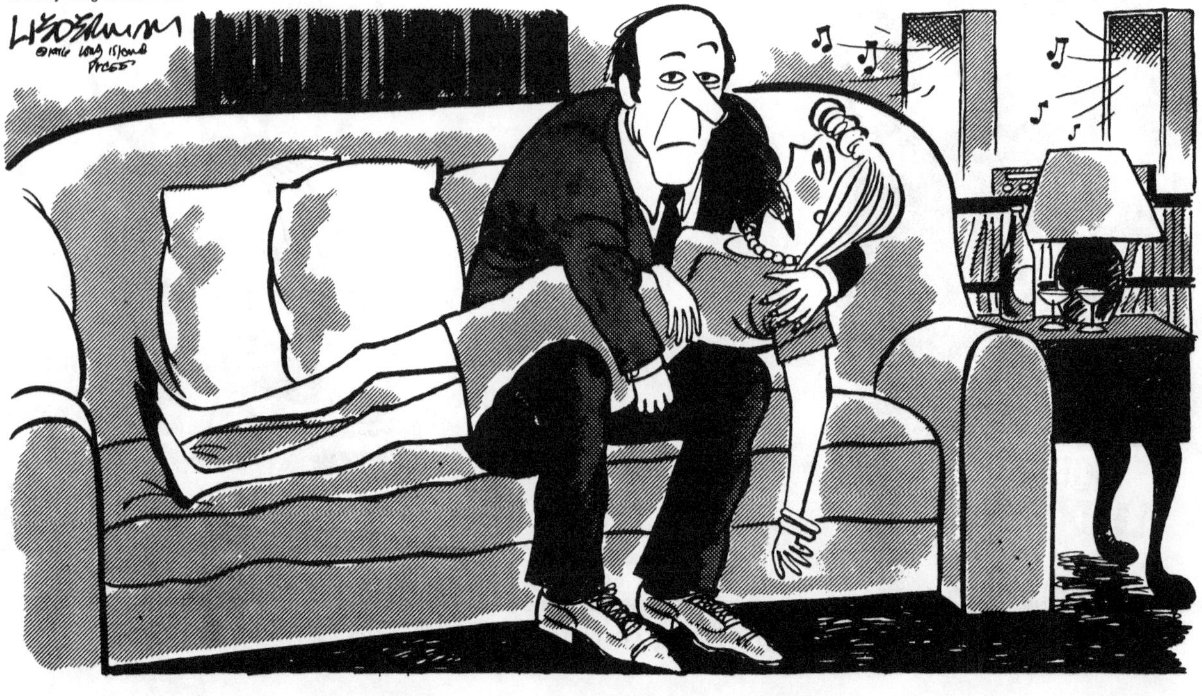

'I must warn you, I'm writing a book.'

ERIC SMITH
Courtesy Capital-Gazette (Md.) Newspapers

JIM ORTON
Courtesy Roll Call

'YOU'LL HAVE TO LEARN TYPING — I CAN'T READ YOUR SCRIPT'

EUGENE PAYNE
Courtesy WSOC-TV, Charlotte

JIM LANGE
The Daily Oklahoman
©The Oklahoma Publishing Co.

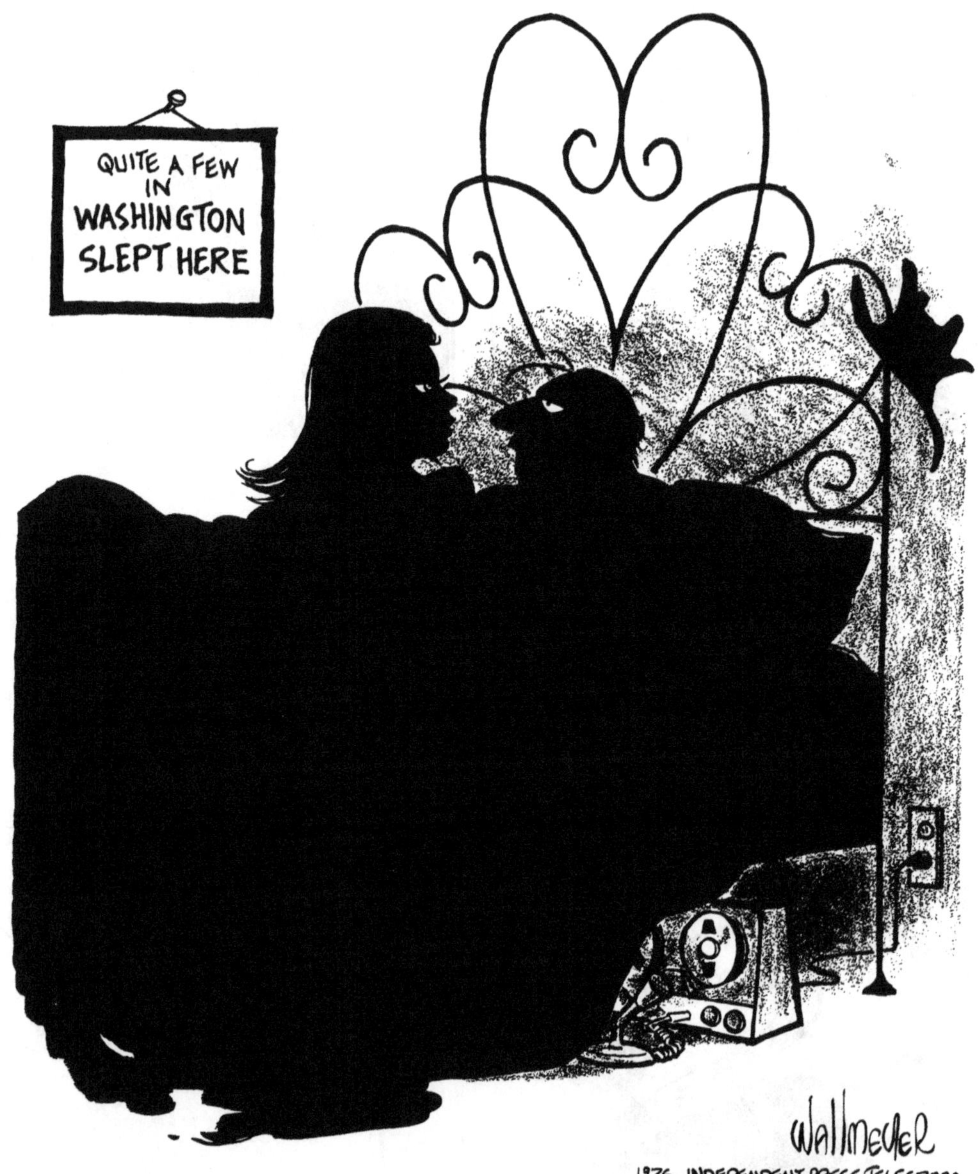
QUITE A FEW
IN
WASHINGTON
SLEPT HERE
Wallmeyer
1976, INDEPENDENT, PRESS-TELEGRAM

DICK WALLMEYER
Long Beach Press-Telegram
©Register and Tribune Syndicate

Playboy Magazine

The Democratic campaign received a severe jolt on September 20 when details of an interview with Jimmy Carter by *Playboy* magazine were made public. The wide-ranging interview was scheduled to appear in the November issue to be released shortly before the election.

Throughout the campaign Carter had emphasized the fact that he was a Baptist deacon, Sunday school teacher, and a person of deep religious convictions. At the conclusion of the *Playboy* interview, however, he said, "I've looked on a lot of women with lust. I've committed adultery in my heart many times. This is something that God recognizes I will do—and I have done—and God forgives me for it."

The incident created a storm of controversy in religious circles and apparently dealt a damaging blow to Carter in the preelection polls.

Adding to his woes after the interview was his statement that President Lyndon Johnson had been guilty of "lying, cheating and distorting the truth." He quickly apologized to the late president's widow for his remarks.

ALL THINGS TO ALL PEOPLE

CHARLES BROOKS
Courtesy Birmingham (Ala.) News

DAVID SIMPSON
Courtesy Tulsa Tribune

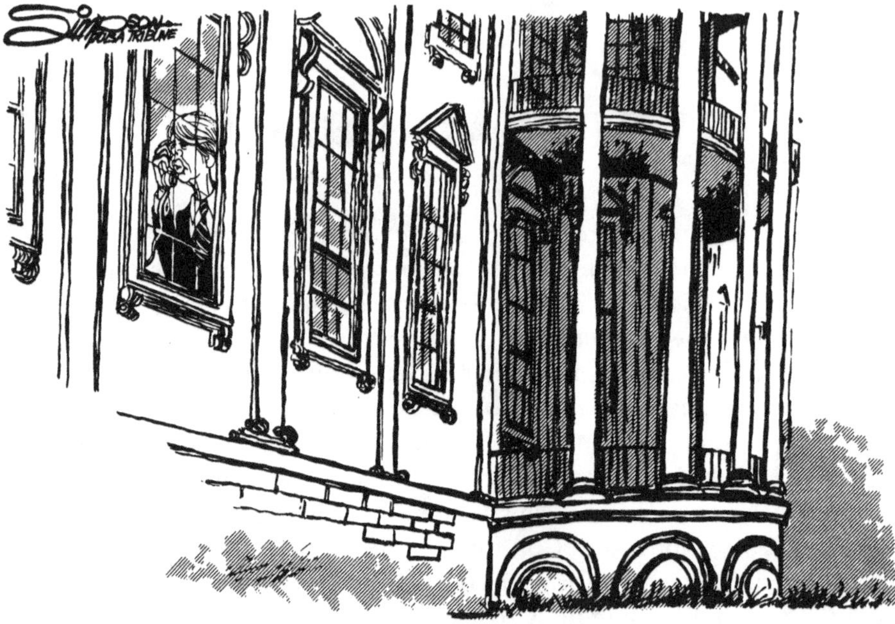
SIMPSON TULSA TRIBUNE

"No, Hefner . . . I will not turn the East Wing into a Bunny Club!"

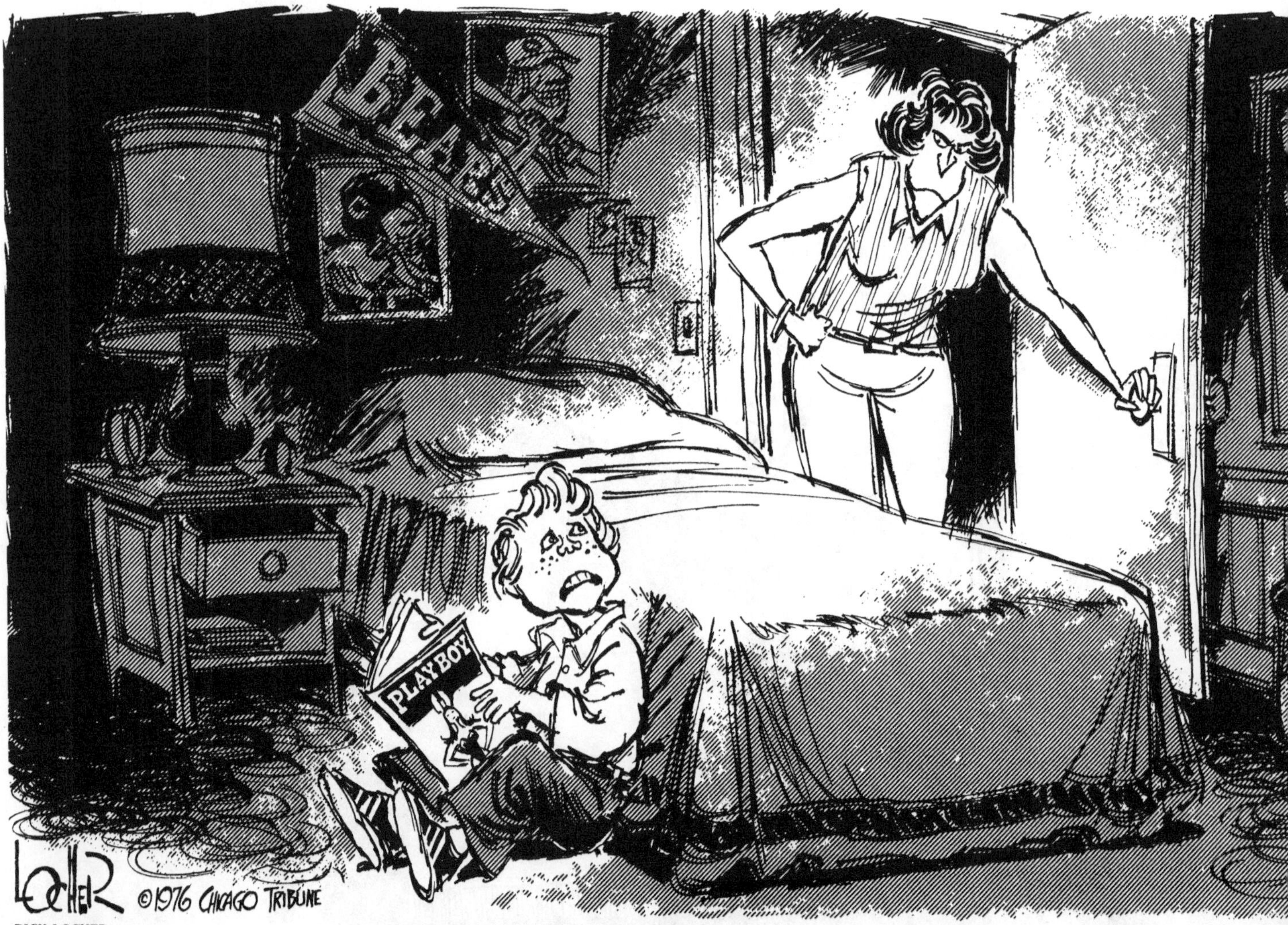
BEARS
PLAYBOY
LOCHER ©1976 CHICAGO TRIBUNE

DICK LOCHER
Courtesy Chicago Tribune

"Honest, Mom...., I was just brushing up on my political philosophy!"

FRANK INTERLANDI
©Los Angeles Times Syndicate

"Ford has a monkey on his back with Watergate!"

'...Read All About It!'

ELDON PLETCHER
Courtesy New Orleans

American Gothic

ELDON PLETCHER
Courtesy New Orleans
Times-Picayune

JIM BERRY
©NEA

"JIMMY CARTER can think about lust — why can't YOU think about lust?"

'DON'T LOOK AT ME LIKE THAT, YOU YOUNG WHIPPERSNAPPER! I KNOW WHAT YOU'RE THINKING!'

CRAIG MACINTOSH
Courtesy Minneapolis Star

LEW HARSH
Courtesy Scranton Times

CHARLES DANIEL
Courtesy Knoxville Journal

MIKE KEEFE
Courtesy Denver Post

'I JUST LOVE IT WHEN YOU TALK DIRTY!'

"If you must know, to keep in touch with U.S. political revelations...and better understand why they sneeze and we get pneumonia."

HUGH HAYNIE
Louisville Courier-Journal
©Los Angeles Times Syndicate

CLYDE PETERSON
Courtesy Houston Chronicle

"IF YOU ASK ME, CARTER IDENTIFIED AND BAGGED HIMSELF A WHOLE NEW VOTING BLOC."

MIKE PETERS
Courtesy Dayton Daily News

Southern Africa

Troubled southern Africa held the attention of the world throughout much of the year. In June Secretary of State Henry Kissinger outlined a plan for peace that called for black-majority rule in Rhodesia and in the buffer state of Namibia, plus more rights for blacks inside South Africa. The plan could succeed only if South Africa's white-majority government, led by Prime Minister John Vorster, cooperated.

In June Kissinger met with Vorster in West Germany to discuss Russian footholds in Mozambique and Angola, as well as growing Soviet naval strength in the Indian Ocean. The Russians were known to be training and arming terrorists for attacks in Rhodesia and Namibia.

The black-to-white population ratios in South Africa and Rhodesia made their policies of apartheid increasingly vulnerable. Of South Africa's 25 million people, only 4.2 million are white. Rhodesia has a population of 6.4 million, with only 270,000 whites.

JERRY BITTLE
Courtesy Albuquerque Tribune

"Henry, old boy . . . you've never explained it quite like this before."

ED GAMBLE
Courtesy Nashville Banner

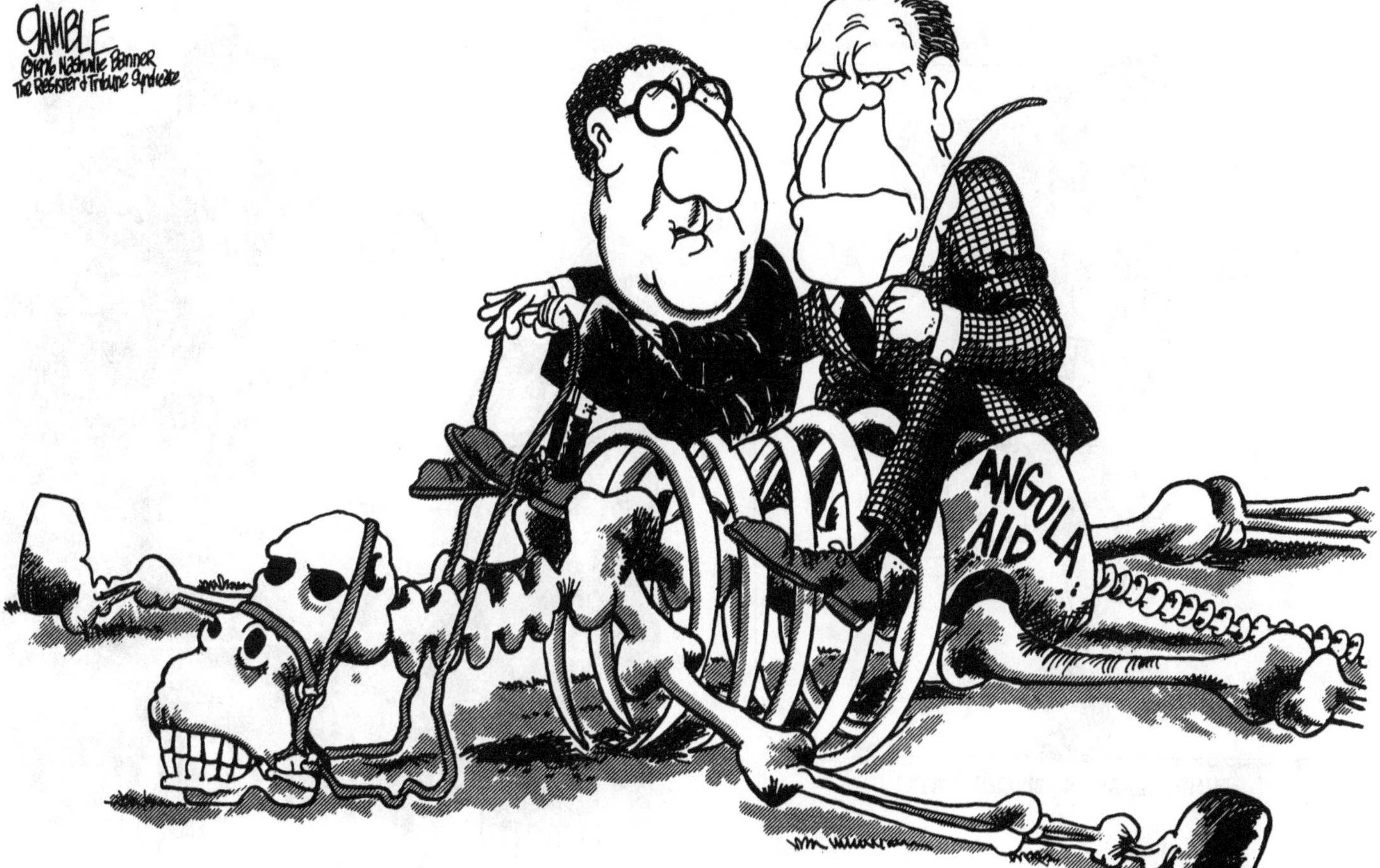
GAMBLE ©1976 Nashville Banner The Register & Tribune Syndicate
ANGOLA AID

"PROD HIM A LITTLE MORE.... I THINK I FELT A TWITCH!"

HUGH HAYNIE
Louisville Courier-Journal
©Los Angeles Times Syndicate

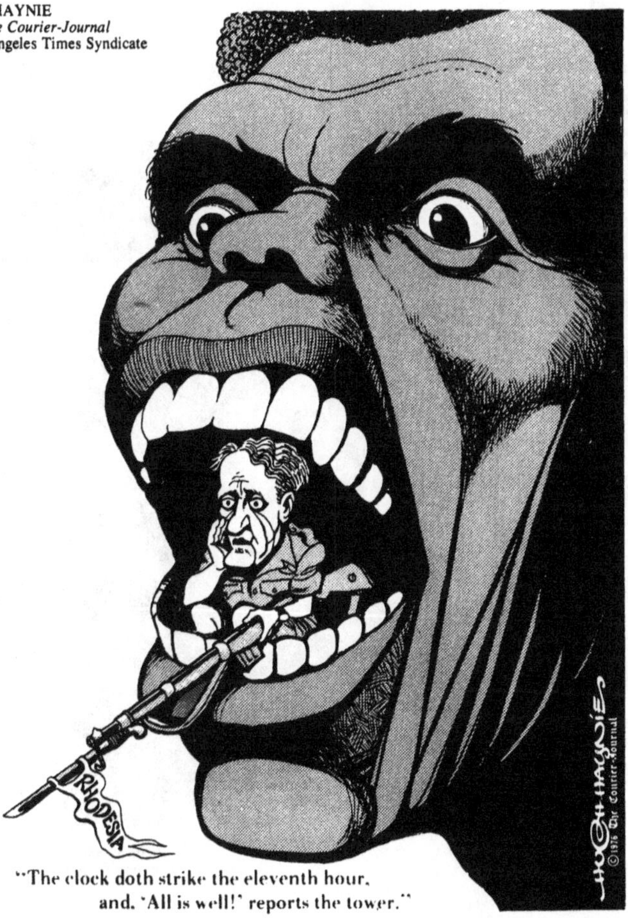
RHODESIA
HUGH HAYNIE
©1976 The Courier-Journal

"The clock doth strike the eleventh hour, and, 'All is well!' reports the tower."

BILL MAULDIN
©Chicago Sun-Times

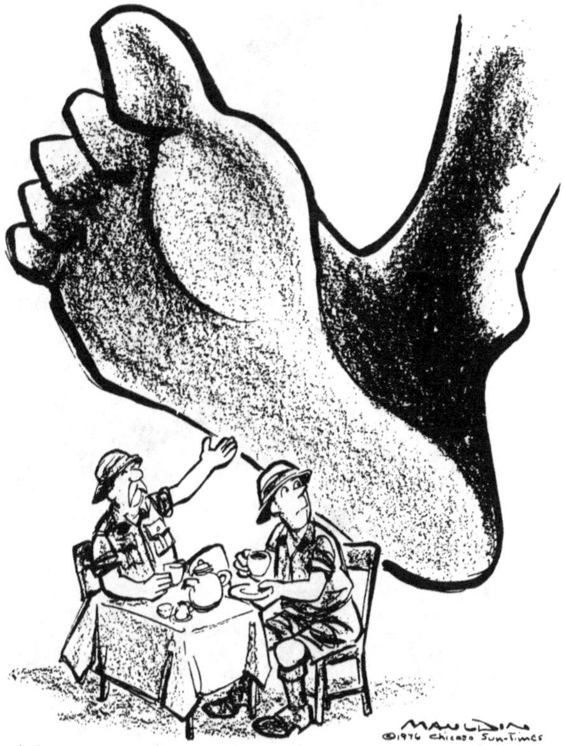
MAULDIN
©1976 Chicago Sun-Times

"It's merely my faithful bearer, Ngumbo, giving me shade."

CLYDE PETERSON
Courtesy Houston Chronicle

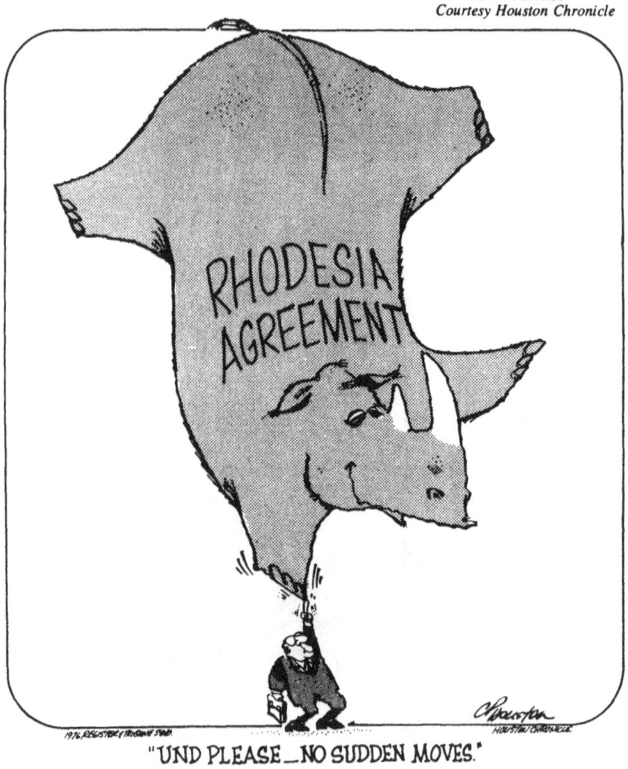
RHODESIA
AGREEMENT

"UND PLEASE_NO SUDDEN MOVES."

'I brought something home . . .'

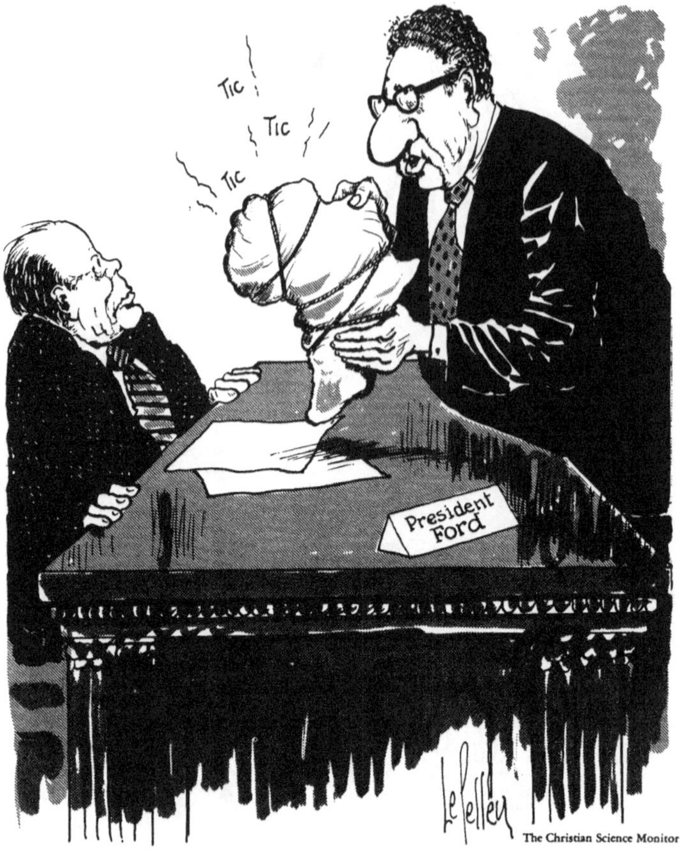
Tic
Tic
Tic
President
Ford
LePelley
The Christian Science Monitor

GUERNSEY LEPELLEY
Courtesy Christian Science Monitor

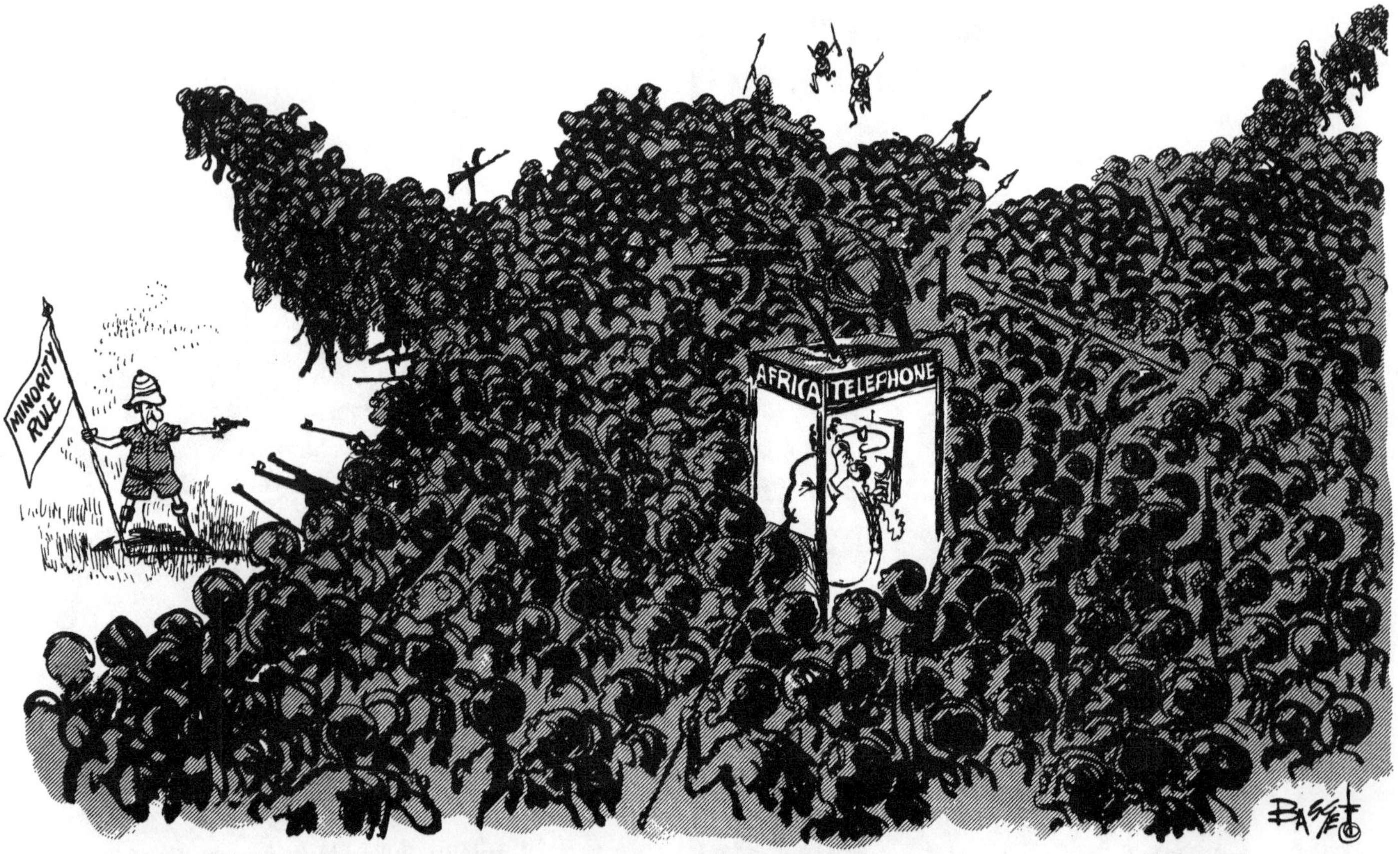
MINORITY
RULE
AFRICA
TELEPHONE

" JERRY, MAYBE IT'S TIME WE BACKED A WINNER"

GENE BASSET
Courtesy Scripps-Howard Newspapers

HARDLY THE TIME FOR A SAUCER OF MILK!

MILT MORRIS
©The Associated Press

DOUG SNEYD
Courtesy Toronto Star

"We're trying to improve transportation for your people, but there are only so many seats one can put on the back of the bus."

DOUGLAS BORGSTEDT
©Copley News Service

JAWS

DENNIS RENAULT
©McClatchy Newspapers

African Clock

JOHN COLLINS
Courtesy Montreal (Can.) Gazette

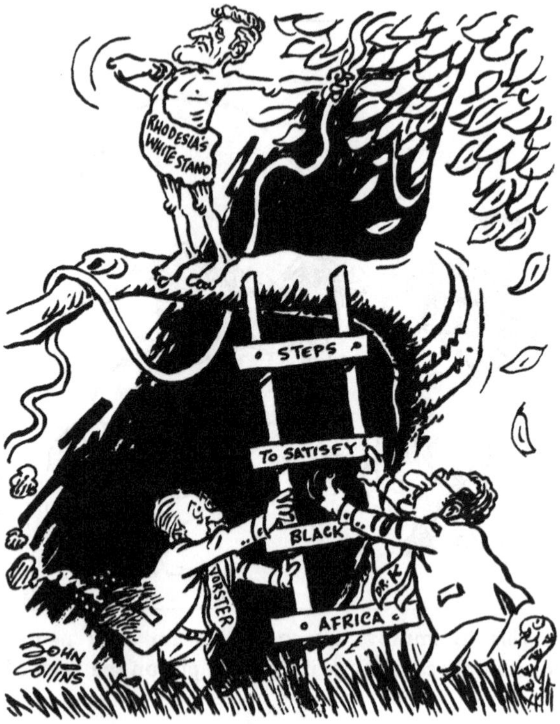
RHODESIA'S WHITE STAND
STEPS
TO SATISFY
BLACK
AFRICA
VORSTER
DR. K
JOHN COLLINS

TRYING TO BRING TARZAN DOWN TO EARTH

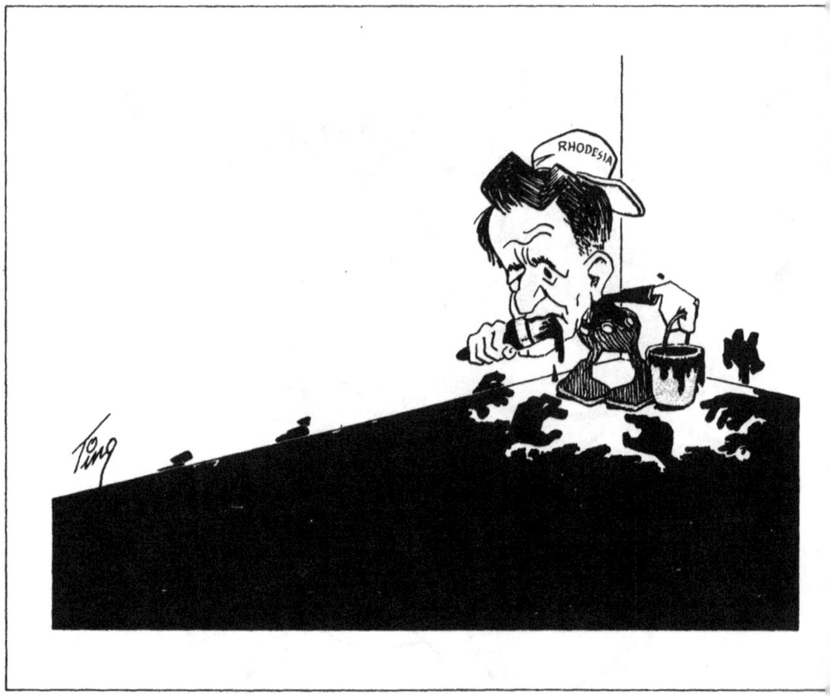
RHODESIA
TING

MERLE TINGLEY
Courtesy London (Can.) Free Pre

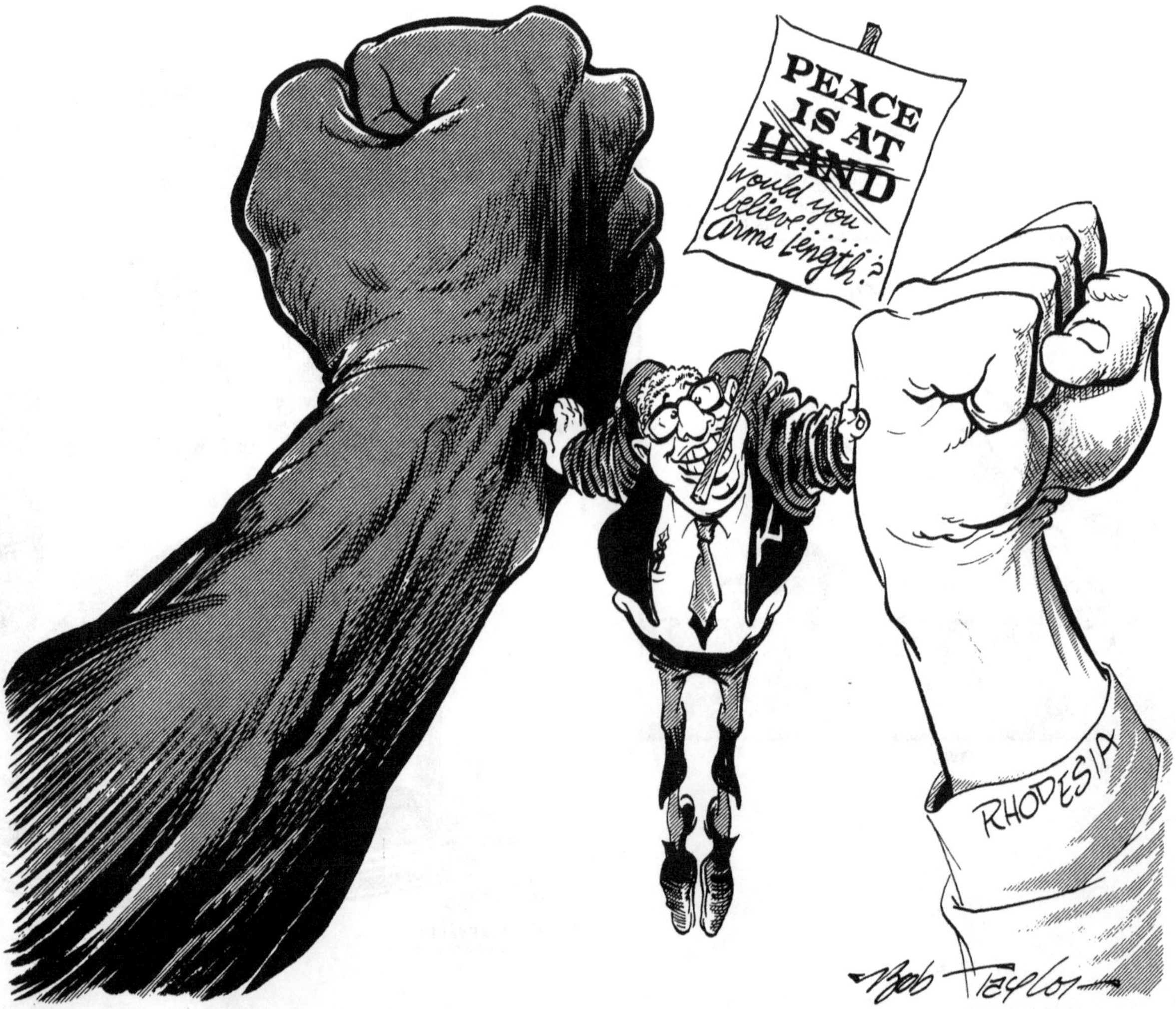
PEACE
IS AT
HAND
would you
believe......
arms length?
RHODESIA
BOB TAYLOR

BOB TAYLOR
Courtesy Dallas Times Herald

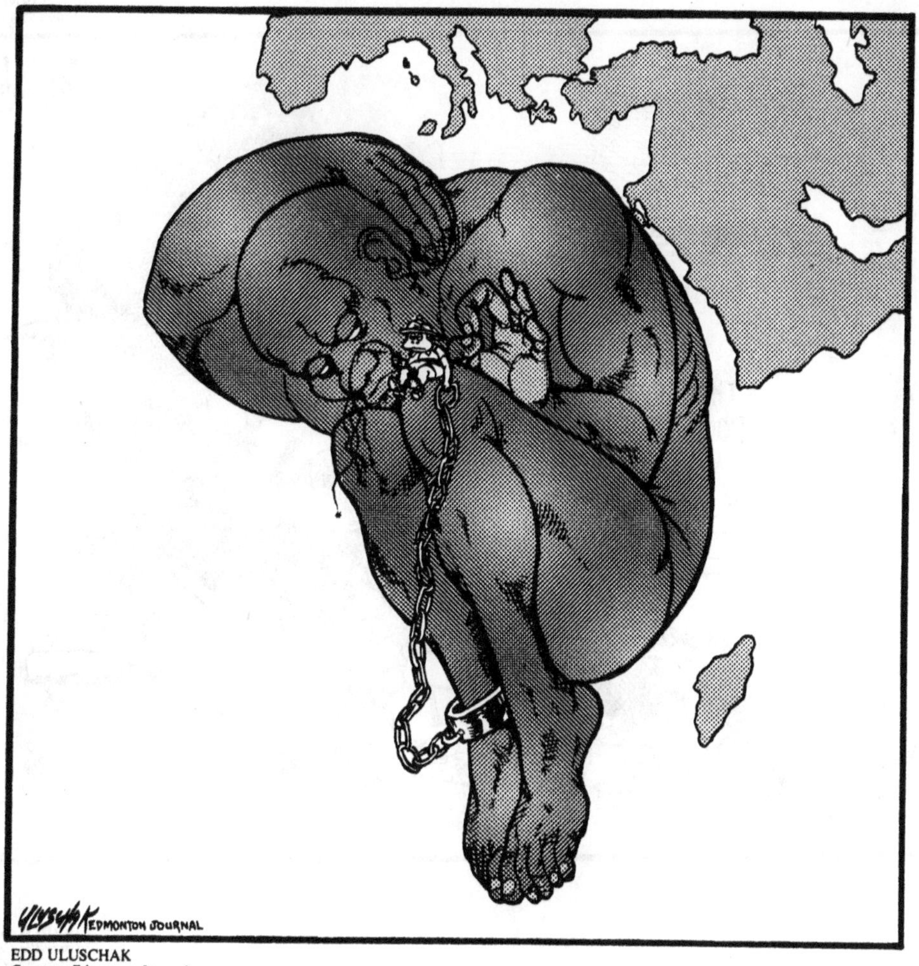
ULUSCHAK EDMONTON JOURNAL

EDD ULUSCHAK
Courtesy Edmonton Journal

HY ROSEN
Courtesy Albany Times-Union

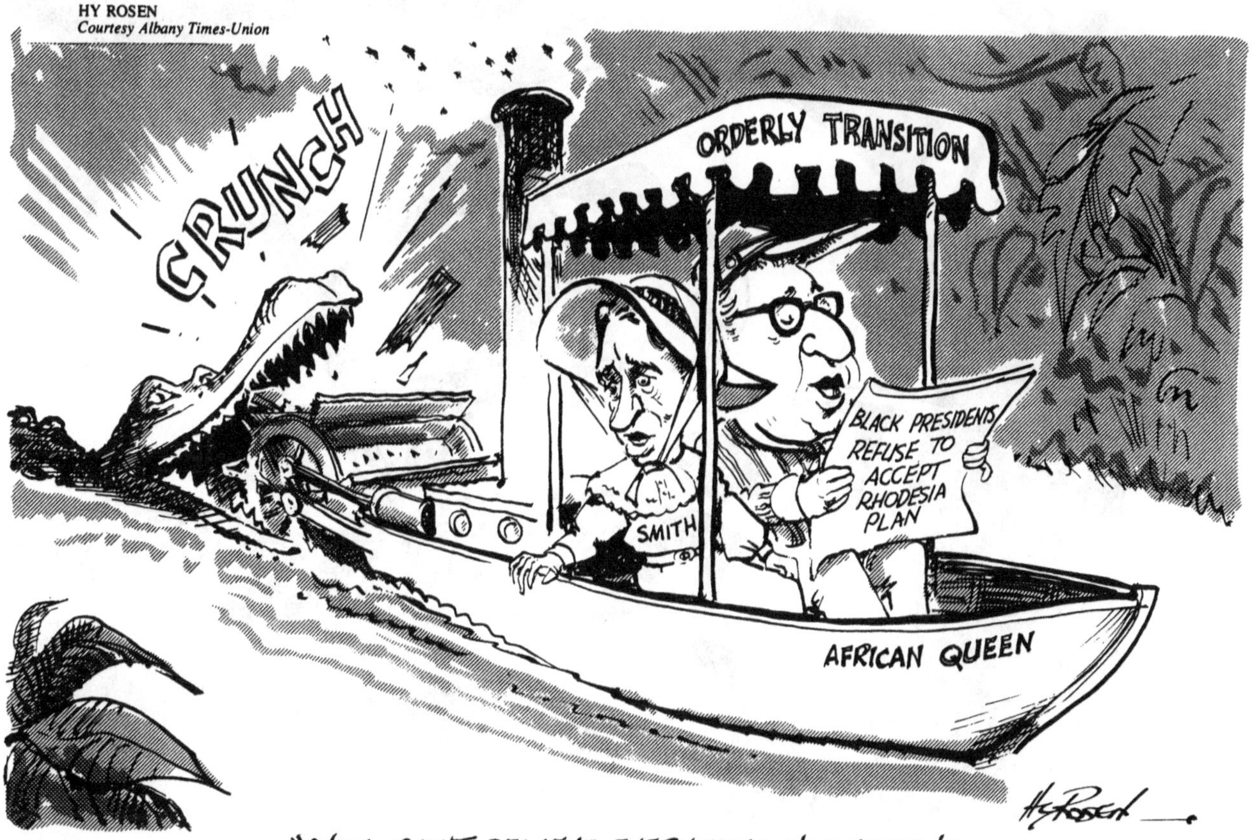
CRUNCH
ORDERLY TRANSITION
SMITH
BLACK PRESIDENTS REFUSE TO ACCEPT RHODESIA PLAN
AFRICAN QUEEN
HY ROSEN

"YOU CAN'T BELIEVE EVERYTHING YOU HEAR!"

BILL GARNER
Courtesy The Commercial Appeal

HUGH HAYNIE
Louisville Courier-Journal
©Los Angeles Times Syndicate

Requiem for an air piracy

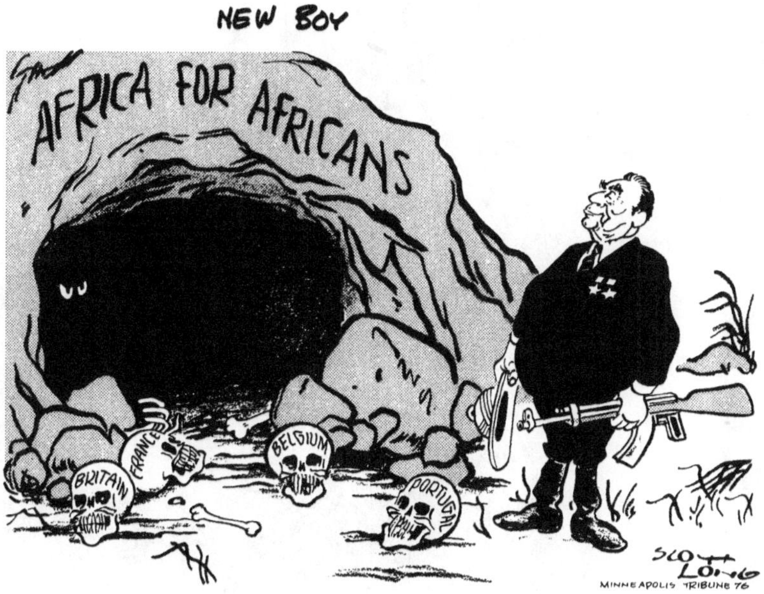
NEW BOY
AFRICA FOR AFRICANS
BRITAIN
FRANCE
BELGIUM
PORTUGAL
MINNEAPOLIS TRIBUNE 76

SCOTT LONG
Courtesy Minneapolis Tribune

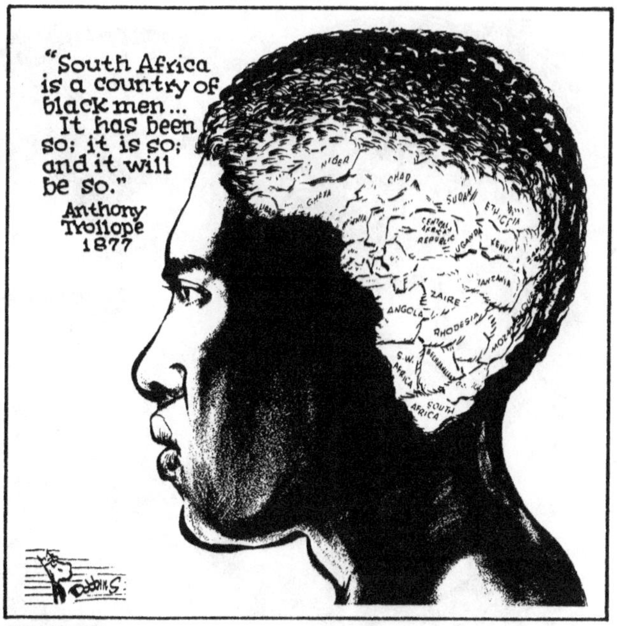
"South Africa is a country of black men... It has been so; it is so; and it will be so."
Anthony Trollope 1877
CHAD
SUDAN
ETHIOPIA
CENTRAL AFRICAN REPUBLIC
UGANDA
KENYA
ZAIRE
TANZANIA
ANGOLA
RHODESIA
S.W. AFRICA
SOUTH AFRICA
DOBBINS

JIM DOBBINS
Courtesy Boston Herald-American

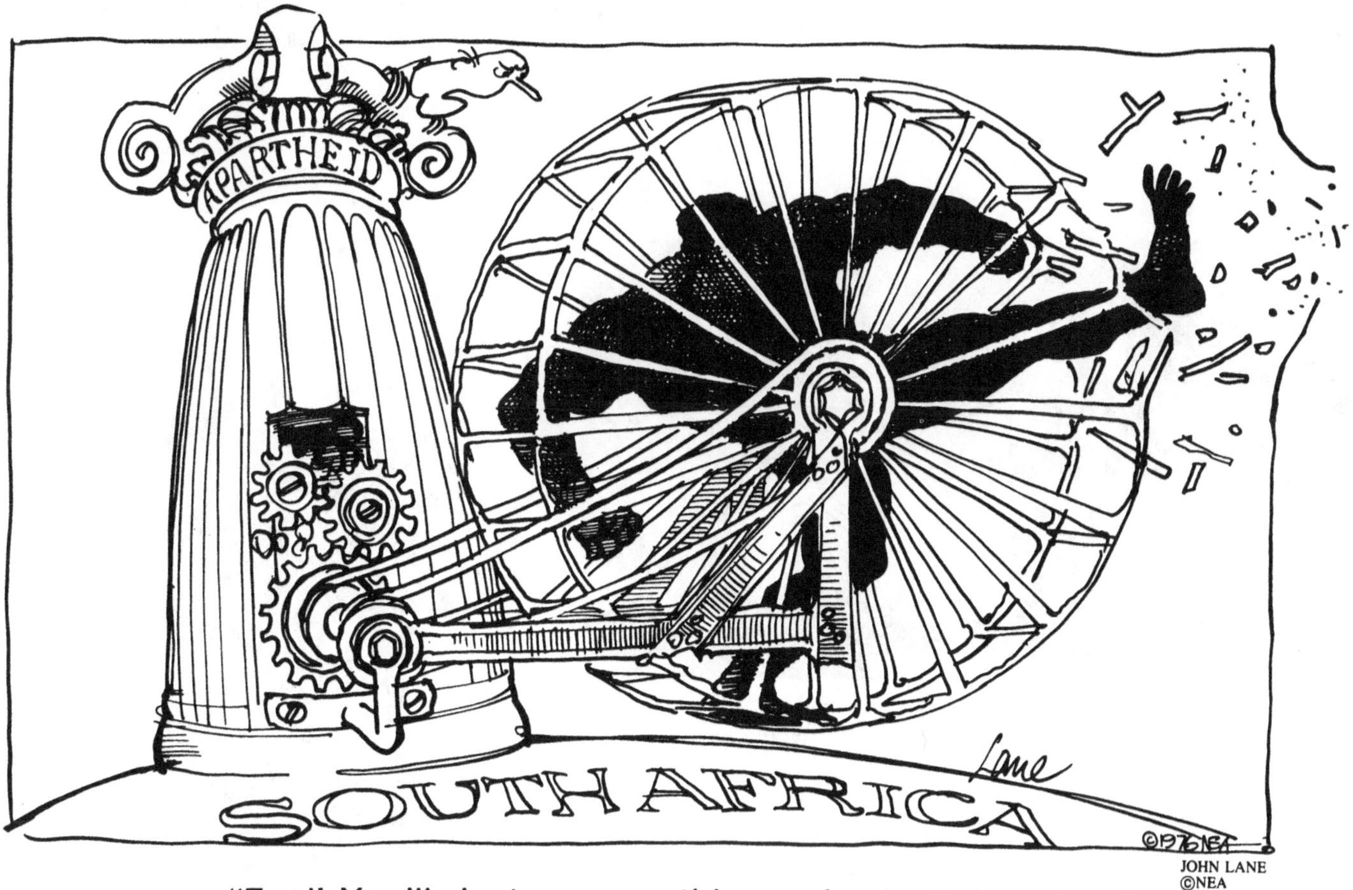
APARTHEID
SOUTH AFRICA
Lane
©1976 NEA

JOHN LANE
©NEA

"Fool! You'll destroy everything we've built together."

'Minstrel Man'

JOHN STAMPONE
Courtesy Army Times

ANTHONY JENKINS
Courtesy Toronto Globe and Mail

WHEN YOU'RE NO. 2 YOU TRY HARDER

AL LIEDERMAN
Courtesy Long Island Press

'Start With... the Imperialist Forces of the U.S....'

CHESTER COMMODORE
Courtesy Chicago Daily Defender

Bicentennial Celebration

On July 4, 1976, America celebrated its two hundredth birthday. It was a long, noisy, enthusiastic party from coast to coast, and in Hawaii and Alaska as well. Major bicentennial events were staged in or around Washington, D. C., Philadelphia, Boston, and New York City.

In New York City, more than six million citizens turned out for the most spectacular and highly publicized event—Operation Sail. Planned for five years, the occasion brought together 225 sailing vessels from thirty-one countries, the largest sailing armada assembled since the Battle of Navorina, fought off the coast of Greece in 1827. The majestic fleet took part in a three-hour parade into New York harbor and up the Hudson River. Heading the procession were sixteen "tall ships," square-riggers with masts more than 127 feet high. Leading the way was the U. S. Coast Guard bark *Eagle*.

Heads of government and royalty visiting during the bicentennial included President Valery Giscard d'Estaing of France, King Juan Carlos I and Queen Sofia of Spain, Queen Margrethe II of Denmark, King Carl XVI Gustaf of Sweden, and Queen Elizabeth II of the United Kingdom.

EUGENE PAYNE
Courtesy WSOC-TV, Charlotte

JAMES MORGAN
Courtesy Spartanburg Herald-Journal

Two giant steps for mankind!

"NO COMRADE IT IS NOT A REVOLUTION; IT'S A CELEBRATION"

CHARLES WERNER
Courtesy Indianapolis Star

JERRY DOYLE
Courtesy Philadelphia Daily News

FRANK INTERLANDI

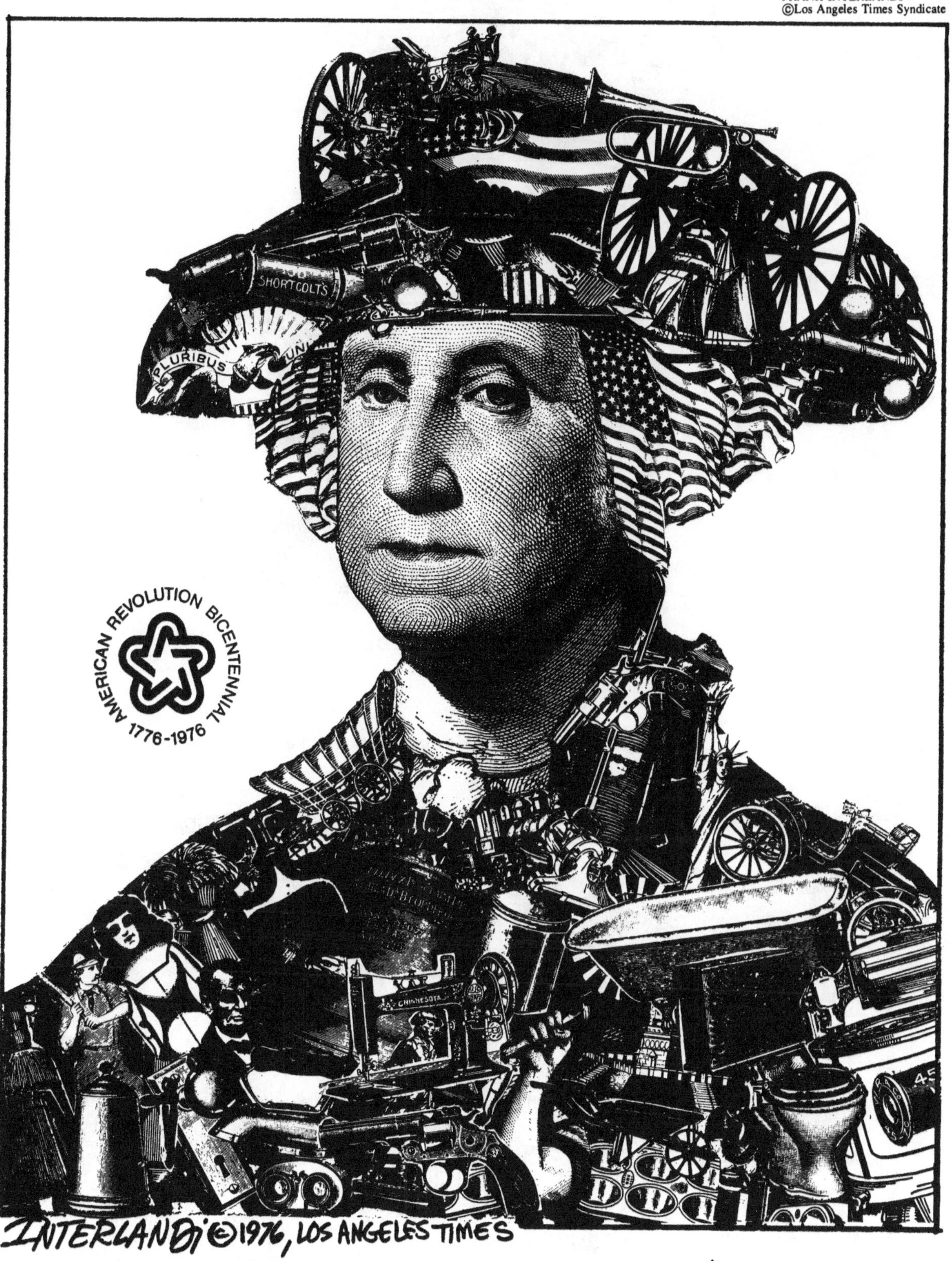
SHORT COLTS
PLURIBUS
UN
AMERICAN REVOLUTION BICENTENNIAL
1776-1976
INTERLANDI ©1976, LOS ANGELES TIMES

HAPPY BIRTHDAY, AMERICA!

Bicentennial Touch

Gas Was Only 59.9 Cents a Gallon Compared to $15.50 today!

JACK BENDER
Waterloo Courier
©Rothco Cartoons, Inc.

VIC CANTONE
©Editor and Publisher

GUERNSEY LEPELLEY
Courtesy Christian Science Monitor

The Christian Science Monitor

Energy and World Resources

The year brought a major increase in the demand for petroleum and a continued decline in domestic crude oil production. Because of an astronomical increase in imports, the United States became even more dependent on foreign oil than it had been prior to the oil embargo of 1973-1974.

U. S. dependence on oil from the Middle East continued to grow at a rapid pace, with about 30 per cent of America's oil imports coming from that area. Near the year's end the OPEC nations voted to raise the price of oil by 10 per cent. One dissenter, Saudi Arabia, the world's leading producer, split with its partners and limited its increase to 5 per cent.

Disposal of radioactive wastes emerged as a major issue during the year. Traces of plutonium and radioactive cesium were discovered in the ocean off the east and west coasts of the U. S., apparently the result of dumping steel drums filled with radioactive waste.

The United Nations sponsored a world food conference and established the International Fund for Agricultural Development to help deal with growing food problems around the globe. Under the program, small landowners would be encouraged to increase crop yields, and more effective fertilizers would be developed.

TOM FLANNERY
Courtesy Baltimore Sun

TOM DARCY
Newsday
©Los Angeles Times Syndicate

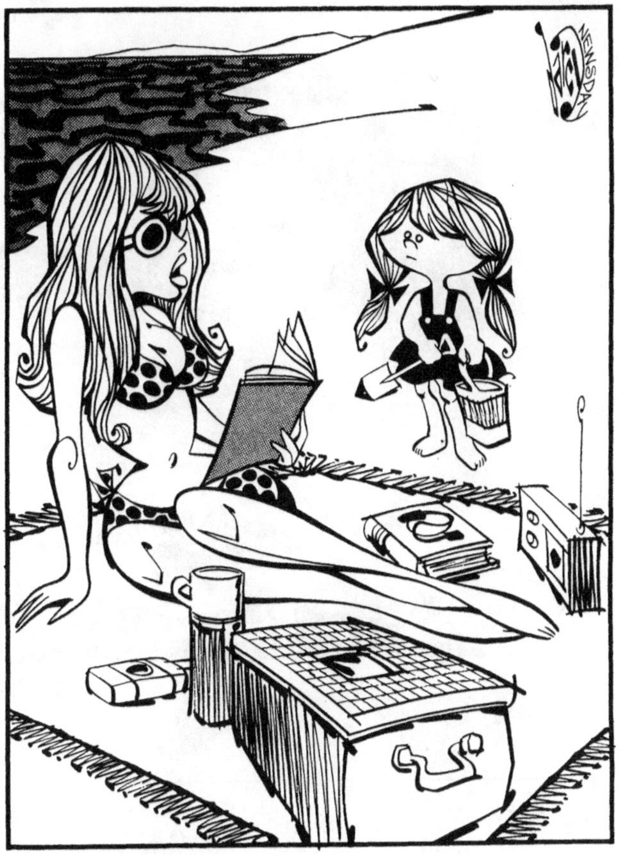

'SAND CASTLES, OKAY... SLUDGE CASTLES ARE A NO-NO'

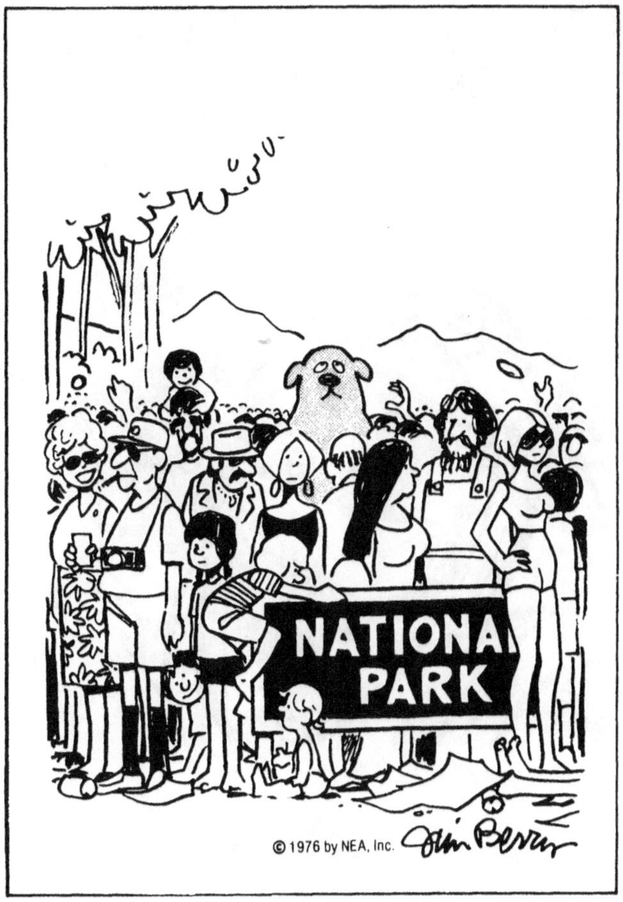
NATIONA
PARK
© 1976 by NEA, Inc.
Jim Berry

JIM BERRY
©NEA

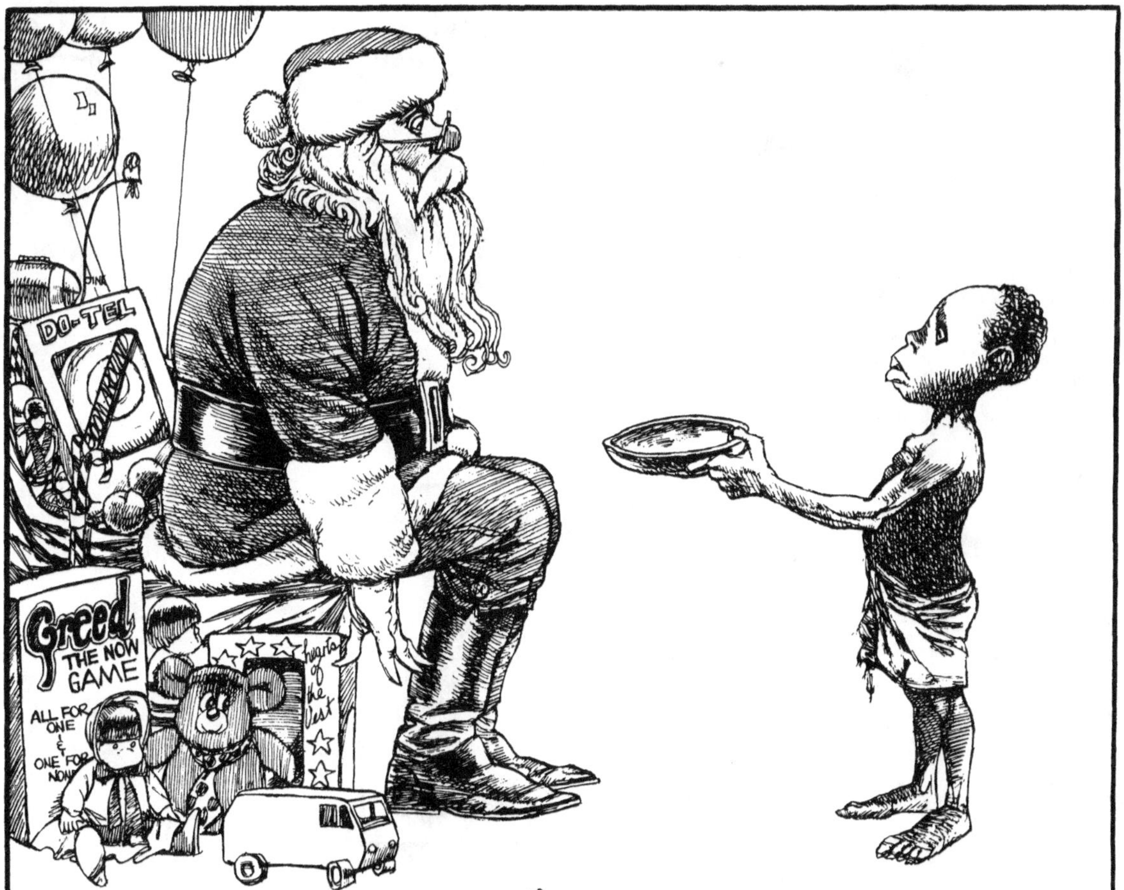
DO-TEL
Greed
THE NOW GAME
ALL FOR ONE & ONE FOR NONE
PILSWORTH TORONTO STAR

GRAHAM PILSWORTH
Courtesy Toronto Star

BERT WHITMAN
Courtesy Phoenix Gazette

DAMOCLES HAD A SWORD TO WORRY ABOUT!

MILT MORRIS
©The Associated Press

JERRY FEARING
Courtesy St. Paul Dispatch

PAT McCARTHY
Courtesy Amarillo News-Globe

ED ASHLEY
Courtesy Toledo Blade

CLYDE PETERSON
Courtesy Houston Chronicle

"It's just until I get my strength up, you understand."

Merrily We Roll Along...

CARL LARSEN
Courtesy Richmond Times-Dispatch

EUGENE CRAIG
Courtesy Columbus (O.) Dispatch

JERRY BARNETT
Courtesy Indianapolis News

SCOTT LONG
Courtesy Minneapolis Tribune

C. F. MORSE
©Hearst Newspapers

SCOTT LONG
Courtesy Minneapolis Tribune

TOM ENGELHARDT
Courtesy St. Louis Post-Dispatch

JOHN LANE
©NEA

Time Capsule

BOB BECKETT
Courtesy Burlington County (N.J.) Times

ROY CARLESS
Courtesy Steel Labor U.S.W.A., Canada

OPERATION RIPOFF!

LOU ERICKSON
Courtesy Atlanta Journal

'Can I grant your every wish? You might be dead right!'

The Middle East

The savage civil war in Lebanon overshadowed all other news from the Middle East during the year. Syrian intervention in the struggle deeply divided the Arab world and took the spotlight off the threat to Israel for a time.

Syria expressed deep concern over the possibility of a left-wing takeover in Lebanon. Its officials reasoned that such a development would make radicals more eager to move against Israel, thus increasing instability throughout the region. In past wars, Syria had been able to count Lebanon as a neutral.

After fierce fighting throughout the summer, Christians, with the help of Syria, gained the upper hand over the Moslems. By late 1976, the Palestinians controlled only about one-fifth of Lebanon. As a result, Russia's influence was weakened substantially in the area.

In other developments, Egypt sought closer ties with the United States, the Palestine Liberation Organization found its prestige diminished, and Saudi Arabia gained stature in Mideastern politics.

RAY OSRIN
Courtesy Cleveland Plain Dealer

"OH, PRAISE ALLAH, AN ISRAELI... FOR A MINUTE I THOUGHT YOU WERE A SYRIAN."

ETTA HULME
Courtesy Ft. Worth Star-Telegram

"TO HOLD THIS POSITION WE'LL NEED MORE AMMO, MORE RATIONS ..... AND A CALCULATOR"

WAYNE STAYSKAL
Courtesy Chicago Tribune

"SOMETIMES I WISH WE WOULD HAVE JUST SENT MISSIONARIES!"

VERN THOMPSON
Courtesy Lawton (Okla.) Constitution

HY ROSEN
Courtesy Albany Times-Union

"THANKS, I NEEDED THAT!"

ED FISCHER
Courtesy Omaha World-Herald

JERRY DOYLE
Courtesy Philadelphia Daily News

Reflection of Another World Degenerate

ART POINIER
© United Feature Syndicate

Death of Mao

Mao Tse-tung, leader of more than 800 million Chinese, died on September 9 at the age of eighty-two, ending an epoch in world history and leaving his nation to face an uncertain future. Premier Chou En-lai, Mao's deputy for decades, had died earlier in the year.

Organizing a guerrilla band in 1939, Mao had fought the Japanese, had won a civil war in a bitter struggle against Chiang Kai-shek, and in 1949 had become absolute ruler of mainland China, where he firmly implanted communism. After collectivizing farms and nationalizing all industry, Mao in 1958 launched his Great Leap Forward, a massive, regimented effort designed to transform China into an industrial giant. The plan failed, leading to a nationwide depression and widespread food shortages.

In 1966, another of Mao's experiments, the Great Proletarian Cultural Revolution, sent millions of youthful Red Guards rampaging through the streets of China's major cities. The party was rent asunder, and moderates were eliminated by the radicals. The wily Mao survived it all.

Over the years Mao attacked and often banished in disgrace many of his closest aides. He is believed to have caused the slaughter of hundreds of thousands—perhaps millions—of Chinese who wouldn't bend to his will.

Shortly after Mao's death, his widow, Chiang Ch'ing, a radical with high political ambitions, was arrested as part of the Gang of Four, who were accused of plotting to seize power.

TOM CURTIS
Courtesy Milwaukee Sentinel

"Greater than Hitler! Greater than Stalin! A truly great man!"

JERRY BARNETT
Courtesy Indianapolis News

ERIC SMITH
Courtesy Capital-Gazette (Md.) Newspapers

The Long March—Destination Unknown

SANDY CAMPBELL
Courtesy The Tennessean

ROBERT GRAYSMITH
Courtesy San Francisco Chronicle

THE LONG MARCH!

JIM DOBBINS
Courtesy Boston Herald-American

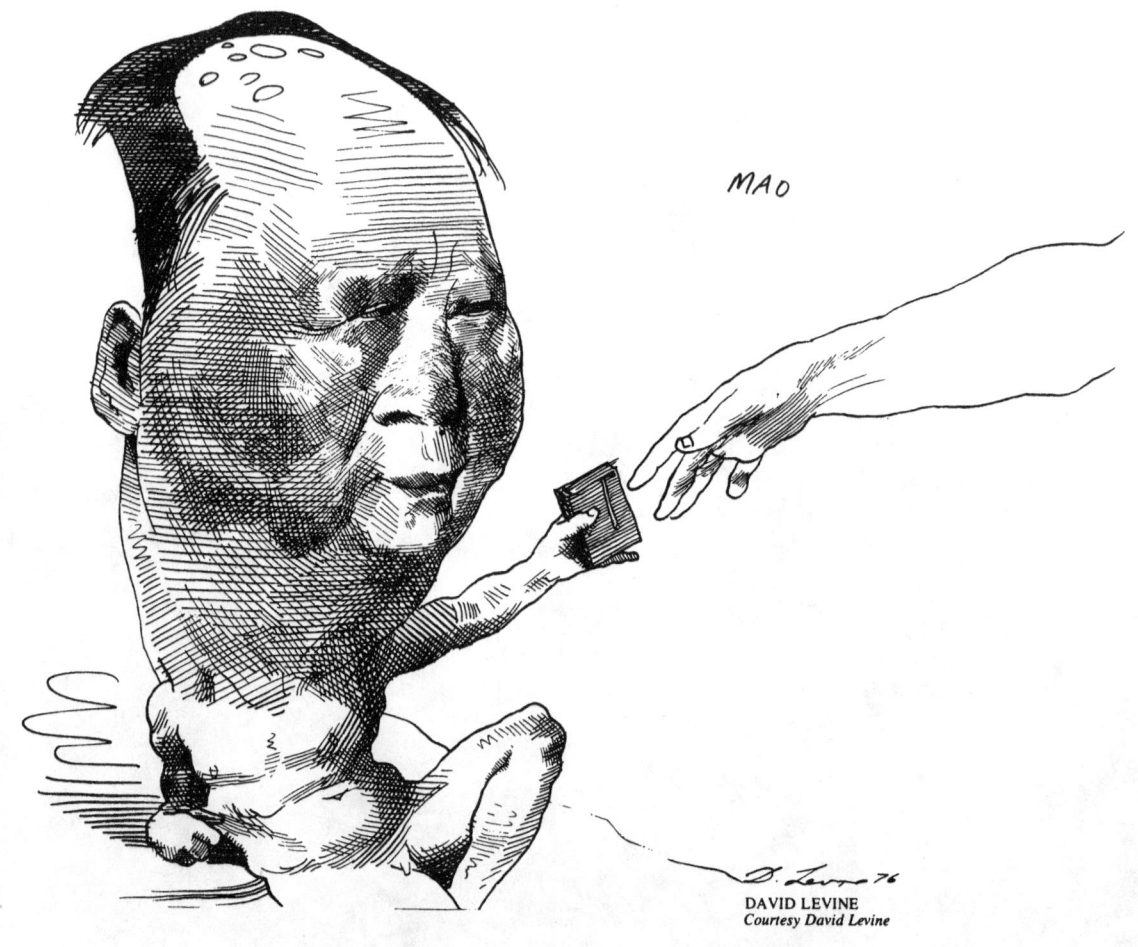

DAVID LEVINE
Courtesy David Levine

'Dick's my boy!'
DENNIS RENAULT
©McClatchy Newspapers

FACE

JIM IVEY
Orlando Sentinel Star
©Rothco Cartoons, Inc

JOHN FISCHETTI
Courtesy Chicago Daily News

"THEY WANT ME BACK ON THE MAINLAND"

Viking I and II

A historic event occurred on July 20 when *Viking I* made a successful landing on the surface of the planet Mars. Two Viking spacecraft had been launched in the summer of 1975, with one scheduled to land July 4 as part of America's bicentennial celebration. After the first had orbited the planet, however, two possible landing sites were rejected as unsuitable, and the landing came two weeks late.

Both vehicles transmitted black-and-white and color photographs of the landscape back to Earth, made meteorological observations, analyzed the soil for possible life, and investigated the atmosphere. In September *Viking II* set down near the northern polar cap, which was found to be made up totally of water ice. The detailed photographs, from almost a half-billion miles away in space, were remarkable in clarity. Neither mission, however, found any evidence of life on Mars.

CHARLES WERNER
Courtesy Indianapolis Star

"Well, there goes the neighborhood!"

ART BIMROSE
Courtesy Portland Oregonian

KEN ALEXANDER
Courtesy San Francisco Examiner

ROBERT GRAYSMITH
Courtesy San Francisco Chronicle

JOHN LANE
©NEA

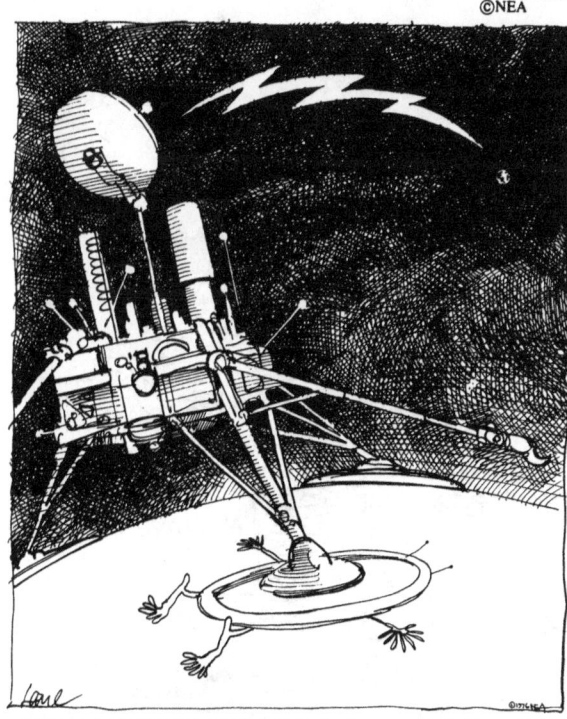

"Viking Lander regrets there is no trace of intelligent life on Mars!"

BOB PALMER
Courtesy Springfield (Mo.)
Leader-Press

LEW HARSH
Courtesy Scranton Times

BYRON HUMPHREY
Courtesy New Orleans States-Item

International Affairs

Britain was hit hard in 1976 by the worst economic crisis in its history as the pound fell to record lows. Troubles piled up: double-digit inflation, high unemployment, a huge foreign debt, slowed industrial output, and the back-breaking cost of maintaining a welfare state. As a stopgap measure, the beleaguered nation obtained a six-month $5.3 billion line of credit from an eleven-nation consortium, which included the U. S. The value of the pound kept plummeting, and in September the British government went looking for another $3.9 billion from the International Monetary Fund.

Canada spent much of the year trying to escape from the shadow of the United States. For years, the nation had chafed under American economic, political, and cultural domination, and the Ottawa government began steps to change that state of affairs. Oil exports to the U. S., for example, would be phased out within two years.

On November 15, a party committed to the secession of the providence of Quebec gained power in national elections. For many of Canada's twenty-three million citizens, the separatist movement repre-

DICK LOCHER
Courtesy Chicago Tribune

INTERNATIONAL AFFAIRS

sented a potentially devastating problem. The biggest fear was that, if Quebec gained independence, a chain reaction of independence-seeking provinces might result.

Jose Lopez became president of Mexico amid a hoard of escalating problems. A sagging economy and land seizures by poor peasants raised the possibility of a military coup.

The government of Prime Minister Indira Gandhi of India acted on several fronts to extend its authoritarian control. Censorship was formally sanctioned by legislation, and basic civil rights were suspended. More than thirty thousand citizens were imprisoned for political reasons.

Italy, too, continued in the grip of political and economic turmoil. Although the threat of a Communist party victory in the June elections did not materialize, the value of the lira declined 24 per cent.

The value of French currency also dropped, but West Germany continued as a model of economic stability, with unemployment at a low 4.5 per cent.

TOM DARCY
Newsday
©Los Angeles Times Syndicate

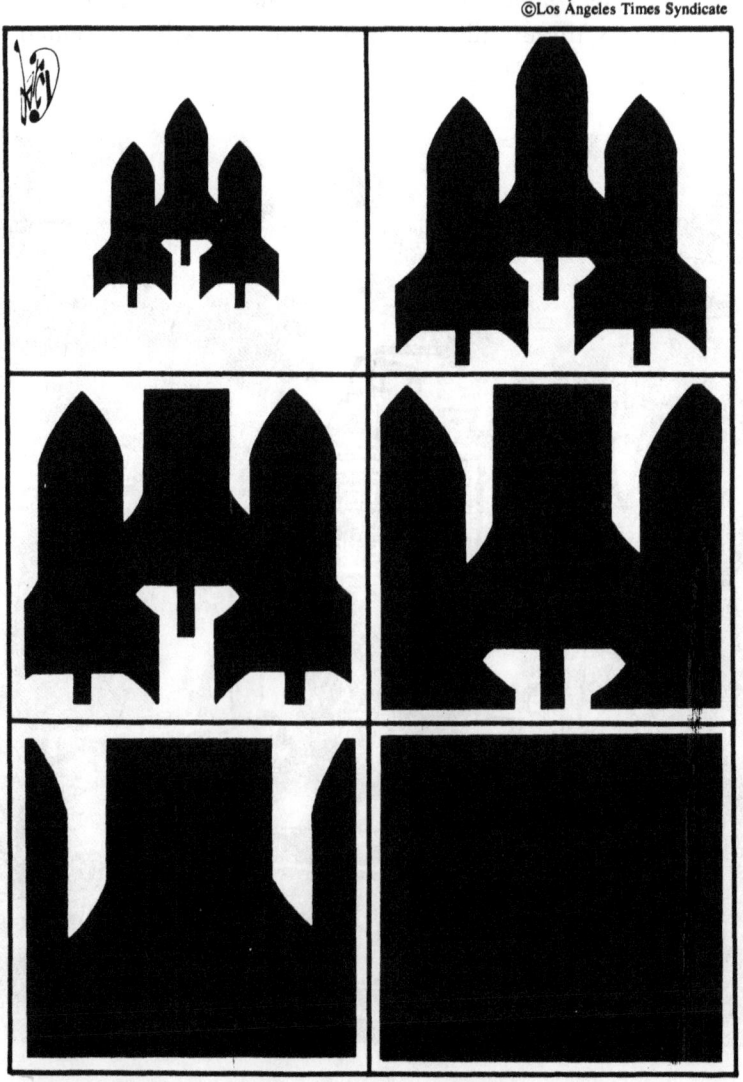

The Arms Race

"WHAT'S YER PLEASURE? POLITICS, RELIGION, MURDER?"

LOU GRANT
Oakland Tribune
©Los Angeles Times Syndicate

KATE PALMER
Courtesy Greenville (S.C.) News

'I FEEL SO AT HOME HERE!'

JERRY BARNETT
Courtesy Indianapolis News

JACK McLEOD
Courtesy Buffalo Evening News

'I'VE DECIDED! LET'S SIT OUT INDIA'S '76 ELECTIONS'

'Didn't the Illustrious Mahatma Always Have His Spinning Wheel?'

CHARLES BISSELL
Courtesy Nashville Tennessean

INDIAN ROPE TRICK

LOU GRANT
Oakland Tribune
©Los Angeles Times Syndicate

'Wonder What's The Critical Mass?'

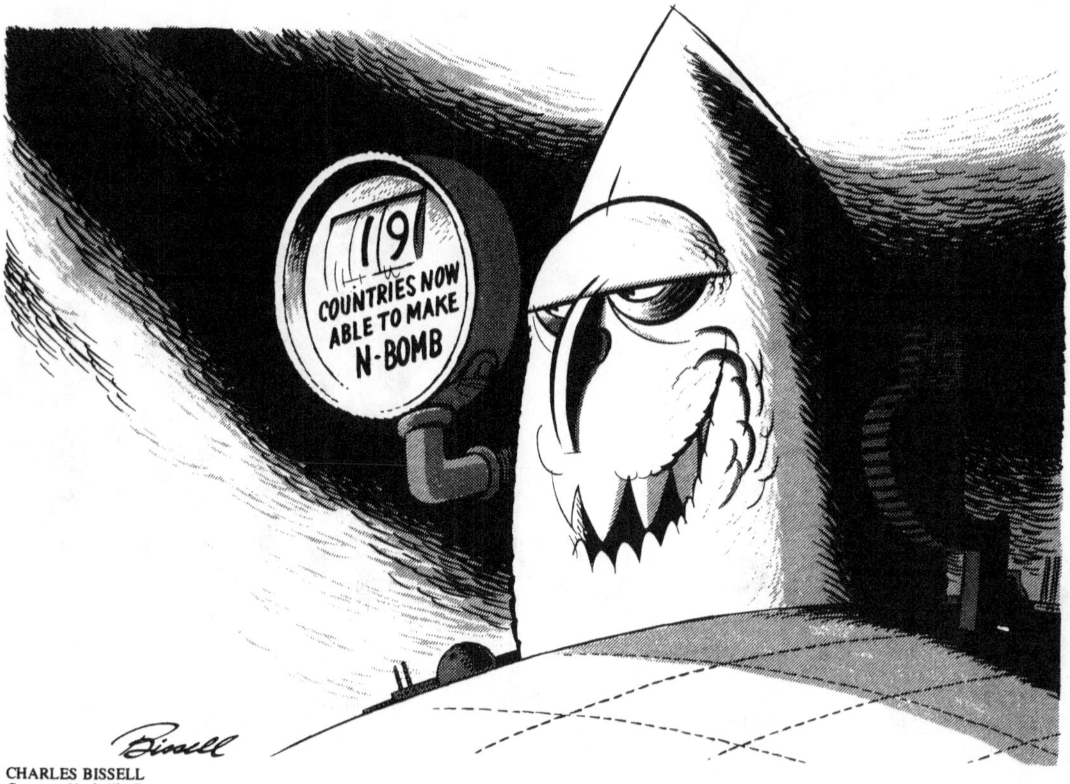
19
COUNTRIES NOW ABLE TO MAKE N-BOMB
Bissell

CHARLES BISSELL
Courtesy Nashville Tennessean

HY ROSEN
Courtesy Albany Times-Union

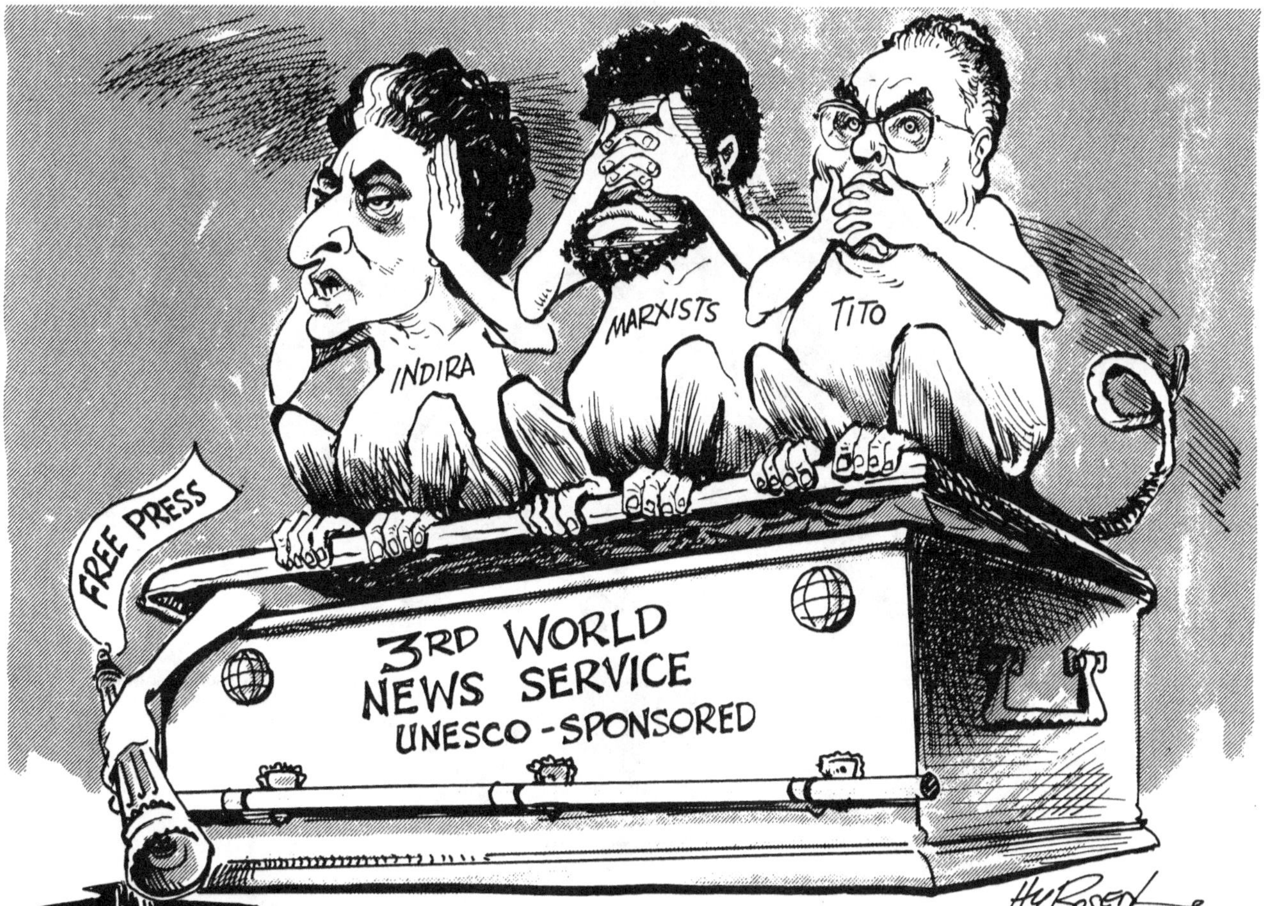
INDIRA
MARXISTS
TITO
FREE PRESS
3RD WORLD NEWS SERVICE UNESCO-SPONSORED
Hy Rosen

ROY PETERSON
Courtesy Vancouver Sun

THE PETERSON PORTFOLIO

ANDY DONATO
Courtesy Toronto Sun

RENE LEVESQUE, SEPARATIST PREMIER OF QUEBEC

"THE MAIN PURPOSE OF THESE CABINET CHANGES GENTLEMEN IS TO HEIGHTEN OUR PUBLIC IMAGE!"

ROY PETERSON
Courtesy Vancouver Sun

The Bionic Man

V. ROSCHKOV
Courtesy Windsor Star

CANADA'S FORIEGN POLICY

JOHN COLLINS
Courtesy Montreal (Can.) Gazette

PETER KUCH
Courtesy Winnipeg Free Press

OTTAWA NEWSBOY

DOUG SNEYD
Courtesy Toronto Star

"The way I understand it, if the communists rule Italy, we would still have nothing, but we would all share it equally."

HANOI: "VIETNAM IS ONE"

ART BIMROSE
Courtesy Portland Oregonian

ART BIMROSE
Courtesy Portland Oregonian

WHILE WE DISCUSS DEFENSE CUTS

JOHN STAMPONE
Courtesy Army Times

'I Believe in Reciprocal Trade'

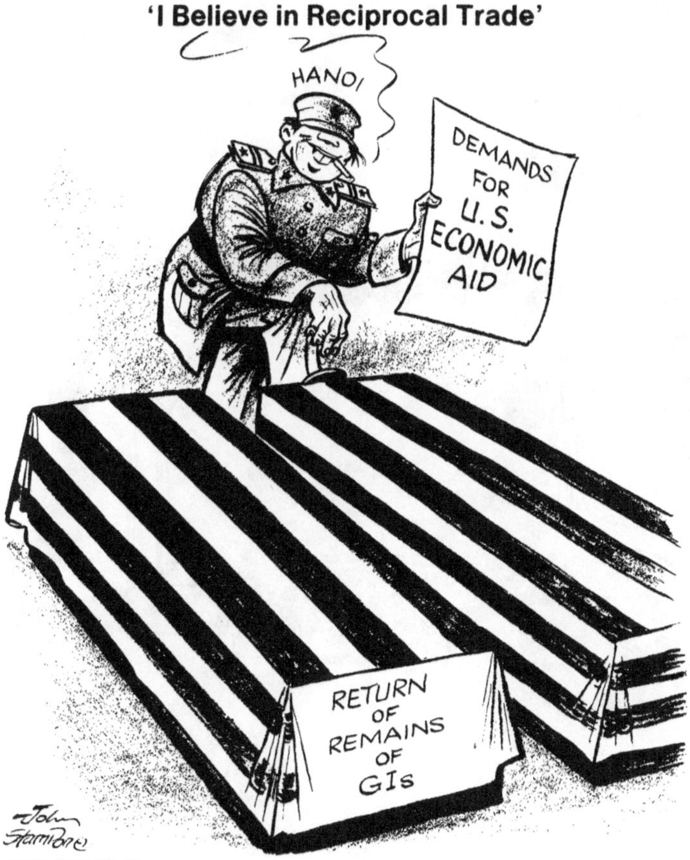
HANOI
DEMANDS FOR U.S. ECONOMIC AID
RETURN OF REMAINS OF GIs

JOHN STAMPONE
Courtesy Army Times

'Forward . . .'

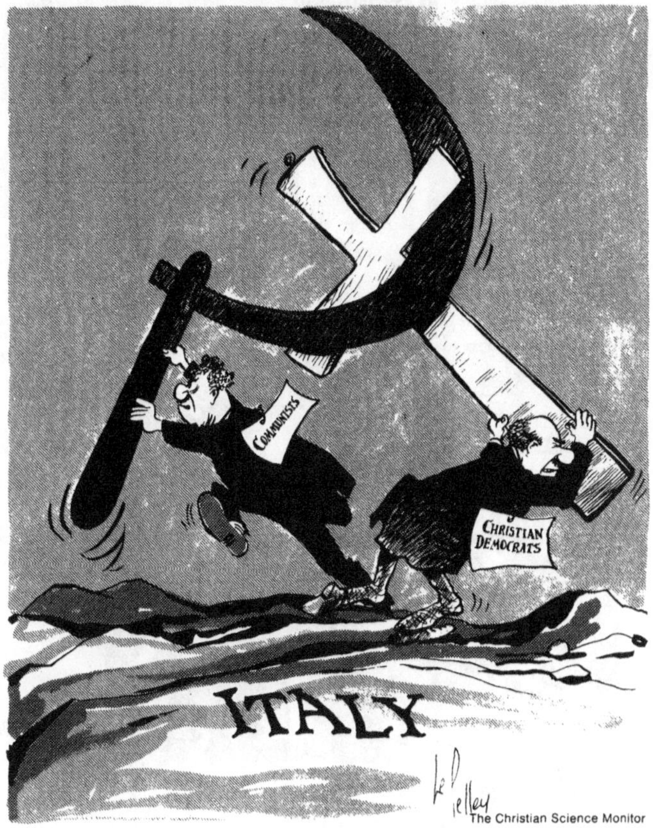
COMMUNISTS
CHRISTIAN DEMOCRATS
ITALY
The Christian Science Monitor

GUERNSEY LEPELLEY
Courtesy Christian Science Monitor

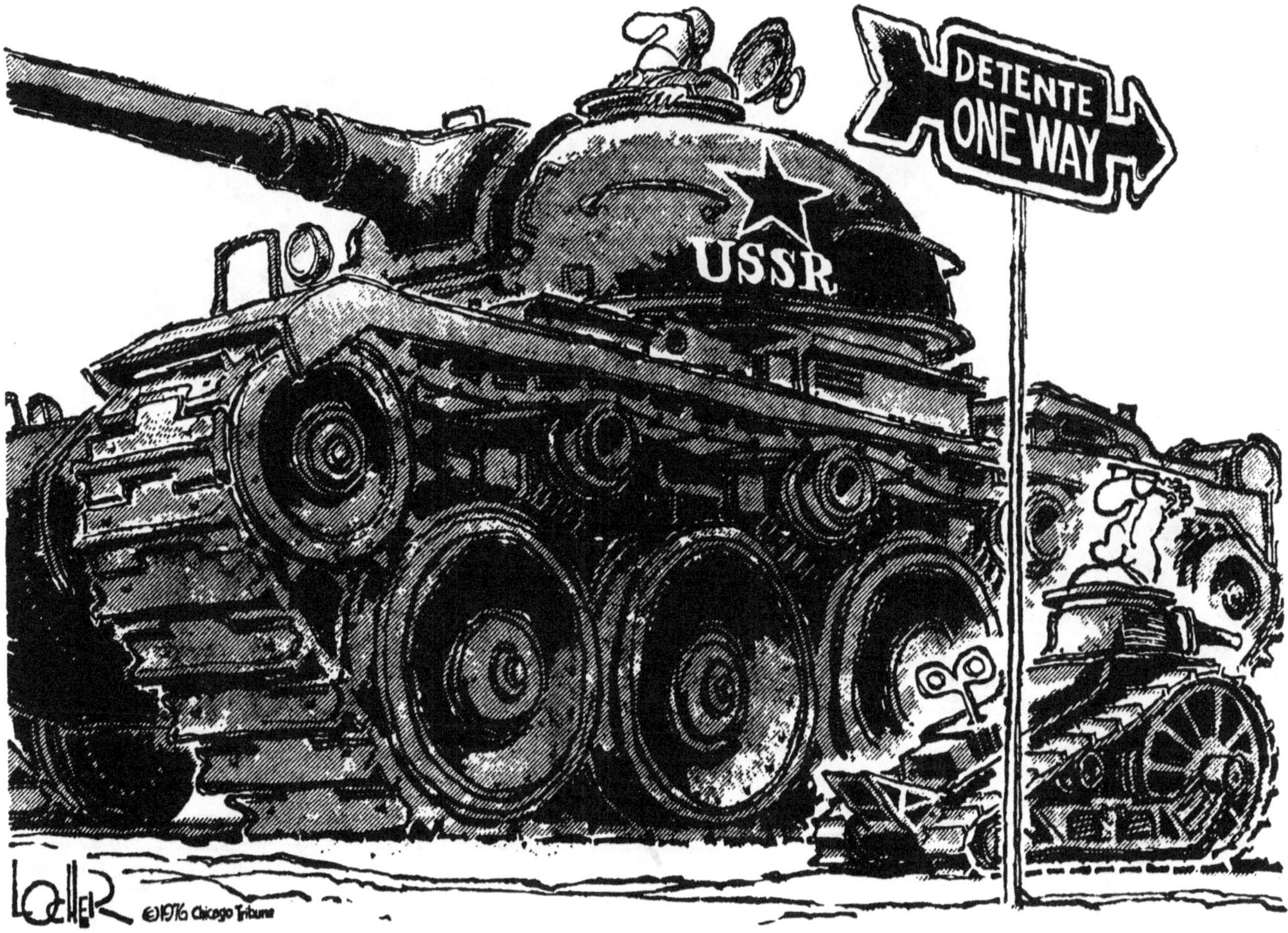
DETENTE
ONE WAY
USSR
©1976 Chicago Tribune

DICK LOCHER
Courtesy Chicago Tribune

PATCHWORK

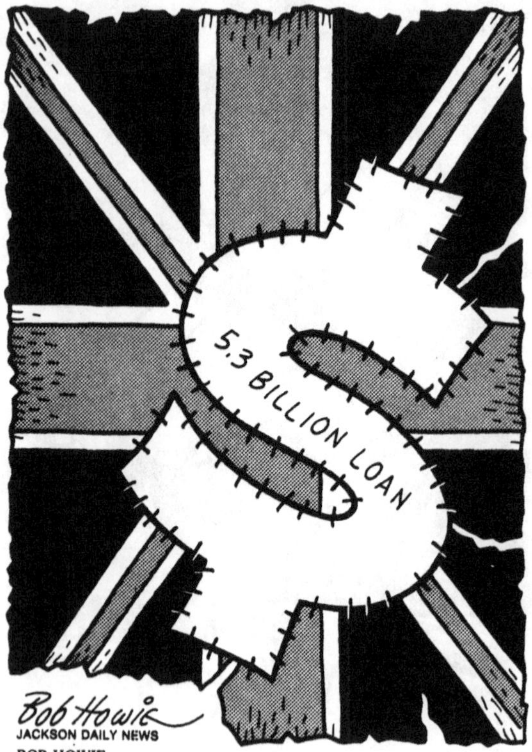
5.3 BILLION LOAN
Bob Howie
JACKSON DAILY NEWS

BOB HOWIE
Courtesy Jackson (Miss.) Daily News

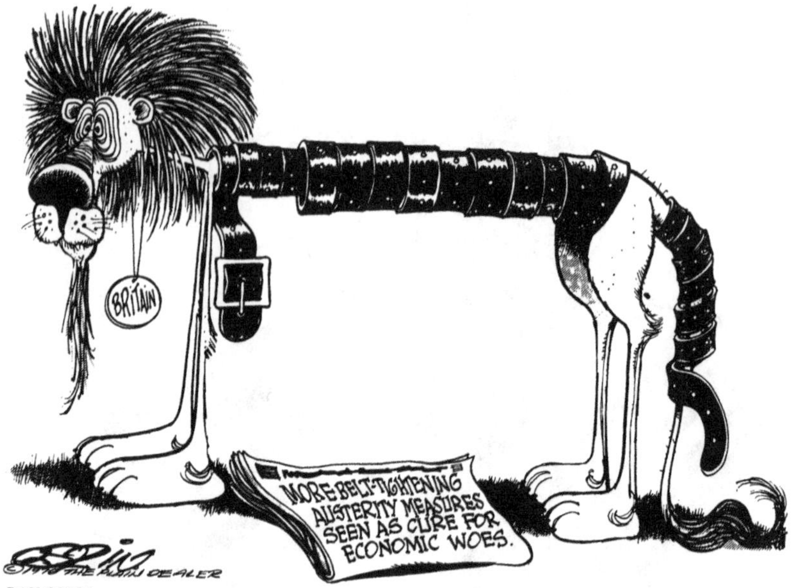
BRITAIN
MORE BELT-TIGHTENING AUSTERITY MEASURES SEEN AS CURE FOR ECONOMIC WOES.

RAY OSRIN
Courtesy Cleveland Plain Dealer

"Bong . . . Bong . . . Bong . . .Bong . . . Clink . . ."

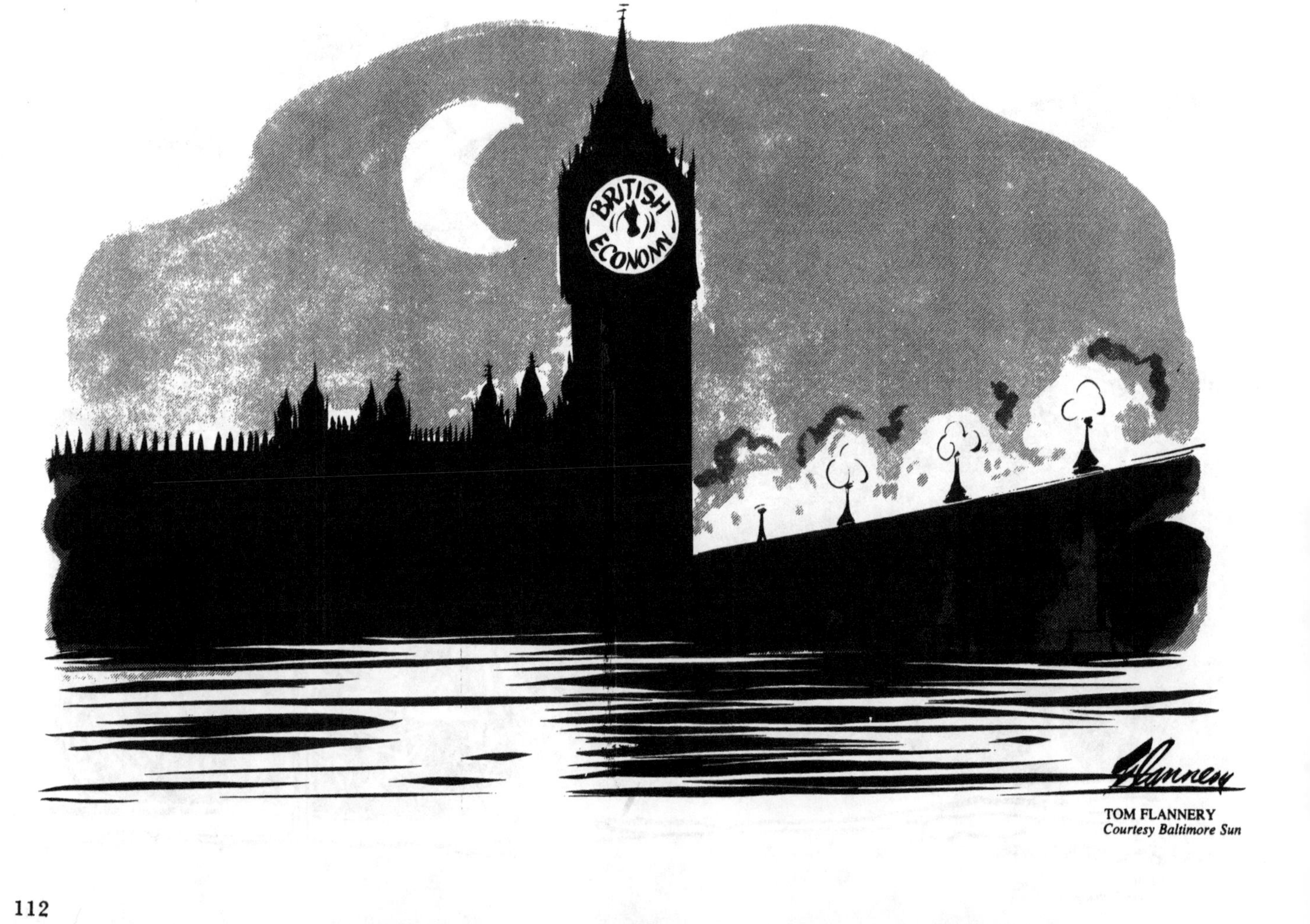
BRITISH ECONOMY

TOM FLANNERY
Courtesy Baltimore Sun

BEASTLY WEATHER, WHAT?

JACK JURDEN
Courtesy Wilmington Evening
Journal-News

"I'VE INITIATED THIS MEETING IN ORDER TO DISCUSS NORMALIZING RELATIONS"

CHARLES BROOKS
Courtesy Birmingham (Ala.) News

UNRAVELLING?

EUGENE CRAIG
Courtesy Columbus (O.) Dispatch

113

Medicaid and Malpractice Charges

The public received a shock when stories of fraud running into billions of dollars and shoddy medical care for millions of citizens were brought to light. These startling facts emerged from hearings in August before the Senate Subcommittee on Long-Term Care. One of the panel's investigators charged, "Rampant fraud and abuse exist among practitioners participating in the medicaid program, matched by an equivalent degree of error and maladministration by government agencies."

Senate investigators found that from one-fourth to one-half of the $15 billion spent for medicaid was drained off by fraud or by poor and often unnecessary medical services. Scores of physicians were found to be drawing medicaid payments of more than $100,000 annually.

Medical malpractice insurance remained a serious problem, as premiums continued to skyrocket. Annual premiums of more than $30,000 for surgeons were not uncommon. The rising costs inevitably led to increased patient fees, and hospital charges also soared. Some companies simply stopped issuing malpractice insurance.

WAYNE STAYSKAL
Courtesy Chicago Tribune

"YES, YES, I CHEATED ON MEDICAID... BUT I ONLY DID IT TO, SOB, PAY FOR MY MALPRACTICE INSURANCE!"

MIKE KEEFE
Courtesy Denver Post

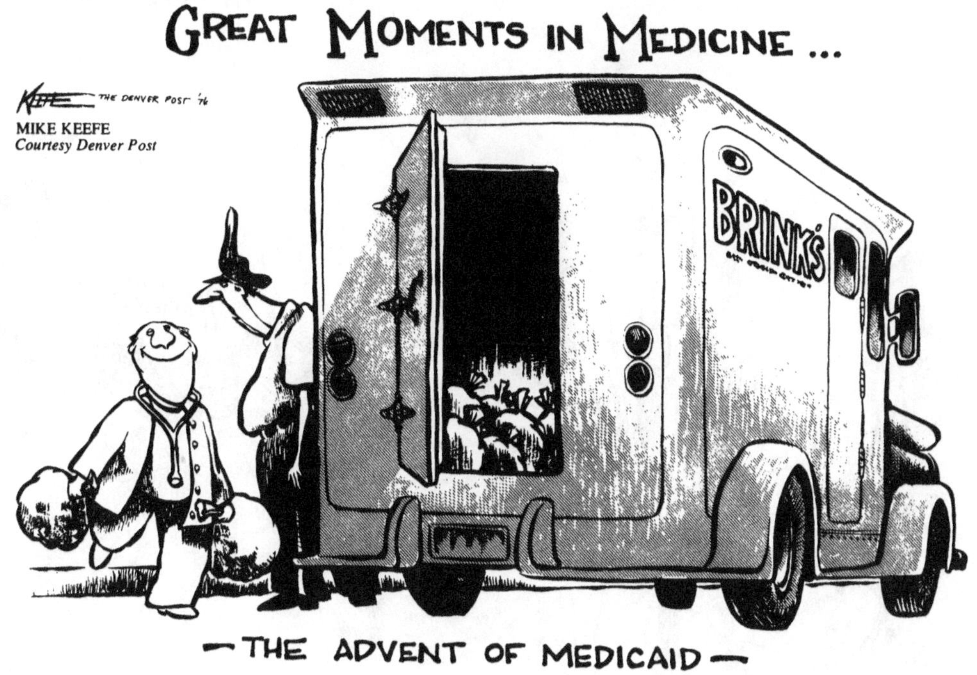
GREAT MOMENTS IN MEDICINE ...
BRINK'S
— THE ADVENT OF MEDICAID —

KATE PALMER
Courtesy Greenville (S.C.) News

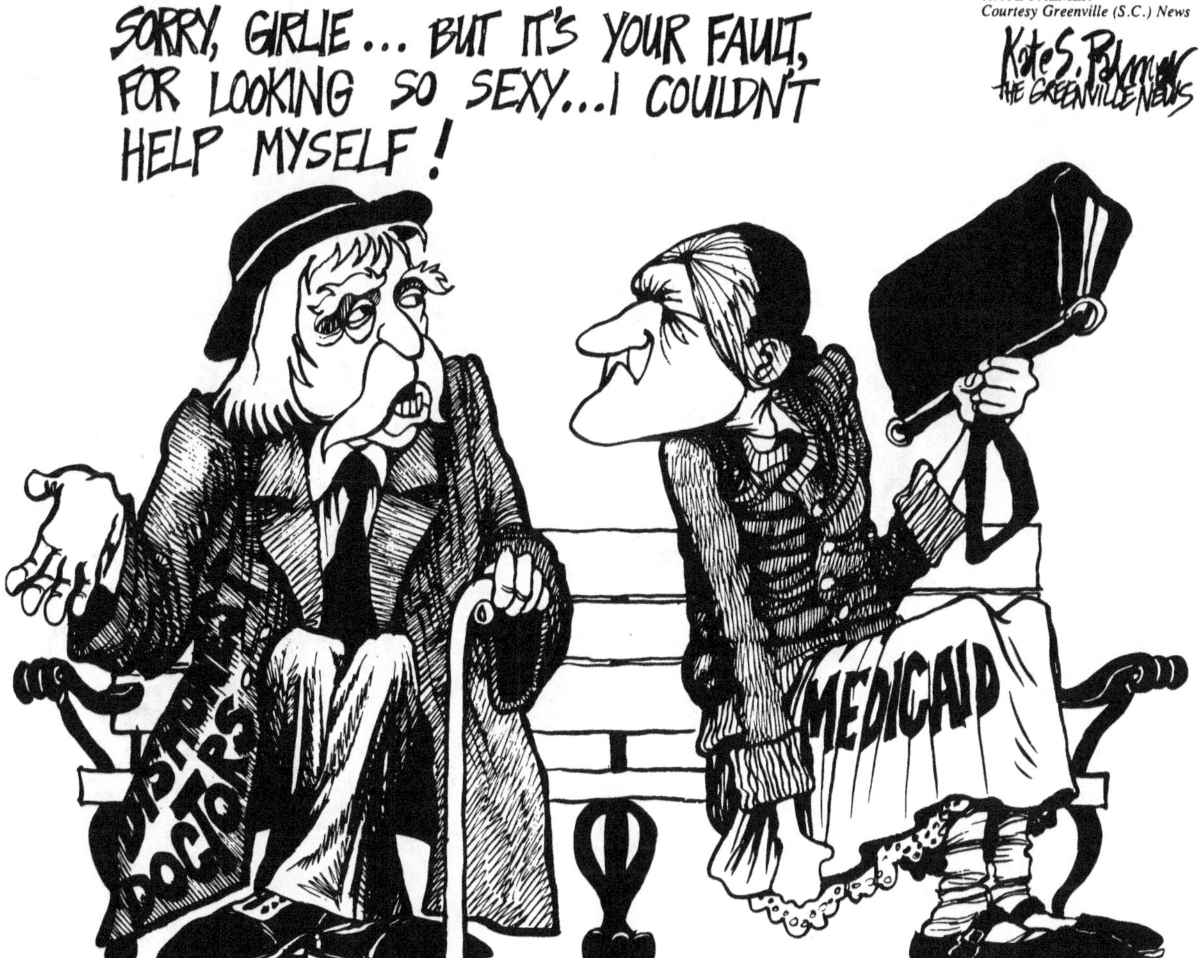
SORRY, GIRLIE ... BUT IT'S YOUR FAULT, FOR LOOKING SO SEXY ... I COULDN'T HELP MYSELF!
MEDICAID

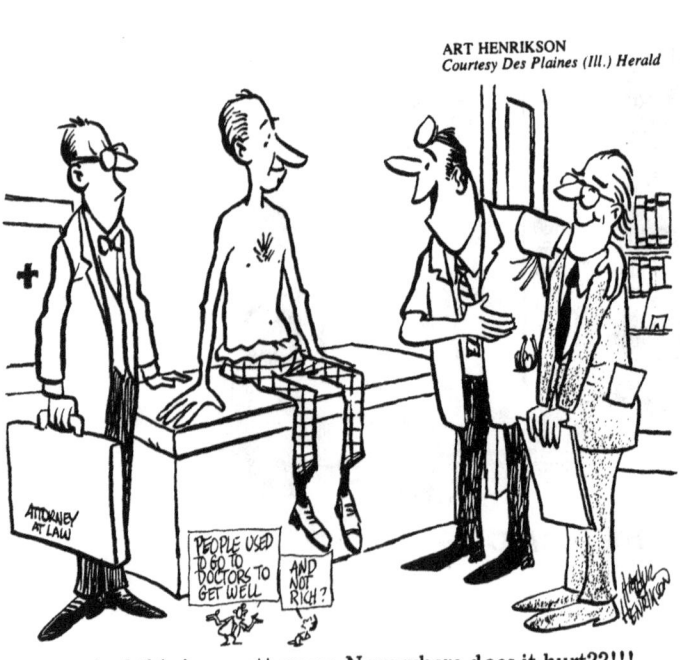

ART HENRIKSON
Courtesy Des Plaines (Ill.) Herald

... And this is my attorney. Now where does it hurt??!!!

REG MANNING
Courtesy Arizona Republic

ROBERT A. DUNN
Courtesy Buffalo Courier-Express

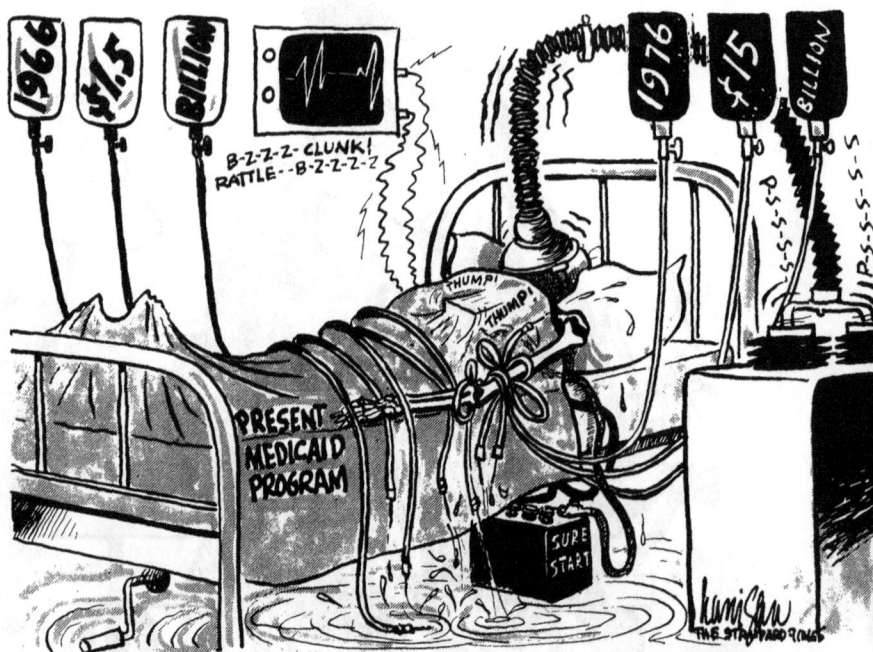

JACK LANIGAN
Courtesy New Bedford Standard-Times

Crime

Illegal and improper activities at the highest levels of big business and involving other nations were disclosed during the year. Through the media, the public became aware of widespread white-collar crime such as bribes and payoffs.

The Lockheed Aircraft Corporation was one of the first large companies to admit making payoffs. Its spokesmen stated that $22 million had been paid to foreign officials since 1970 as a "tax" for doing business. The disclosures had quick and severe repercussions in Japan and the Netherlands. Lockheed's president announced that Prince Bernhard, husband of Queen Juliana of the Netherlands, had been paid $1.1 million. A Senate subcommittee disclosed that Yoshio Kodama, an ultra-right militarist, had served as sales agent for Lockheed in Japan and had received more than $7 million in secret payments.

Crimes against business—shoplifting, credit manipulations, and other forms of theft—continued to increase sharply. Government and industries estimated the cost of such crimes at from $23 to $40 billion annually. According to official estimates, 500,000 Americans were "career criminals," with the overall price tag for fighting and controlling crime being nearly $100 billion a year.

LEONARD NORRIS
Courtesy Vancouver (Can.) Sun

"...and business being what it is these days, I can well understand your interest in one that's booming..."

"JUST YELL IF YOU'RE THREATENED BY FOREIGN AGGRESSORS!"

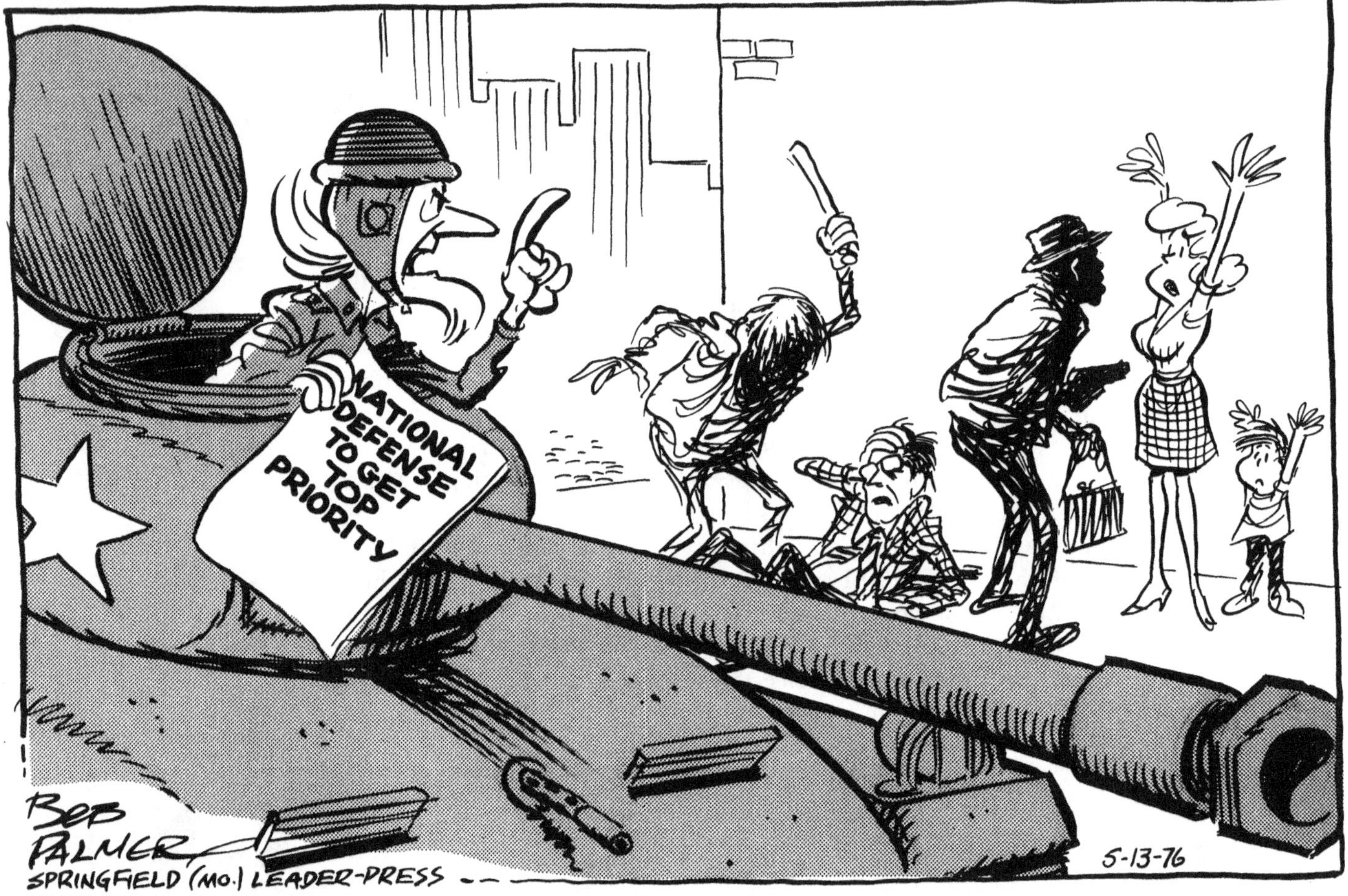

NATIONAL DEFENSE TO GET TOP PRIORITY
BOB PALMER
SPRINGFIELD (MO.) LEADER-PRESS
5-13-76

BOB PALMER
Courtesy Springfield (Mo.) Leader-Press

JERRY BITTLE
Courtesy Albuquerque Tribune

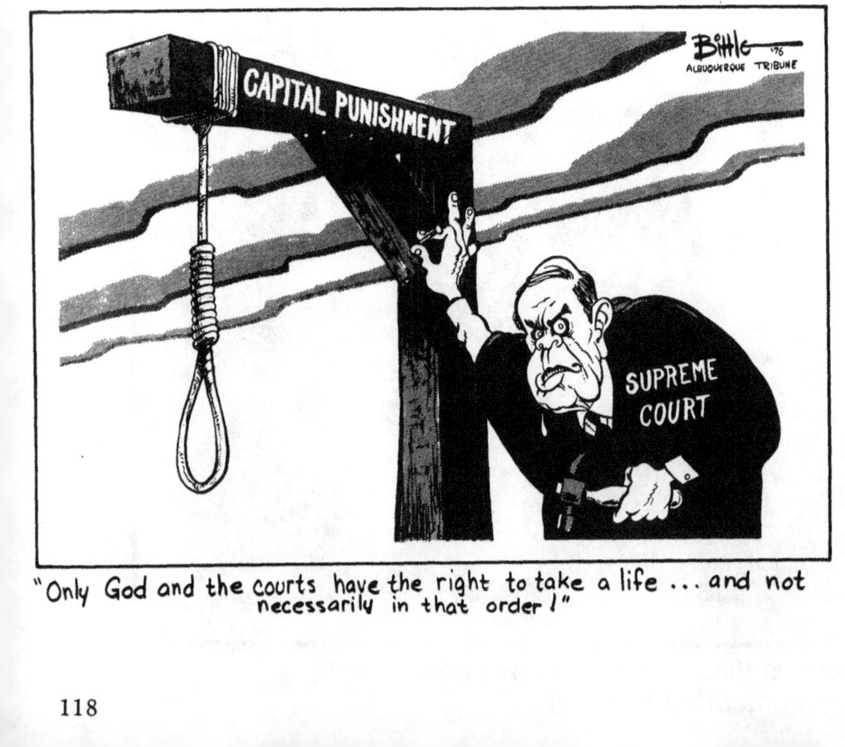

Bittle '76
ALBUQUERQUE TRIBUNE
CAPITAL PUNISHMENT
SUPREME COURT

"Only God and the courts have the right to take a life ... and not necessarily in that order!"

JOHN LANE
©NEA

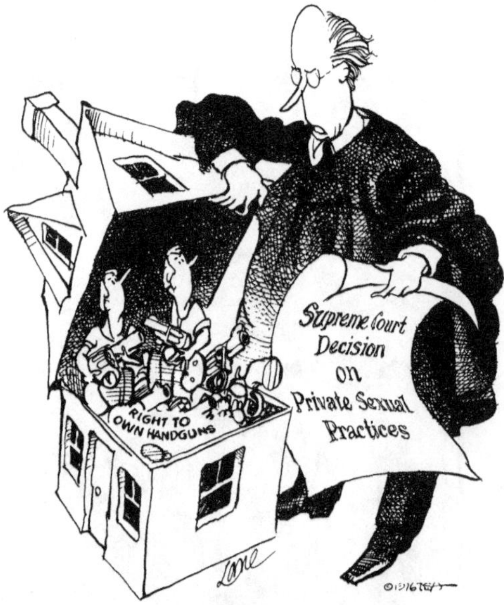

Supreme Court Decision on Private Sexual Practices
RIGHT TO OWN HANDGUNS
Lane

"That's okay! Just don't make love!"

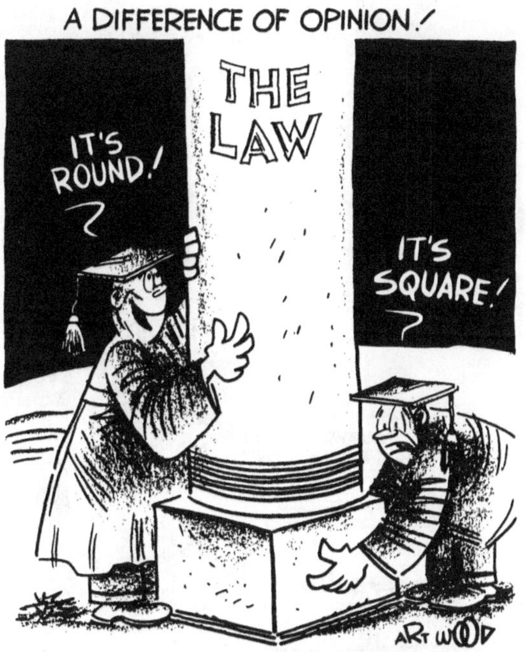
A DIFFERENCE OF OPINION!
THE LAW
IT'S ROUND! ?
IT'S SQUARE! ?
ART WOOD

ART WOOD
Courtesy U. S. Independent Telephone Assn.

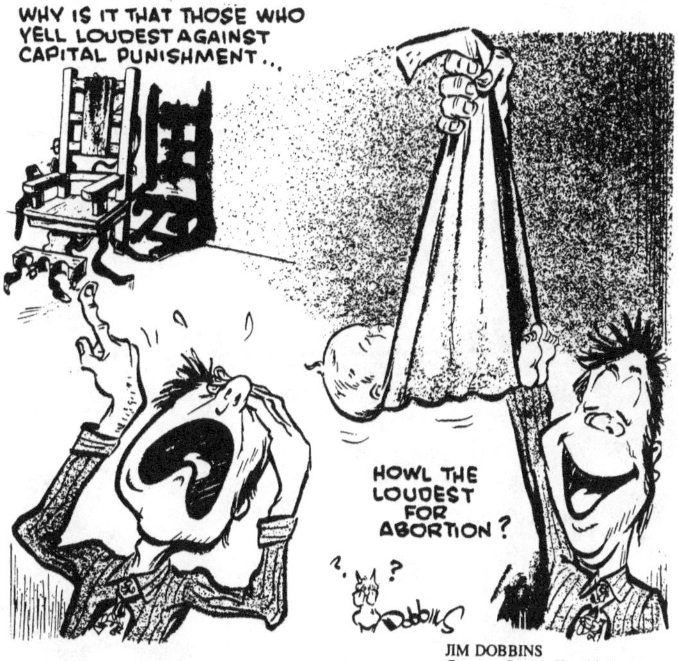
WHY IS IT THAT THOSE WHO YELL LOUDEST AGAINST CAPITAL PUNISHMENT...
HOWL THE LOUDEST FOR ABORTION?
DOBBINS

JIM DOBBINS
Courtesy Boston Herald-American

HERC FICKLEN
Courtesy Dallas Morning News

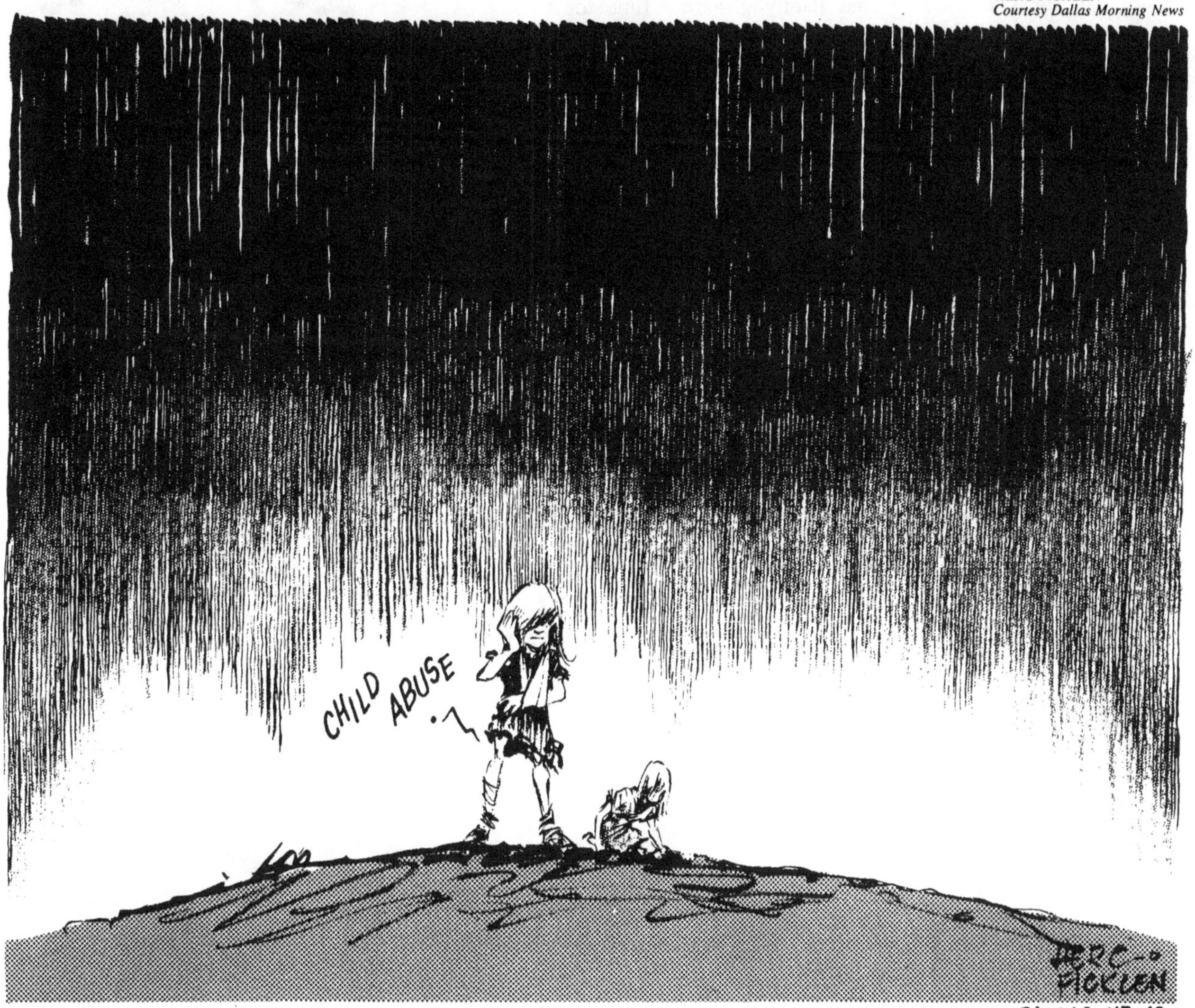
CHILD ABUSE.
HERC-O FICKLEN
DALLAS NEWS
SPEAKING OF ISSUES —

EDD ULUSCHAK
Courtesy Edmonton Journal

"Out on bail for two weeks?—That hardly gives me time for enough bank jobs to pay my lawyer!"

JACK BENDER
Waterloo Courier
©Rothco Cartoons, Inc

LOU ERICKSON
Courtesy Atlanta Journal

'Gentlemen of the board, something must be done to stop this awful crime in the streets'

Russia

While the Ford administration was promoting détente, the Soviet Union continued to outrace the United States in an all-out buildup of military capability. By mid-1977, Russia was expected to lead America in strategic missiles by more than 600 and in land-based missiles by some 450. The Soviets were replacing older land-based missiles with newer models, and their submarines were being armed with the new SSN-8 missile, with twice the range of the best American version. Soviet ground forces increased to 1.7 million troops, with a total military strength estimated at 4.4 million men.

But, while upgrading their military machine, the Soviets were struggling to avert a blowup of the Red empire. In East Germany an estimated 150,000 discontented citizens applied for exit visas. In Poland a powerful combination of intellectuals, workers, and the Catholic church began challenging the Communist regime. The Communist satellite Romania seemed determined to preserve its independence in foreign policy, despite Russian growls.

Communist Empire

CARL LARSEN
Courtesy Richmond Times-Dispatch

MIDEAST BUMP

JOHN RIEDELL
Courtesy Peoria Journal

CALVIN GRONDAHL
Courtesy Deseret News

That's Funny, this sandwich wasn't toasted when I packed it this morning.

RAY OSRIN
Courtesy Cleveland Plain Dealer

WARREN KING
Courtesy N.Y. Daily News

Olympics

The 1976 Olympic games held in Montreal may have been the best in history from a competitive standpoint, but the economic and political problems that accompanied them made many people wonder if they were worth it. An environmental and financial debate first led the winter games to be moved from Denver, Colorado, to Innsbruck, Austria. Then came a dispute over the participation of Taiwan in the Montreal games.

A week before the opening ceremonies, the Canadian government announced that it would not permit Taiwanese athletes to compete under the flag, anthem, or name of the Republic of China. Canada had put politics ahead of the pledge it made when it was designated the host

TOM DARCY
Newsday
©Los Angeles Times Syndicate

OLYMPICS

country. Many African athletes pulled out because New Zealand's national rugby team had toured South Africa at a time when black students were rioting in Johannesburg.

The brightest stars of the games were the ice skater Dorothy Hamill and the gymnast Nadia Comaneci, whose flawless performances provided a stark contrast to the machinations of some of the governments involved.

MERLE TINGLEY
Courtesy London (Can.) Free Press

JACK McLEOD
Courtesy Buffalo Evening News

'LAST CHANCE TO DEFECT TILL 1984'

BEN SARGENT
Courtesy Austin American

JOHN COLLINS
Courtesy Montreal (Can.) Gazette

UNOFFICIAL GUIDE TO THOSE OLYMPIC SYMBOLS

ANTHONY JENKINS
Courtesy Toronto Globe and Mail

BOB ALEXANDER
Courtesy Lawrence (Mass.) Eagle-Tribune

The Post Office

During the year a resident of Elizabeth, New Jersey, received a Christmas card, postmarked December 10, 1975, on Valentine's Day. A real estate agent in Coral Gables, Florida, complained that a letter he mailed took five days to travel exactly five blocks. Everyone seemed to have a horror story of snail's-pace mail service during the year.

Higher costs and less efficiency seemed to be the problems. A new rate increase went into effect, raising the cost of a first-class letter to thirteen cents, more than twice the six-cent stamp of 1970.

Despite the rate increase and cutbacks in service, the U. S. Postal Service was saddled with a deficit totaling $1.4 billion. The General Accounting Office predicted that, if the agency were to achieve self-sufficiency without further major cutbacks in service, a first-class letter might cost thirty-two cents by 1984.

There was one obvious reason for the post office deficit; from 1970 to 1975, employee wages rose by 60 per cent, considerably more than the cost of living.

LEW HARSH
Courtesy Scranton Times

" A DIRECTIVE, MAILED FROM WASHINGTON TWO MONTHS AGO, JUST ARRIVED! IT SAYS 'CLOSE YOUR POST OFFICE AND GO HOME'!"

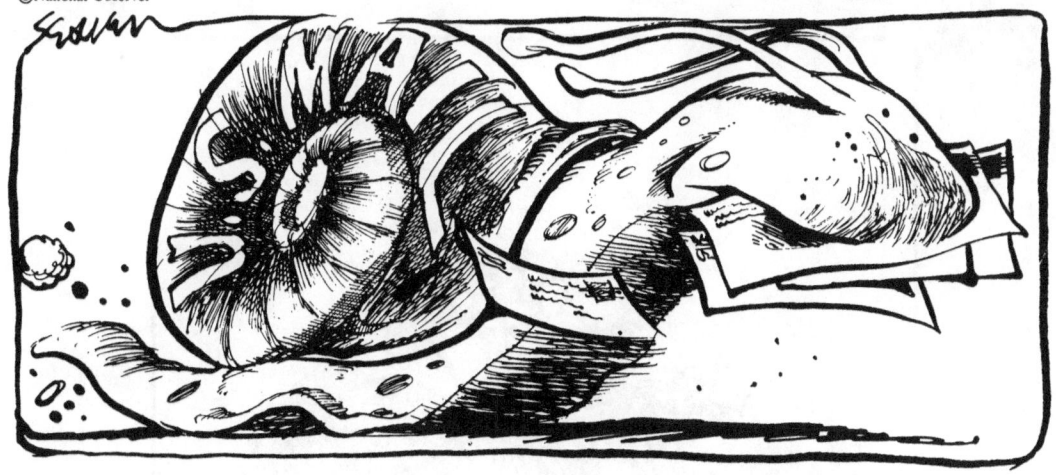

DAVID SEAVEY
©National Observer

"I'M AMAZED THAT, WITH ALL THOSE TRUTH-IN-ADVERTISING LAWS, WE HAVEN'T BEEN ORDERED TO STOP CALLING IT FIRST-CLASS MAIL."

LARRY WRIGHT
Courtesy Detroit News

DICK LOCHER
Courtesy Chicago Tribune

"Hello, Congress?...about that billion dollar subsidy to the post office..., please send it over by cab! You know how unreliable mail delivery is today!"

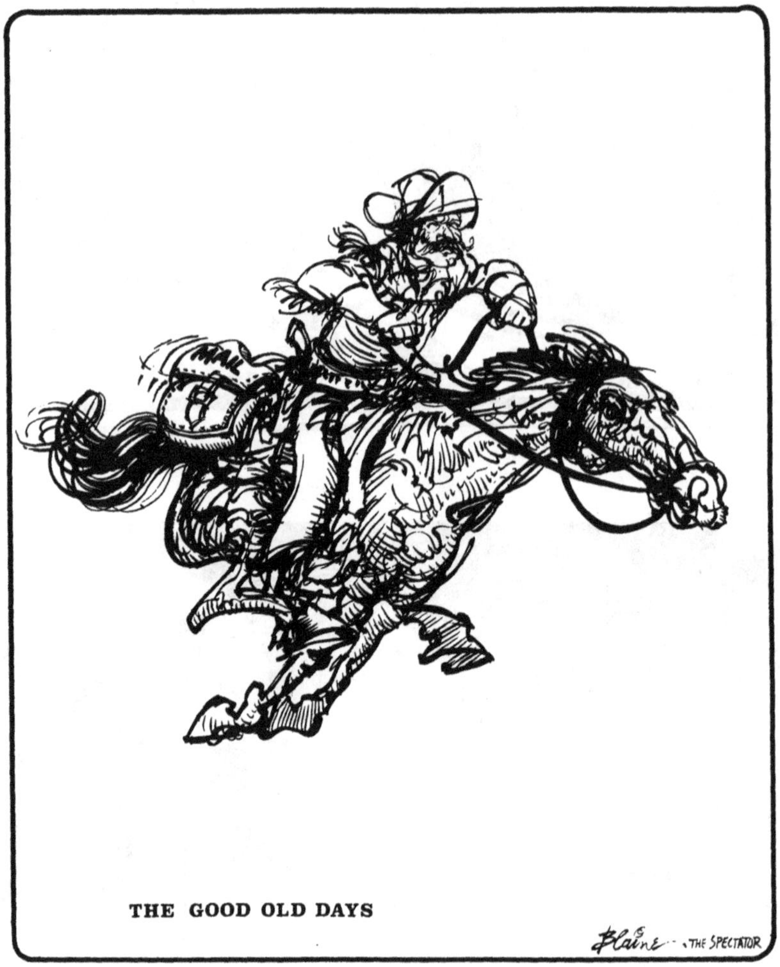
THE GOOD OLD DAYS
MAIL
Blaine THE SPECTATOR

BLAINE
Courtesy The Spectator, Canada

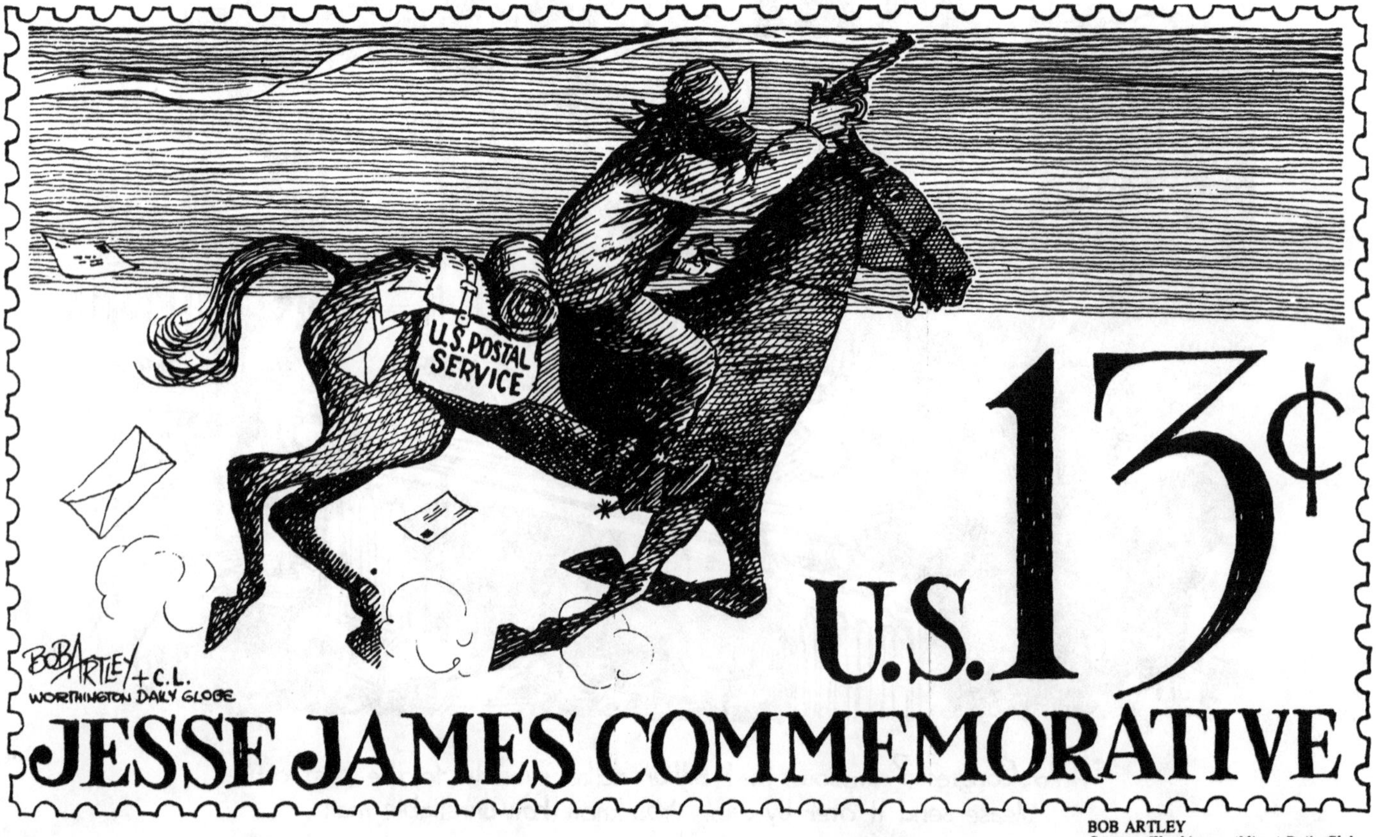
U.S. POSTAL SERVICE
U.S. 13¢
BOB ARTLEY + C.L.
WORTHINGTON DAILY GLOBE
JESSE JAMES COMMEMORATIVE

BOB ARTLEY
Courtesy Worthington (Minn.) Daily Globe

Morality

Sex scandals were not the only evidences of questionable morality linked to Congress during the year. An investigation by the Justice Department turned up evidence that congressmen and other highly placed American officials may have accepted large gifts and campaign contributions from agents of the South Korean government. These payments allegedly were made in an effort to influence American policy toward South Korea. According to investigators, as many as ninety members of Congress may have been involved.

Senator Frank Church's subcommittee on multinational corporations created a stir in February when it disclosed that the Lockheed Aircraft Corporation had paid millions to influence top governmental officials of foreign nations. Egypt opened an investigation of charges that highly placed persons in its state-owned airline had taken commissions on aircraft purchases from the Boeing Corporation.

Under U. S. law, bribery of foreign officials was not a criminal offense.

"...OKEY, EVERYBODY OUT!..."

BALDY
Courtesy Atlanta Constitution

IT'S CALLED SUCTION

KARL HUBENTHAL
Courtesy Los Angeles Herald-Examiner

ROY PETERSON
Courtesy Vancouver Sun

"... is only a wild theory, Comrad Captain, but is looking like a long-range surveillance aircraft of the Lockheed configuration..."

GARRY APGAR
Courtesy Roanoke Times and World-News

The ugly American

GEORGE FISHER
Courtesy N. Little Rock Times

DICK WALLMEYER
Long Beach Press-Telegram
©Register and Tribune Syndicate

"YOU THINK *YOU* GOT TROUBLES?..."

'A CADET WILL NOT LIE, CHEAT OR STEAL, OR TOLERATE THOSE WHO DO'

CRAIG MACINTOSH
Courtesy Minneapolis Star

TOM ENGELHARDT
Courtesy St. Louis Post-Dispatch

'Atta Boy, Poochie—You Certainly Are Congressmen's Best Friend'

CHARLES BROOKS
Courtesy Birmingham (Ala.) News

MILT MORRIS
©The Associated Press

ART POINIER
© United Feature Syndicate

DENNIS RENAULT
©McClatchy Newspapers

'Your honor, my client believes that campaign spending limitations are a curb on free speech because everybody knows money talks!'

Another double standard

REG MANNING
Courtesy Arizona Republic

LOU ERICKSON
Courtesy Atlanta Journal

U.S. Defense

While the United States and Russia ended 1976 virtually even in the nuclear arms race, the Soviets retained a strong advantage in numbers and weight of long-range missiles. Alarmed, the U. S. Air Force issued a statement saying that, as the size, number, and accuracy of Soviet missiles continued to increase, America's one thousand Minuteman missiles would be in danger of a knockout punch.

The Soviets began massive hardening programs of possible military and industrial targets. This broad-scale program to protect military installations and industries in the event of an all-out nuclear war seemed to put the U. S. S. R. in a highly advantageous position. America's naval position shifted from one of clear superiority to one of approximate balance with the Soviet Union.

U. S. leadership in technology appeared to deteriorate further as

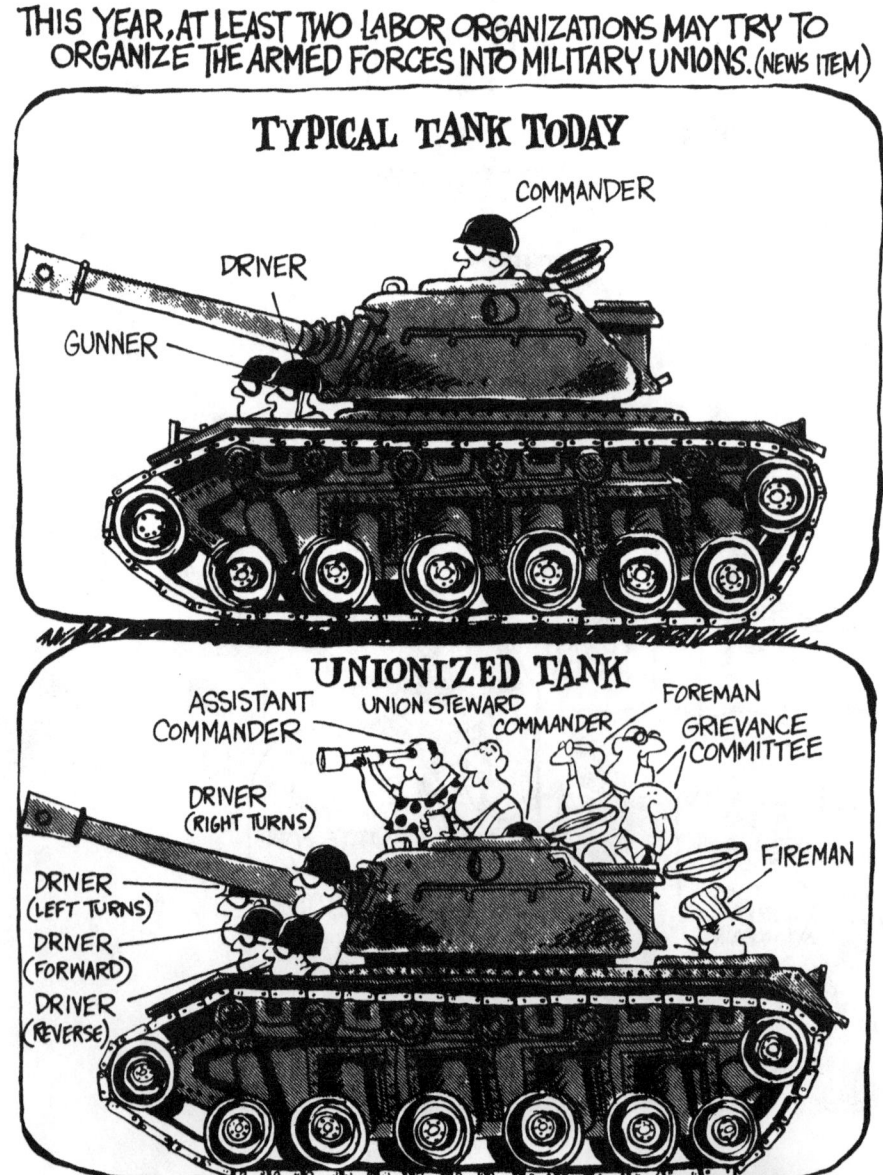

BOB ENGLEHART
Courtesy Dayton Journal Herald

U. S. DEFENSE

Russia escalated its military research and development program. Although NATO was believed to be currently strong enough to dissuade a potential aggressor, the supreme commander of NATO forces warned that the present trend was not favorable.

The Ford administration submitted to Congress the largest defense budget in history and later proposed additional defense budget increases.

"It's Our 1977 Economy Model!"

DEFENSE SPENDING
BYRON HUMPHREY

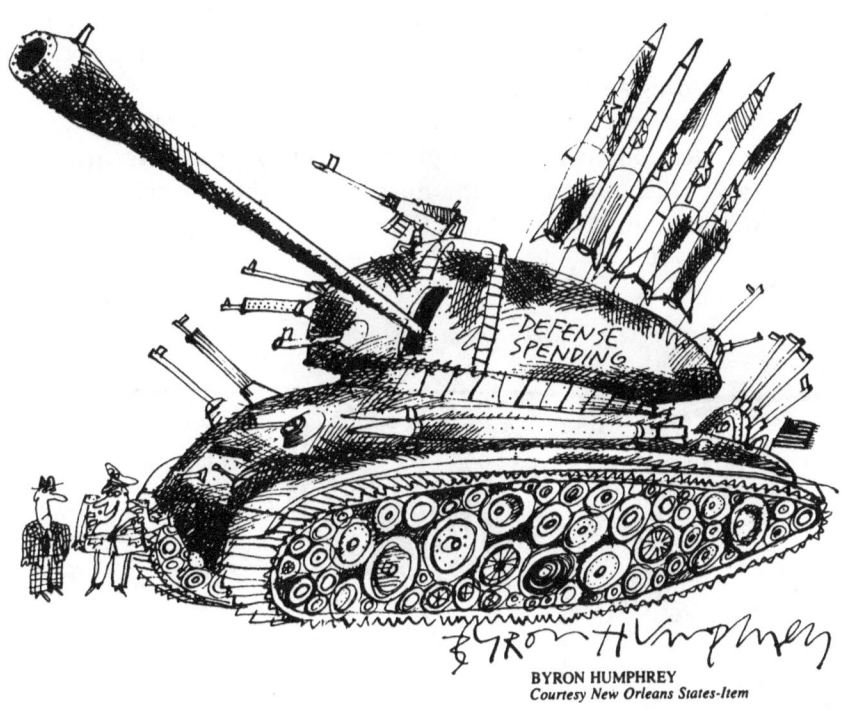

BYRON HUMPHREY
Courtesy New Orleans States-Item

BILL ANDREWS
THIS TOWN AIN'T BIG ENOUGH FOR BOTH OF US!
'DEFENSE' CONTRACTORS
USA
HEALTH EDUCATION AND WELFARE

BILL ANDREWS
Courtesy New York Daily World

Education

Busing to achieve racial integration in public schools remained a touchy issue in many cities across the United States. Incidents flared in Boston and Louisville, and potentially serious conflicts simmered in Omaha, Dallas, and Dayton. For the first time, whites were a minority in Boston's embattled schools. About 24,000 Boston students were being bused.

School programs were also the target of growing criticism. New reports on student proficiency showed a continued decline in test scores over the past thirteen years. Factors cited were a lack of parental guidance and discipline, fear of competition, and insufficient practice in developing reading and writing skills.

The U. S. Supreme Court ruled that the Civil Rights Act of 1866 prohibited private nonsectarian schools from denying admission on the basis of race. Unanswered was the question of whether private schools could still discriminate on the basis of religion or sex.

"You really don't want to get on that bus, do you, kid?"

OLLIE HARRINGTON
Courtesy New York Daily World

CLYDE WELLS
Courtesy Augusta (Ga.) Chronicle

The Economy

Following a recession low of 8.9 per cent in May, 1975, the rate of unemployment had been trimmed to 7.8 per cent, or 7.4 million persons, by September, 1976. Over the past thirty years, the unemployment rate averaged about 4.9 per cent.

Economists contended that a sizable part of the unemployed consisted of women and teen-agers, categories that typically suffered from high unemployment rates. The number of women entering the labor force rose by 11.3 million, or 41.4 per cent, since 1966. Teen-agers faced increased competition for jobs since the draft was ended and the armed forces were reduced in size.

Automobile sales enjoyed a strong year, with 10.2 million units sold. Housing starts totaled about 1.5 million. The rate of inflation was reduced to 4.8 per cent by the end of the year.

Economists predicted a steady climb in industrial output during 1977, a renewed surge in consumer spending, and a strong increase in capital outlay.

ROB LAWLOR
Courtesy Philadelphia Daily News

"HERE COMES ANOTHER GROUP OF LEADING ECONOMIC INDICATORS"

AT THE END OF THE ASSEMBLY LINE

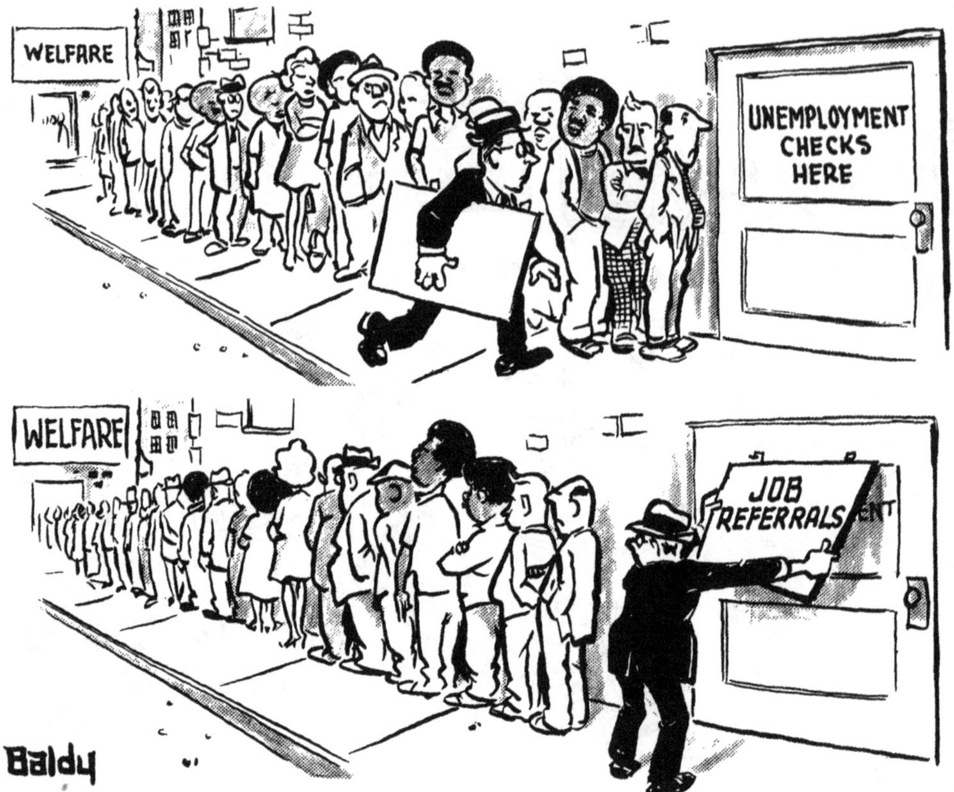
WELFARE
UNEMPLOYMENT CHECKS HERE
WELFARE
JOB REFERRALS
Baldy

BALDY
Courtesy Atlanta Constitution

SIGNS OF THE TIMES

LEONARD NORRIS
Courtesy Vancouver (Can.) Sun

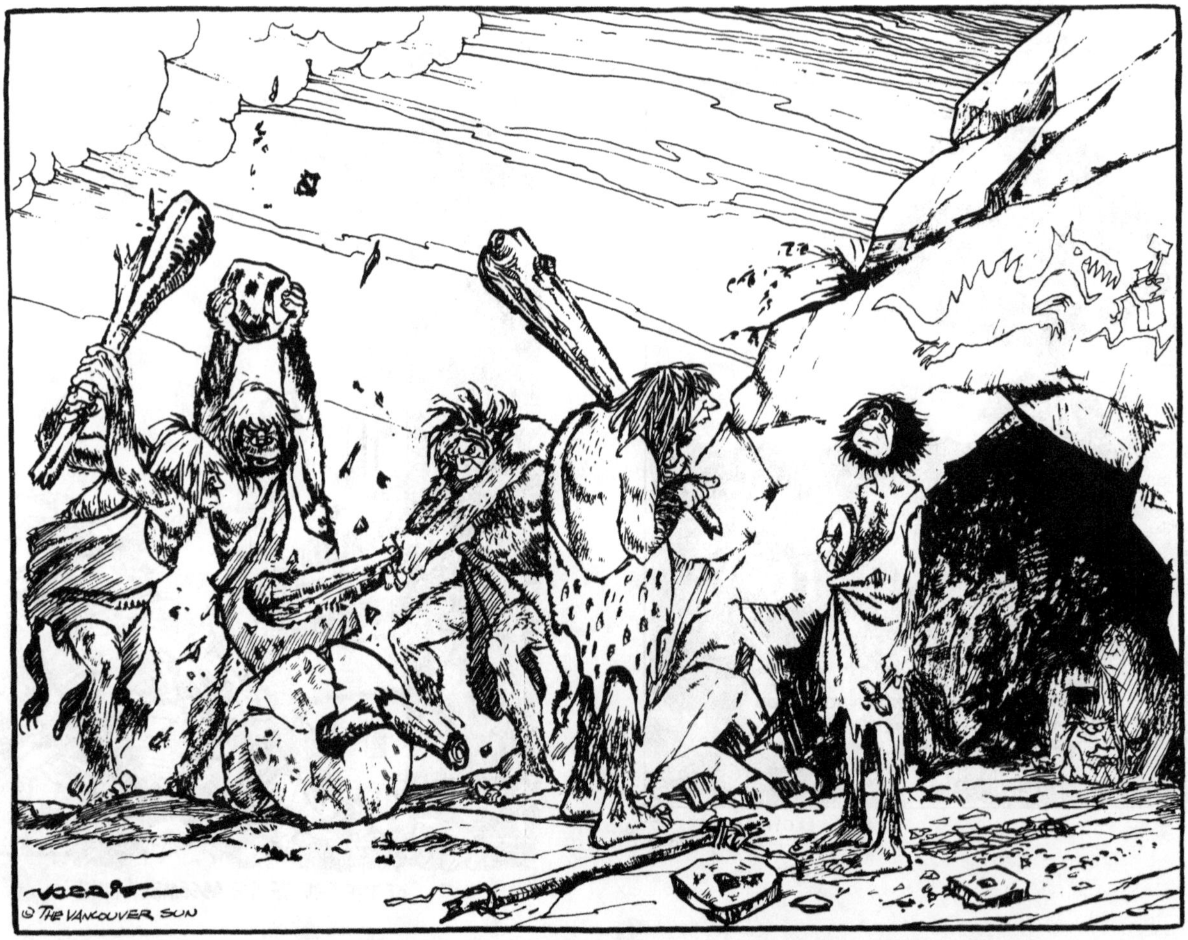
© THE VANCOUVER SUN

"You can call it a wheel if you like... we call it automation."

"Whadda ya mean who won the election? Both candidates was our guy!"

OLLIE HARRINGTON
Courtesy New York Daily World

"Ten years ago your budget would have gotten you a nice little house, but at 1976 prices, well..."

BOB BECKETT
Courtesy Burlington County (N.J.) Times

JOHN CRAWFORD
Courtesy Alabama Journal

FRANK INTERLANDI
©Los Angeles Times Syndicate

GOOD NEWS! THE TAXMAN SAYS YOUR HOME IS WORTH $3,000 MORE THIS YEAR!

LEE JUDGE
Courtesy Sacremento Union

Swine Flu

The threat of a nationwide epidemic of swine flu, the same strain that killed more than half a million Americans in 1918-1919, stirred public health officials to action during the year. In March President Ford announced a national swine flu vaccination program aimed at stopping the expected epidemic, and Congress earmarked $135 million for the campaign.

When insurance companies refused to offer liability coverage to pharmaceutical companies producing the vaccine, Congress passed legislation obligating the federal government to assume the cost of any malpractice suits resulting from the mass inoculations.

In October some thirty-five persons died within forty-eight hours of inoculation, and many states suspended the program. Still later, several persons contracted a rare form of paralysis, and health officials warned that the vaccine might have caused it. By the end of the year the inoculation program was at a standstill.

SLEEPING GIANT —

HERC FICKLEN
Courtesy Dallas Morning News

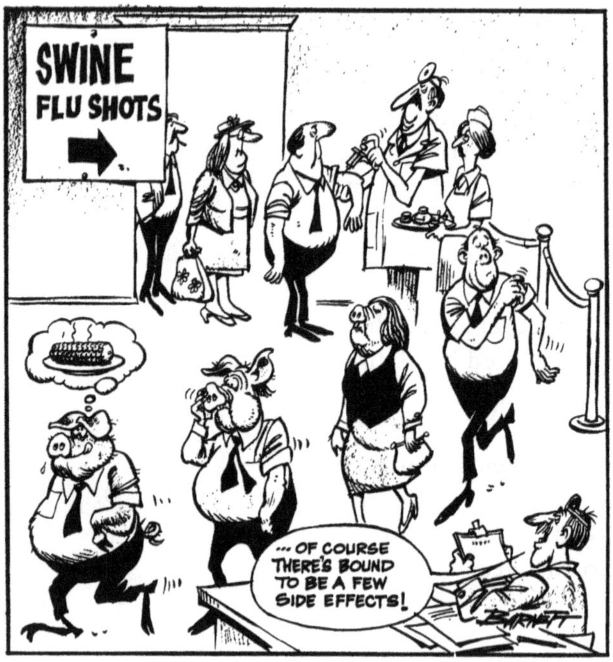
SWINE FLU SHOTS
...OF COURSE THERE'S BOUND TO BE A FEW SIDE EFFECTS!
BARNETT

JERRY BARNETT
Courtesy Indianapolis News

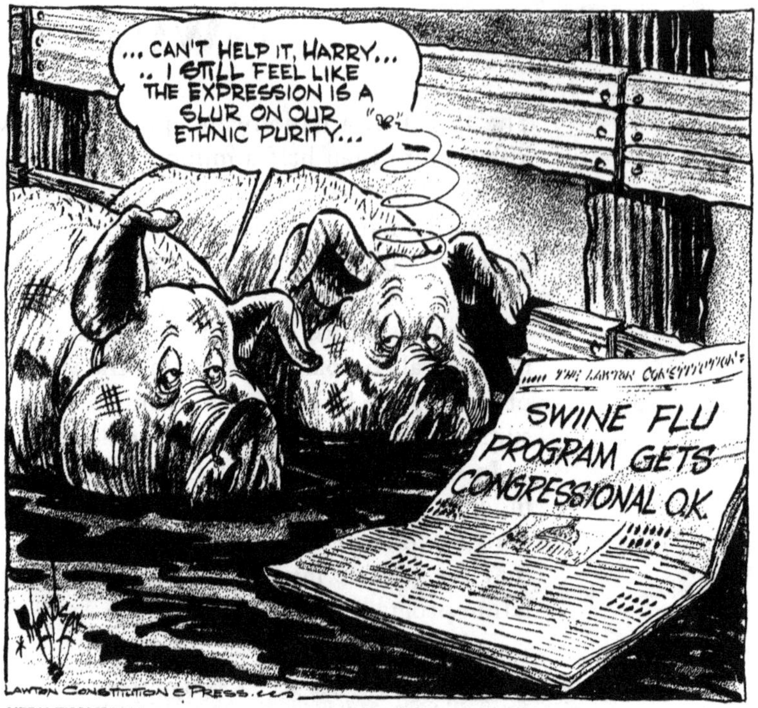
...CAN'T HELP IT, HARRY... .. I STILL FEEL LIKE THE EXPRESSION IS A SLUR ON OUR ETHNIC PURITY...
THE LAWTON CONSTITUTION
SWINE FLU PROGRAM GETS CONGRESSIONAL O.K.
LAWTON CONSTITUTION & PRESS

VERN THOMPSON
Courtesy Lawton (Okla.) Constitution

'You know, I'm really enjoying this'

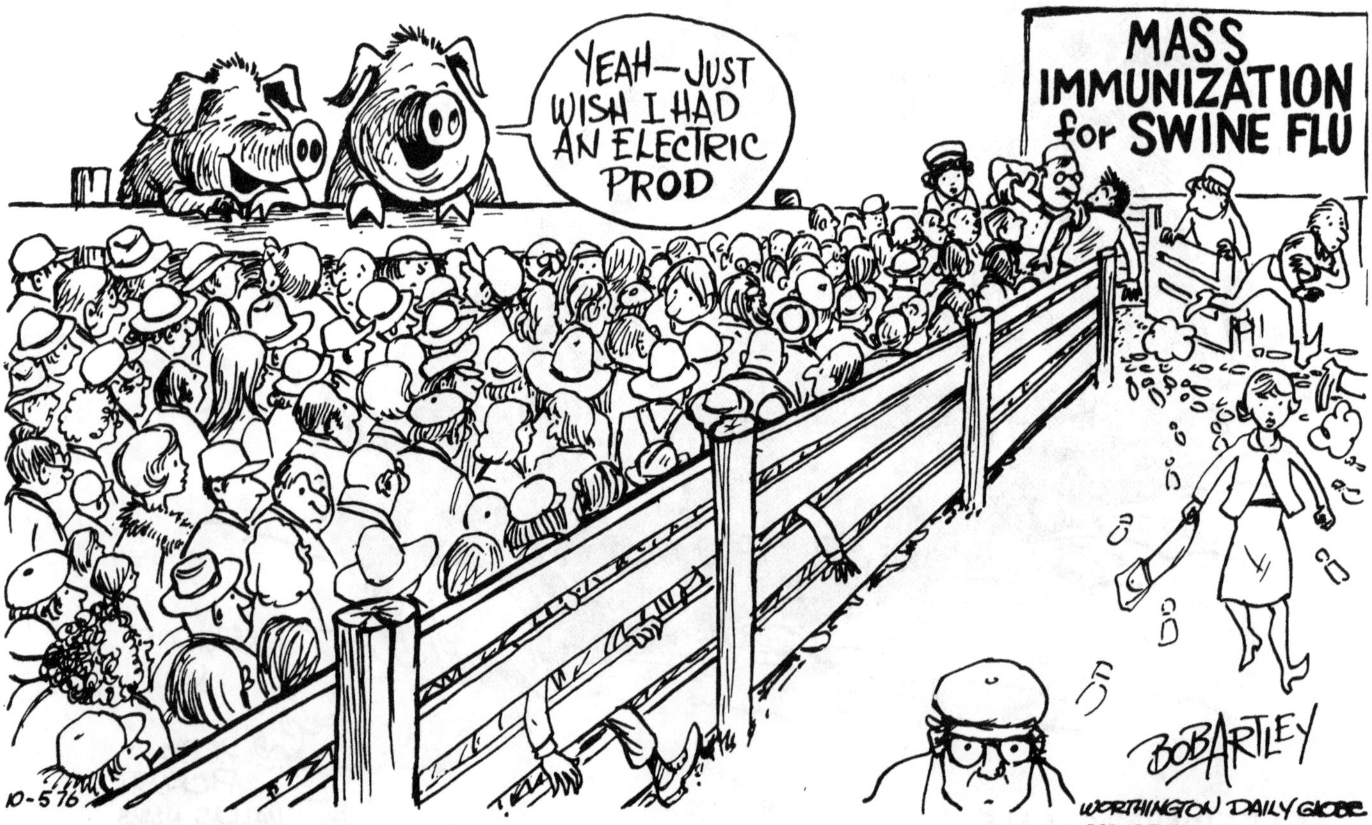
YEAH—JUST WISH I HAD AN ELECTRIC PROD
MASS IMMUNIZATION for SWINE FLU
10-5-76
BOB ARTLEY
WORTHINGTON DAILY GLOBE

BOB ARTLEY
Courtesy Worthington (Minn.) Daily Globe

Earl Butz

Secretary of Agriculture Earl Butz, a staunch advocate of Ford administration farm policies whose outspoken views had landed him in hot water before, spoke candidly once too often—and it cost him his job. The Watergate figure John Dean, who had covered the Republican National Convention for *Rolling Stone* magazine, quoted Butz as having made obscene and derogatory remarks in a joke about blacks. According to Dean, Butz's comment came in response to a question about how the GOP might appeal to black voters.

After the story made page-one news throughout the country, it seemed apparent that Butz had to go. Although most farmers liked Butz and his farm program, many consumers did not. Following several days of official silence, Ford, "with my deep regret," allowed Butz to resign.

'EARL BUTZ! IS THERE A FORMER SECRETARY BUTZ HERE?'

CRAIG MACINTOSH
Courtesy Minneapolis Star

JOHN FISCHETTI
Courtesy Chicago Daily News

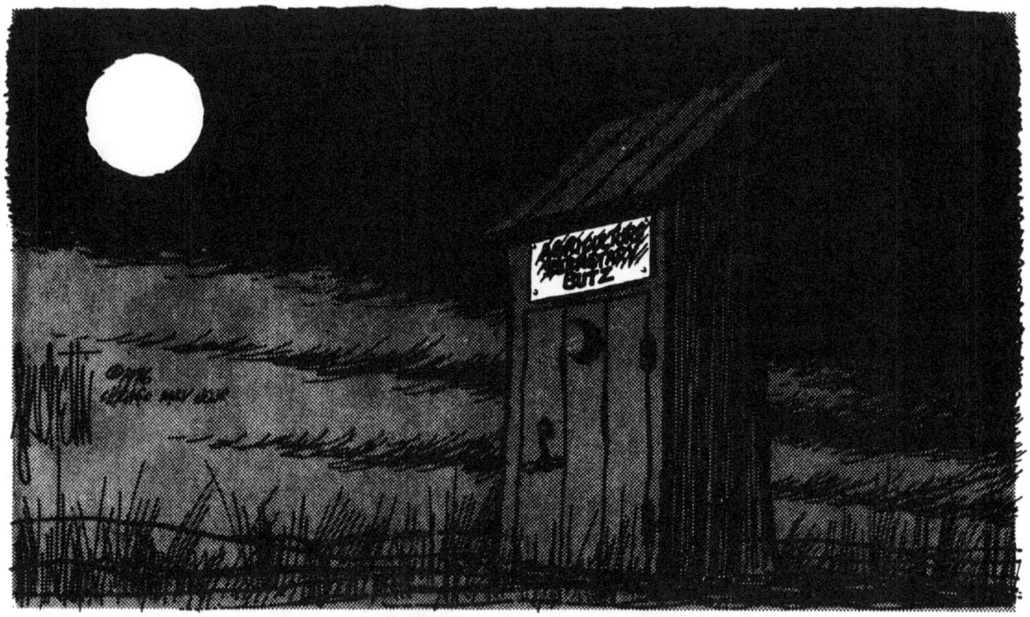
BUTZ

THE LITTLE HOUSE ON THE PRAIRIE

CHARLES BISSELL
Courtesy Nashville Tennessean

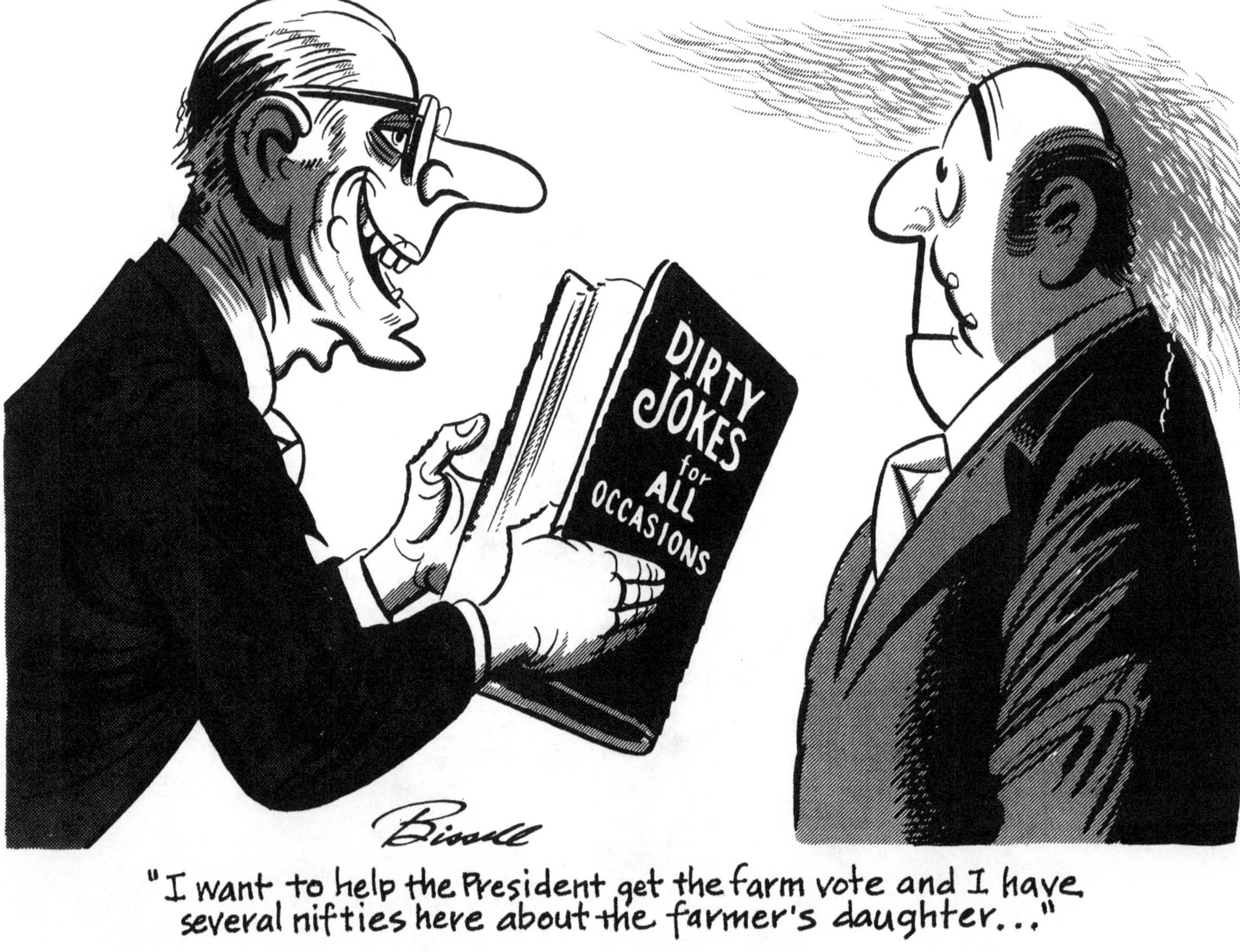
DIRTY JOKES for ALL OCCASIONS
Bissell

"I want to help the President get the farm vote and I have several nifties here about the farmer's daughter..."

PAUL SZEP
Courtesy Boston Globe

"BEING EARL BUTZ MEANS NEVER HAVING TO SAY YOU'RE SORRY"

RACIAL POISON

ROB LAWLOR
Courtesy Philadelphia Daily News

DOUG SNEYD
Courtesy Toronto Star

"It's a job offer, Mr. Butz...from the producers of *All in the Family.*"

TIMOTHY ATSEFF
Courtesy Syracuse Herald-Journal

. . . And Other Issues

American prestige, which had suffered on a variety of fronts in previous years, was bolstered by the announcement of the 1976 Nobel prizes. Americans swept all five categories awarded—medicine, physics, chemistry, economics, and literature.

The Department of Health, Education, and Welfare should have won a prize of some sort for its bizarre ruling that father-and-son banquets and all-boy choirs were patently discriminatory and therefore illegal. As a result of the ruling, choirs were forced to disband in several states.

The Anglo–French Concorde remained one of the best airplanes flying, but it had difficulty finding places to land. Landing rights at JFK Airport in New York were denied until air pollution and noise level studies could be made.

Howard Hughes, one of the world's richest men, died April 5, and more than thirty wills reputed to be his quickly turned up.

A bedroom-bugging incident marred the tranquillity of the household of Governor George Wallace of Alabama, but he passed it off as a domestic matter and refused to discuss it publicly.

EDD ULUSCHAK
Courtesy Edmonton Journal

VIC CANTONE
©Editor and Publisher

THE PRICE OF SILENCE.

"TAKE A BREAK, COMRADE—"

"—THEY'VE JUST SWEPT THE NOBEL PRIZES!"

"SHAME ON AMERICANS" LINE

C. F. MORSE
©Hearst Newspapers

BILL GARNER
Courtesy The Commercial Appeal

CORNELIA— THERE'S A BUG IN MY GRITS!

MIKE PETERS
Courtesy Dayton Daily News

ART HENRIKSON
Courtesy Des Plaines (Ill.) Herald

All out for New York — and thanks for flying Concorde.

FRAME OF REFERENCE

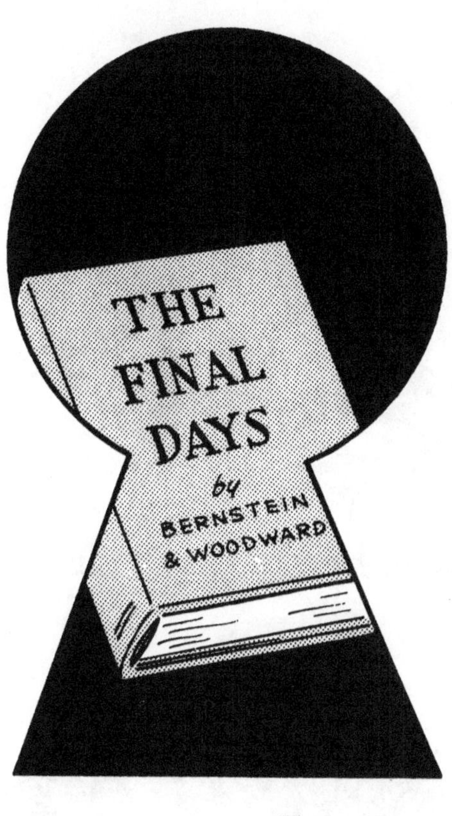
THE FINAL DAYS
by BERNSTEIN & WOODWARD

BOB HOWIE
Courtesy Jackson (Miss.) Daily News

Bob Howie
JACKSON DAILY NEWS

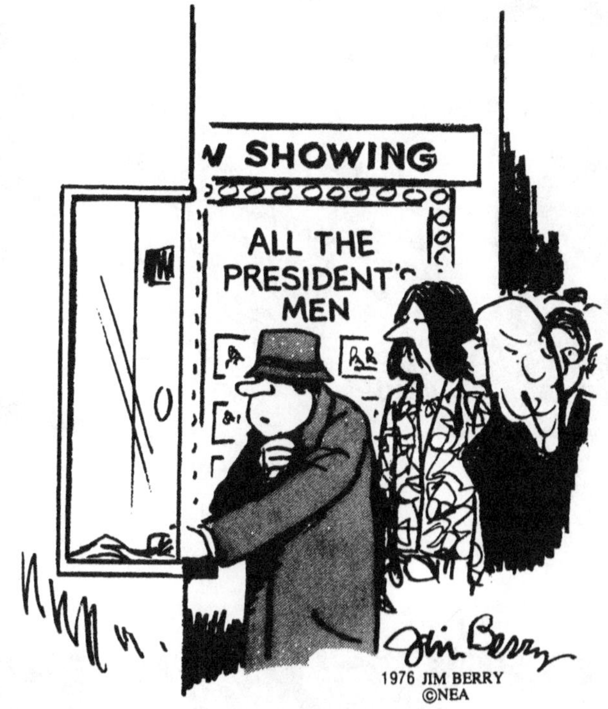
W SHOWING
ALL THE PRESIDENT'S MEN
Jim Berry
1976 JIM BERRY
©NEA

"One!"

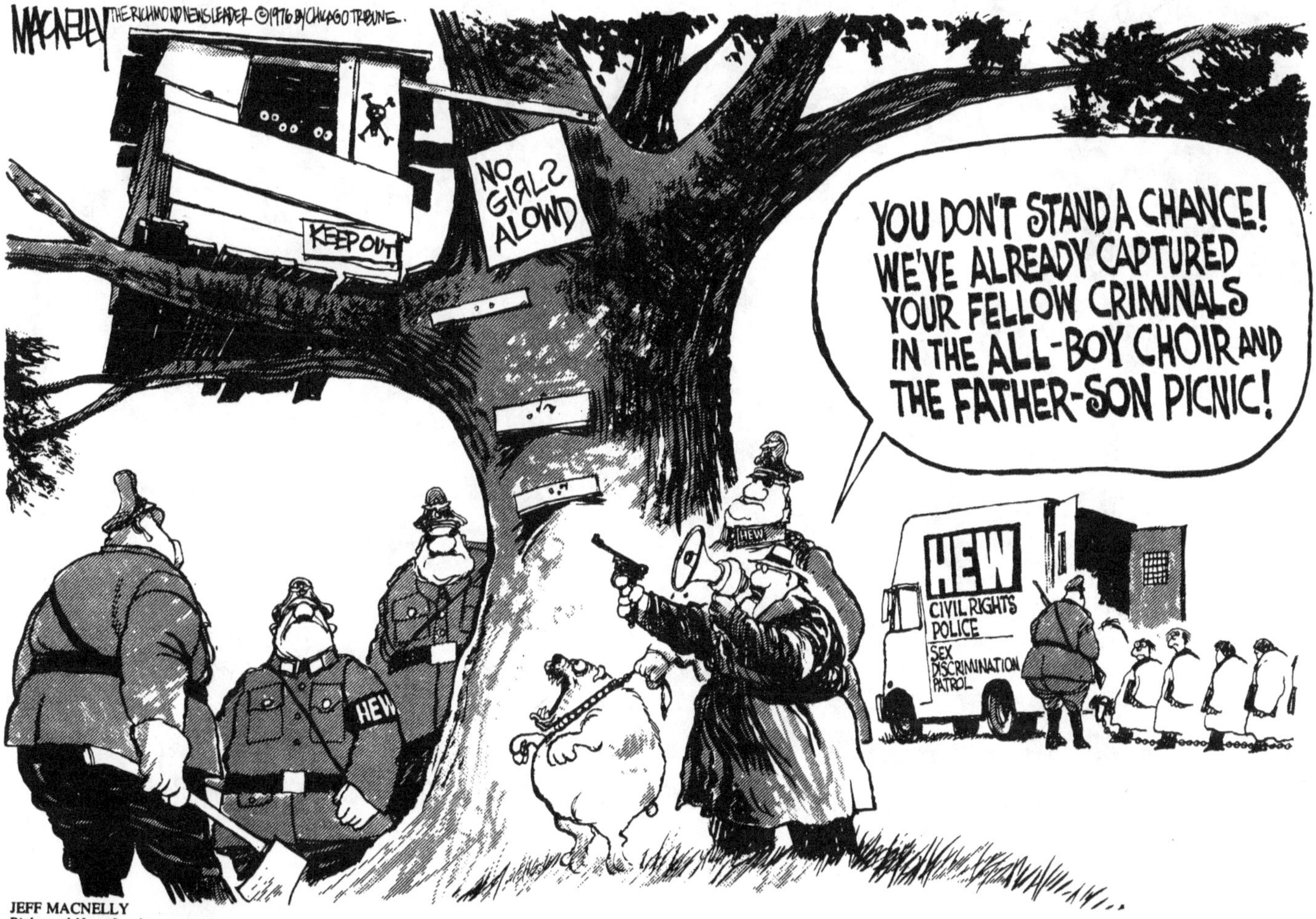
MACNELLY THE RICHMOND NEWS LEADER ©1976 BY CHICAGO TRIBUNE.
KEEP OUT
NO GIRLS ALOWD
YOU DON'T STAND A CHANCE! WE'VE ALREADY CAPTURED YOUR FELLOW CRIMINALS IN THE ALL-BOY CHOIR AND THE FATHER-SON PICNIC!
HEW
HEW
HEW
CIVIL RIGHTS POLICE
SEX DISCRIMINATION PATROL

JEFF MACNELLY
Richmond News Leader
©Chicago Tribune—New York News Syndicate

ED FISCHER
Courtesy Omaha World-Herald

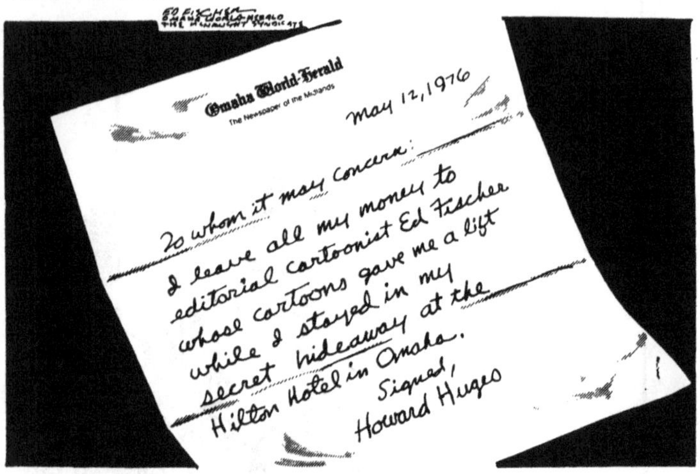
Omaha World-Herald
The Newspaper of the Midlands
May 12, 1976
To whom it may concern:
I leave all my money to editorial cartoonist Ed Fischer whose cartoons gave me a lift while I stayed in my secret hideaway at the Hilton Hotel in Omaha.
Signed,
Howard Huges

The Real Hughes Will

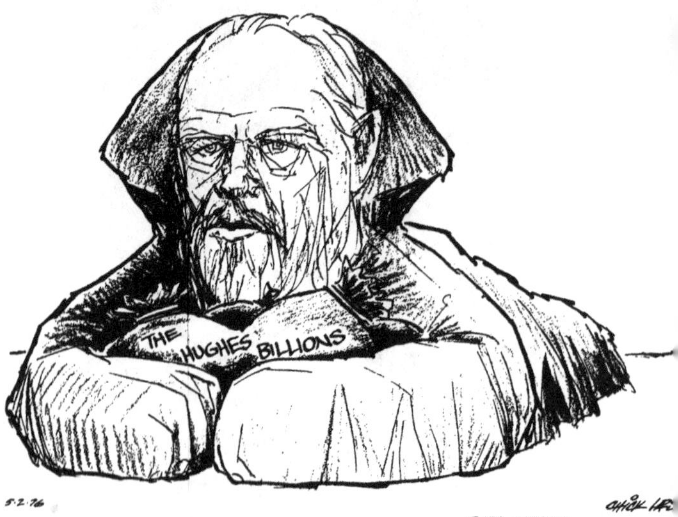
THE HUGHES BILLIONS
5-2-76

CARL LARSEN
Courtesy Richmond Times-Dispa

ED GAMBLE
Courtesy Nashville Banner

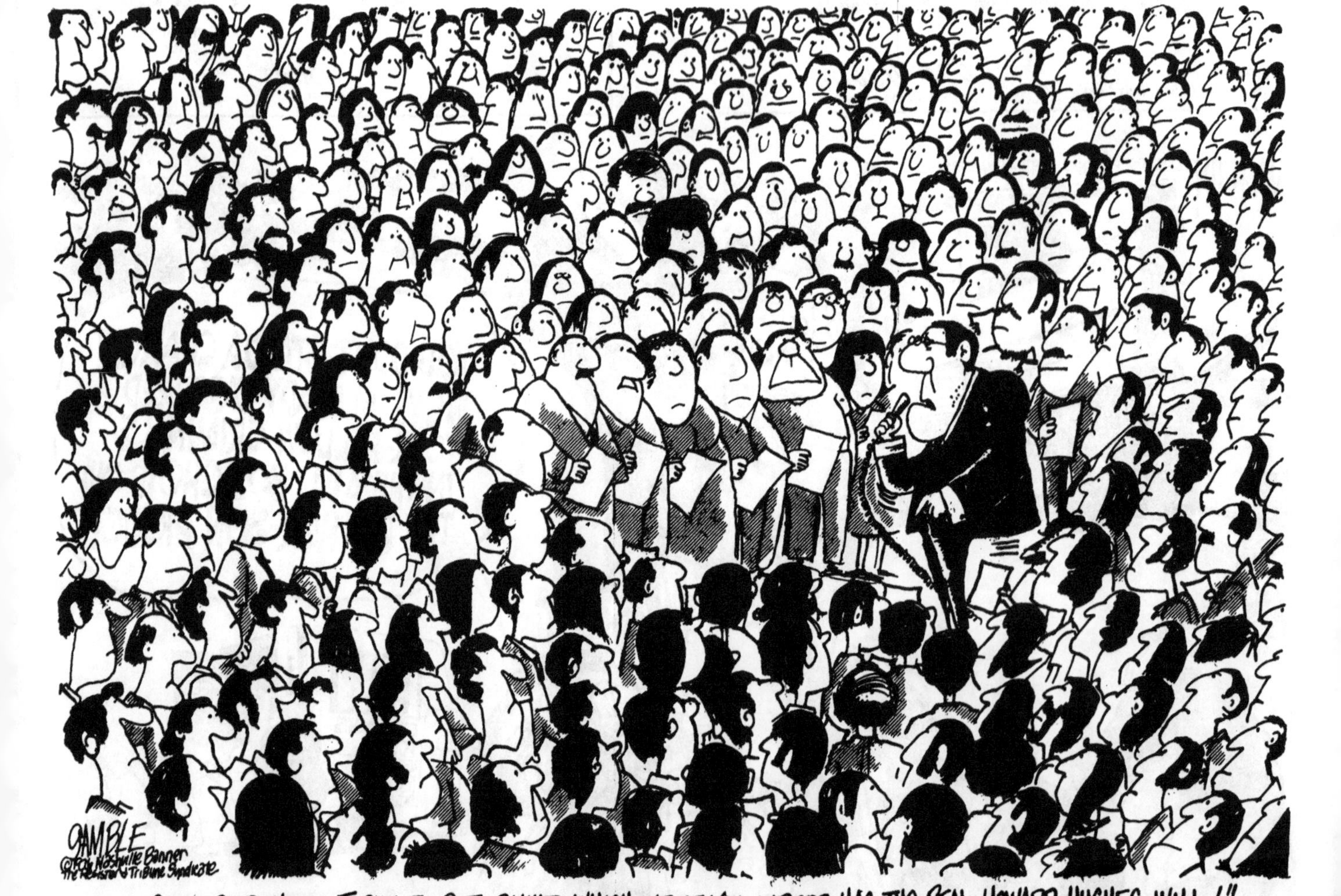
GAMBLE
©1976 Nashville Banner
The Register & Tribune Syndicate

"WE ARE GATHERED HERE TODAY TO DETERMINE WHICH ONE OF YOU, INDEED, HAS THE REAL HOWARD HUGHES WILL!"

LEONARD NORRIS
Courtesy Vancouver (Can.) Sun

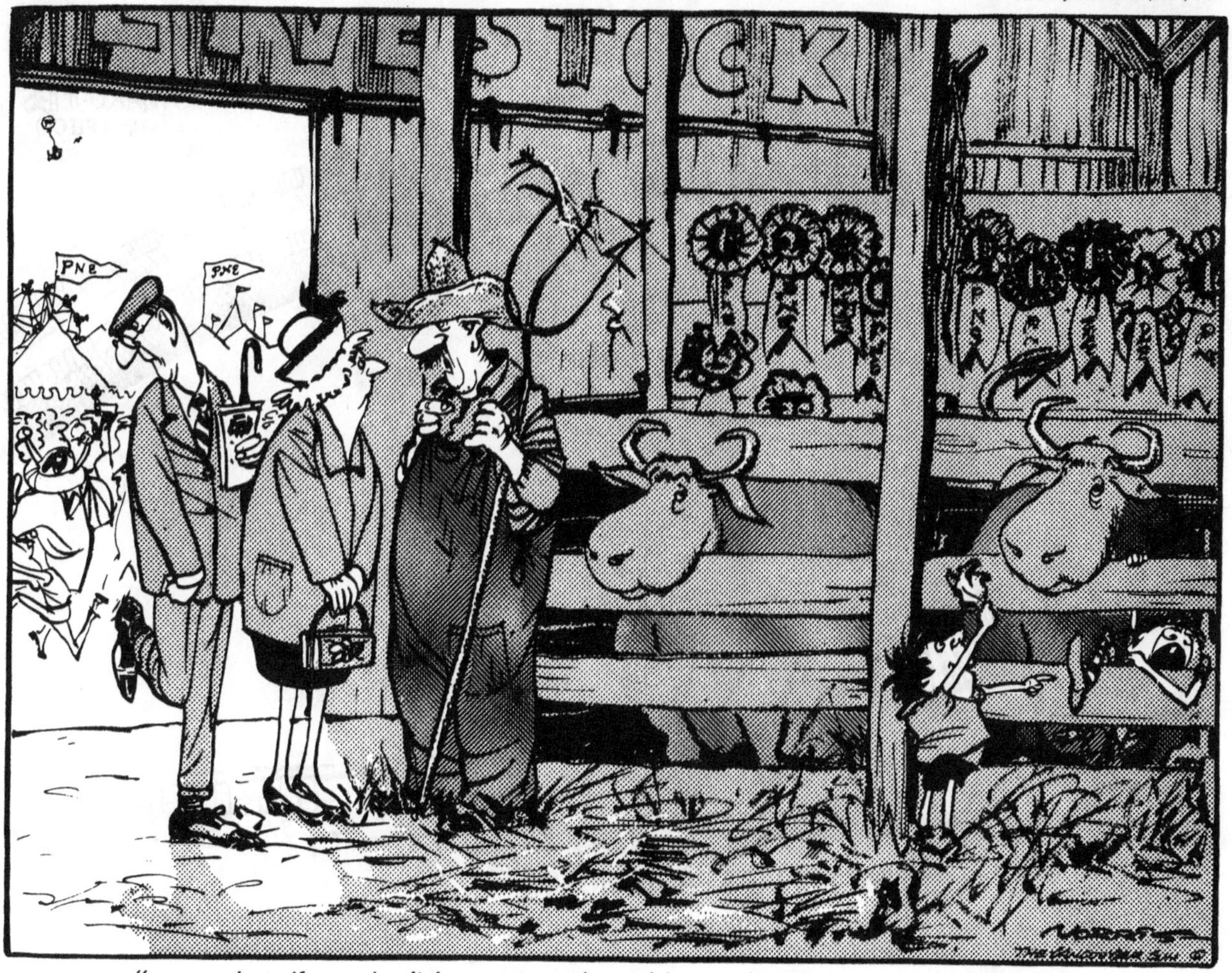
LIVESTOCK
PNE
PNE

". . . and as if we don't have enough problems already, we're going to have to teach them to give litres instead of quarts . . ."

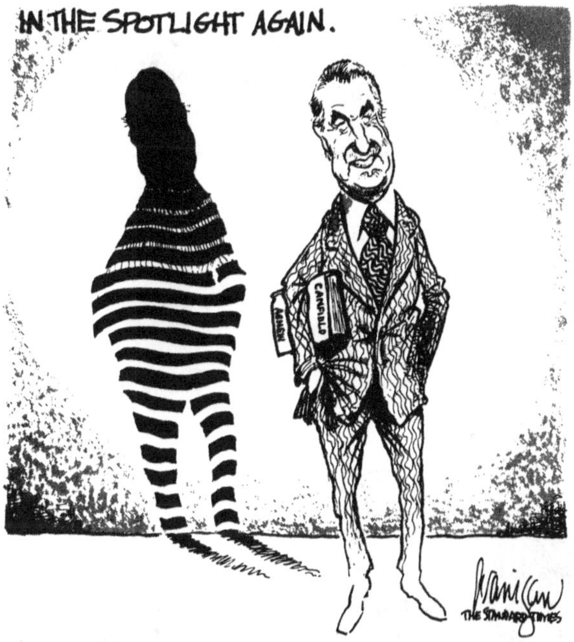
IN THE SPOTLIGHT AGAIN.
CANDIDO
THE STANDARD-TIMES

JACK LANIGAN
Courtesy New Bedford Standard-Times

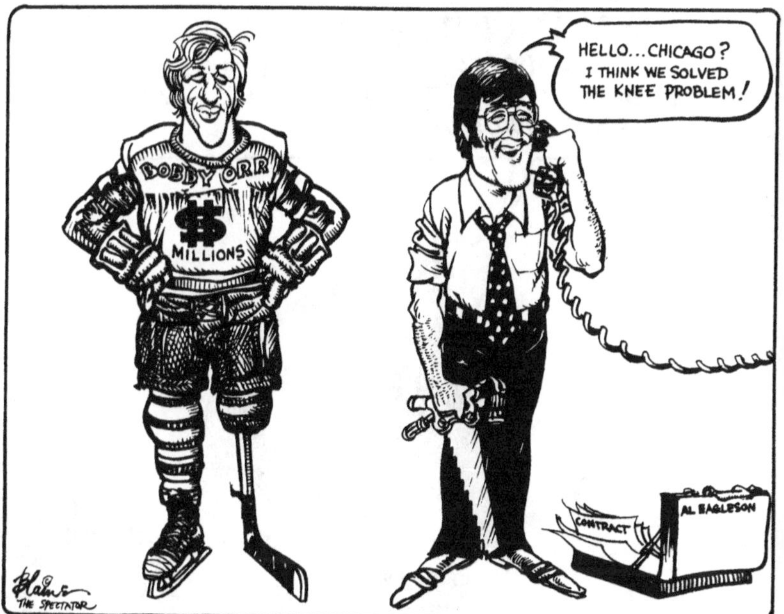
HELLO...CHICAGO?
I THINK WE SOLVED
THE KNEE PROBLEM!
BOBBY ORR
$
MILLIONS
CONTRACT
AL EAGLESON
THE SPECTATOR

BLAINE
Courtesy The Spectator, Canada

JIMMY MARGULIES
©Rothco Cartoons

MARGULIES
ROTHCO
NO ARTIFICIAL COLORING ADDED
"WELL THAT'S REASSURING"

IT'S AN OUTRAGE, I TELL YOU! A MILLION BUCKS A YEAR FOR BARBARA WALTERS— PURE SHOW BIZ! ALL THOSE YEARS IN CONVINCING AMERICA THAT TV NEWS IS ON PAR WITH PRINT JOURNALISM! SHOT!!
INCIDENTLY, WE'RE COUNTERING WITH SAMMY DAVIS JR. & RAQUEL WELCH— HOW ABOUT YOU GUYS?
WE'RE MOVING WALTER OVER TO COMMENTARY & BRINGING IN ROBERT REDFORD & CHER.
NBC NEWS
CBS

CLYDE WELLS
Courtesy Augusta (Ga.) Chronicle

Past Award Winners

PULITZER PRIZE EDITORIAL CARTOON

1922—Rollin Kirby, New York World
1924—J. N. Darling, New York Herald Tribune
1925—Rollin Kirby, New York World
1926—D. R. Fitzpatrick, St. Louis Post-Dispatch
1927—Nelson Harding, Brooklyn Eagle
1928—Nelson Harding, Brooklyn Eagle
1929—Rollin Kirby, New York World
1930—Charles Macauley, Brooklyn Eagle
1931—Edmund Duffy, Baltimore Sun
1932—John T. McCutcheon, Chicago Tribune
1933—H. M. Talburt, Washington Daily News
1934—Edmund Duffy, Baltimore Sun
1935—Ross A. Lewis, Milwaukee Journal
1937—C. D. Batchelor, New York Daily News
1938—Vaughn Shoemaker, Chicago Daily News
1939—Charles G. Werner, Daily Oklahoman
1940—Edmund Duffy, Baltimore Sun
1941—Jacob Burck, Chicago Times
1942—Herbert L. Block, Newspaper Enterprise Association
1943—Jay N. Darling, New York Herald Tribune
1944—Clifford K. Berryman, Washington Star
1945—Bill Mauldin, United Feature Syndicate
1946—Bruce Russell, Los Angeles Times
1947—Vaughn Shoemaker, Chicago Daily News
1948—Reuben L. (Rube) Goldberg, New York Sun
1949—Lute Pease, Newark Evening News
1950—James T. Berryman, Washington Star
1951—Reginald W. Manning, Arizona Republic
1952—Fred L. Packer, New York Mirror
1953—Edward D. Kuekes, Cleveland Plain Dealer
1954—Herbert L. Block, Washington Post
1955—Daniel R. Fitzpatrick, St. Louis Post-Dispatch
1956—Robert York, Louisville Times
1957—Tom Little, Nashville Tennessean
1958—Bruce M. Shanks, Buffalo Evening News
1959—Bill Mauldin, St. Louis Post-Dispatch

PAST AWARD WINNERS

1961—Carey Orr, Chicago Tribune
1962—Edmund S. Valtman, Hartford Times
1963—Frank Miller, Des Moines Register
1964—Paul Conrad, Denver Post
1966—Don Wright, Miami News
1967—Patrick B. Oliphant, Denver Post
1968—Eugene Gray Payne, Charlotte Observer
1969—John Fischetti, Chicago Daily News
1970—Thomas F. Darcy, Newsday
1971—Paul Conrad, Los Angeles Times
1972—Jeffrey K. MacNelly, Richmond News Leader
1974—Paul Szep, Boston Globe
1975—Garry Trudeau, Universal Press Syndicate
1976—Tony Auth, Philadelphia Enquirer

NOTE: Pulitzer Prize Award was not given 1923, 1936, 1960, 1965, and 1973.

SIGMA DELTA CHI AWARDS EDITORIAL CARTOON

1942—Jacob Burck, Chicago Times
1943—Charles Werner, Chicago Sun
1944—Henry Barrow, Associated Press
1945—Reuben L. Goldberg, New York Sun
1946—Dorman H. Smith, Newspaper Enterprise Association
1947—Bruce Russell, Los Angeles Times
1948—Herbert Block, Washington Post
1949—Herbert Block, Washington Post
1950—Bruce Russell, Los Angeles Times
1951—Herbert Block, Washington Post, and Bruce Russell, Los Angeles Times
1952—Cecil Jensen, Chicago Daily News
1953—John Fischetti, Newspaper Enterprise Association
1954—Calvin Alley, Memphis Commercial Appeal
1955—John Fischetti, Newspaper Enterprise Association
1956—Herbert Block, Washington Post
1957—Scott Long, Minneapolis Tribune
1958—Clifford H. Baldowski, Atlanta Constitution
1959—Charles G. Brooks, Birmingham News
1960—Dan Dowling, New York Herald-Tribune
1961—Frank Interlandi, Des Moines Register
1962—Paul Conrad, Denver Post
1963—William Mauldin, Chicago Sun-Times
1964—Charles Bissell, Nashville Tennessean
1965—Roy Justus, Minneapolis Star

PAST AWARD WINNERS

1966—Patrick Oliphant, Denver Post
1967—Eugene Payne, Charlotte Observer
1968—Paul Conrad, Los Angeles Times
1969—William Mauldin, Chicago Sun-Times
1970—Paul Conrad, Los Angeles Times
1971—Hugh Haynie, Louisville Courier-Journal
1972—William Mauldin, Chicago Sun-Times
1973—Paul Szep, Boston Globe
1974—Mike Peters, Dayton Daily News
1975—Tony Auth, Philadelphia Enquirer

NATIONAL NEWSPAPER AWARD/CANADA

1949—Jack Boothe, Toronto Globe and Mail
1950—James G. Reidford, Montreal Star
1951—Len Norris, Vancouver Sun
1952—Robert La Palme, Le Devoir, Montreal
1953—Robert W. Chambers, Halifax Chronicle-Herald
1954—John Collins, Montreal Gazette
1955—Merle R. Tingley, London Free Press
1956—James G. Reidford, Toronto Globe and Mail
1957—James G. Reidford, Toronto Globe and Mail
1958—Raoul Hunter, Le Soleil, Quebec
1959—Duncan Macpherson, Toronto Star
1960—Duncan Macpherson, Toronto Star
1961—Ed McNally, Montreal Star
1962—Duncan Macpherson, Toronto Star
1963—Jan Kamienski, Winnipeg Tribune
1964—Ed McNally, Montreal Star
1965—Duncan Macpherson, Toronto Star
1966—Robert W. Chambers, Halifax Chronicle-Herald
1967—Raoul Hunter, Le Soleil, Quebec
1968—Roy Peterson, Vancouver Sun
1969—Edward Uluschak, Edmonton Journal
1970—Duncan Macpherson, Toronto Daily Star
1971—Yardley Jones, Toronto Sun
1972—Duncan Macpherson, Toronto Star
1973—John Collins, Montreal Gazette
1974—Blaine, Hamilton Spectator
1975—Roy Peterson, Vancouver Sun

Index

Aguila, Danny, 29
Alexander, Bob, 45, 125
Alexander, Ken, 18, 34, 51, 101
Andrews, Bill, 135, 139
Apgar, Garry, 131
Artley, Bob, 128, 144
Ashley, Ed, 89
Atseff, Timothy, 31, 147
Auth, Tony, 12, 13

Baldy (Baldowski), 43, 47, 129, 140
Barnett, Jerry, 90, 97, 106, 144
Basset, Gene, 15, 36, 69, 74
Beckett, Bob, 92, 141
Bender, Jack, 85, 120
Berry, Jim, 16, 67, 87, 151
Bimrose, Art, 101, 110
Bissell, Charles, 106, 107, 146
Bittle, Jerry, 72, 118
Blaine, 128, 153
Borgman, Jim, 49, 60
Borgstedt, Douglas, 27, 75
Brooks, Charles, 55, 65, 113, 132

Campbell, Sandy, 47, 97
Cantone, Vic, 85, 149
Carless, Roy, 92
Collins, John, 76, 109, 125
Commodore, Chester, 34, 60, 80
Craig, Eugene, 90, 113
Crawford, John, 19, 141
Cunnington, Merle, 19
Curtis, Tom, 43, 61, 96

Daniel, Charles, 17, 68
Daniels, Bill, 24, 32, 38
Darcy, Tom, 87, 104, 123
Davies, Lloyd, 139
Dobbins, Jim, 79, 98, 119
Donato, Andy, 49, 51, 108
Doyle, Jerry, 82, 95
Dunn, Robert, 116

Englehart, Bob, 17, 58, 134
Engelhardt, Tom, 84, 91, 132
Erickson, Lou, 92, 120, 133

Fearing, Jerry, 42, 88
Ficklen, Herc, 54, 119, 143
Fischer, Ed, 52, 56, 95, 152
Fischetti, John, 16, 99, 146
Fisher, George, 32, 44, 131
Flannery, Tom, 22, 86, 112

Gamble, Ed, 21, 37, 73, 152
Garner, Bill, 22, 30, 78, 149
Germano, Eddie, 47, 84
Grant, Lou, 25, 39, 105, 106
Graysmith, Robert, 18, 98, 101
Grondahl, Calvin, 20, 26, 122

Harrington, Ollie, 137, 141
Harsh, Lew, 68, 102, 126
Haynie, Hugh, 27, 70, 73, 78
Henrikson, Art, 54, 116, 150
Hill, Draper, 40, 45, 50, 62
Howie, Bob, 112, 151
Hubenthal, Karl, 22, 46, 48, 130
Hulme, Etta, 94, 139
Humphrey, Byron, 102, 135

Interlandi, Frank, 18, 67, 83, 142
Ivey, Jim, 51, 99

Jenkins, Anthony, 80, 125
Judge, Lee, 142
Jurden, Jack, 23, 113

Keefe, Mike, 52, 61, 68, 115
Kennedy, Jon, 19, 29, 42
King, Warren, 17, 27, 122
Konopacki, Michael, 51, 52
Kuch, Peter, 109

Lane, John, 79, 91, 101, 118
Lange, Jim, 38, 56, 63
Lanigan, Jack, 116, 153
Larsen, Chick, 89, 121, 152
Lawlor, Rob, 40, 138, 147
LePelley, Gurnsey, 36, 74, 85, 111
Levine, David, 55, 98
Liederman, Al, 62, 80
Locher, Dick, 66, 103, 111, 127

INDEX

Long, Scott, 39, 79, 90, 91

MacIntosh, Craig, 68, 131, 145
MacNelly, Jeff, 16, 21, 33, 151
McCarthy, Pat, 26, 88
McLeod, Jack, 19, 20, 106, 124

Manning, Reg, 56, 116, 133
Margulies, Jimmy, 154
Mauldin, William, 73
Morgan, Jim, 82
Morris, Milt, 75, 88, 132
Morse, C.F., 54, 91, 149

Norris, Leonard, 69, 117, 140, 152

Orton, Jim, 54, 63
Osrin, Ray, 93, 112, 122

Palmer, Bob, 54, 102, 118
Palmer, Jim, 30, 46
Palmer, Kate, 30, 105, 115
Payne, Eugene, 25, 63, 81
Peters, Mike, 31, 39, 71, 150
Peterson, Clyde, 29, 71, 74, 89
Peterson, Roy, 14, 108, 130
Pilsworth, Graham, 87
Pletcher, Eldon, 67
Poinier, Art, 28, 95, 132
Powell, Dwane, 25, 50, 59

Rawls, S.C., 28, 40
Renault, Dennis, 50, 75, 99, 133
Riedell, John, 122
Robinson, Jerry, 26, 28
Roschkov, V., 20, 35, 109
Rosen, Hy, 57, 77, 94, 107
Runtz, Vic, 55, 58

Sargent, Ben, 36, 45, 124
Seavey, David, 127, 136
Simpson, David, 22, 34, 38, 66
Smith, Eric, 35, 63, 97
Sneyd, Doug, 75, 110, 147
Spangler, Frank, 24, 38
Stampone, John, 80, 110, 111
Stayskal, Wayne, 23, 59, 94, 114
Szep, Paul, 49, 52, 53, 147

Taylor, Bob, 24, 35, 58, 76
Thompson, Vern, 61, 94, 144
Tingley, Merle, 76, 124

Uluschak, Edd, 77, 120, 148

Wallmeyer, Dick, 23, 41, 64, 131
Wells, Clyde, 137, 154
Werner, Charles, 22, 32, 82, 100
Whitman, Bert, 42, 60, 88
Wood, Art, 29, 119
Wright, Larry, 37, 52, 127

www.ingramcontent.com/pod-product-compliance
Lightning Source LLC
Chambersburg PA
CBHW080546170426
43195CB00016B/2698